Joseph J Casey

Personal Names in Hening's Statutes at Large of Virginia and

Shepherd's Continuation

Joseph J Casey

Personal Names in Hening's Statutes at Large of Virginia and Shepherd's Continuation

ISBN/EAN: 9783337815677

Printed in Europe, USA, Canada, Australia, Japan

Cover: Foto ©Andreas Hilbeck / pixelio.de

More available books at **www.hansebooks.com**

PERSONAL NAMES

IN

HENING'S STATUTES
AT LARGE

OF

VIRGINIA,

AND

SHEPHERD'S CONTINUATION

―――

BY

JOSEPH J. CASEY, A. M.

―――

PREFACE.

Published

New York   1896

Having become much interested in tracing the pedigrees of several Virginia families, I was advised to procure a copy of Hening's "Statutes", as a most indispensable adjunct in my researches. A hasty glance through its pages convinced me that it was a mine of genealogical lore. It substantiated with all the authority of Law, many statements of family history, for proof of which I had hitherto searched in vain. If so useful to me why not be made as useful to others?

I had arranged all the names in the original thirteen volumes, and was on the point of giving the manuscript to the Printer, when my attention was called to three supplemental volumes published as a continuation of Hening by Samuel Shepherd, Esq., of Richmond. A copy of Shepherd's book could not be found in New York. Had not assistance come to hand, my ambition to figure on the title page would have been nipped in the bud. W. W. Scott, Esq., Librarian of the State Library at Richmond, heard of my dilemma, and most generously enabled me to complete my work. With that courtesy so distinctive of the Virginian, it mattered not that I was an utter stranger to him. So whatever of praise the book may merit, Mr. Scott must have the greater share.

In the list, the volumes are numbered consecutively from I to XVI, the volumes I to XIII indicating Hening, the volumes XIV to XVI, the three supplemental volumes of Shepherd. The numeral in parenthesis indicates the number of times the name appears on the page. The foot-notes refer to the various spellings of what I have supposed to be the same name. Every name is printed exactly as found in the "Statutes", and discretion in Christian names has not been exercised except in cases where an inference was palpable.

JOSEPH J. CASEY.

26, East 129 St., New York.
2d May, 1896.

DEDICATED

BY PERMISSION

TO THE

SOCIETY OF COLONIAL DAMES

IN THE

STATE OF VIRGINIA.

A

ABBOT, III, 471
ABOTT, George, II, 158
ABOTT, George, VII, 206
  Samuel, XIII, 100(4).
  101
ABERCROMBIE, James, VII,
  371, 373(6), 374
ANKKMAN, Jacob, VII, 184
  John, VII, 184
ABERNETHY, Samuel, XIII,
  171, 581, 582(2)
  William, XIII, 171, 581,
  562(2)
ABET, George, VII, 209
ABNEY, XIV, 156
  Abraham, VI, 495
  William, VII, 201
ABRAHALL,* Robert, I, 530;
  II, 59, 159, 330
ABRAHAM, John, I, 499
ABRELL, Robert, I, 387
AHSTON, John, VII, 269
ABYVON, George, VIII, 454

ACKISS, John, XI, 270
ACRIL, William, V, 119
ACUFF, John, VII, 224

ADAM, David, VII, 212
ADAMS, IV, 267
  Andrew, I, 46
  Francis, XIII, 580(5),
    581; XVI, 168, 305
  George, VII, 207, 208,
    209; XII, 119, 282;
    XIII, 87, 275; XIV,
    267
  James, VIII, 149; XII,
    631, 719
  John, I, 29, 36; XIII,
    590; XVI, 35, 79, 90,
    335
  John, Junior, XV, 334
  Joseph, VII, 218

Nathan, VII, 224(2)
Richard, VII, 61, 224,
  569; VIII, 149(2),
  391, 422, 494; IX, 70;
  X, 313; XIII, 229;
  XV, 419; XVI, 95
ADAMS, Robert, VIII, 132;
  XI, 250; XIII, 583
  Robert, Junior, XI, 134,
    135
  Samuel, I, 36, 46
  Silvester, IX, 386; XIV,
    156?
  Thomas, I, 46; VII, 570;
    VIII, 149
ADDAIR, James, XIV, 321
ADDAMS, Robert, I, 129
ADDISON, IV, 268; V, 364;
  VI, 19(2); XIV, 153
  (2),
ADIE, Hugh, VI, 280(5),
  281
ADKINS, Gardner, VII, 191

AIMS, Moses, VIII, 130
AITCHISON, William, VII,
  435, 437; VIII, 299

ALBEMARLE, II, 528; V, 433
  (3), 434
ALBERT, William, XIV, 426
ALCOCKE, Thomas, I, 36
ALCONN, James, VII, 209
ALDERSON, XV, 168
  Curtis, XIII, 228(3)
  George, XIV, 312, 323
  John, XIV, 408
ALESTON, II, 200
ALEXANDER, XIV, 154
  Alexander John, VII,
    570
  Andrew, XV, 442
  Anne, V, 398(2)
  Archibald, VII, 195;
    XVI, 183

Charles, XV, 123
David, V, 399
Francis, VII, 190
Gerard, VI, 399(2), 400
  (7), 401(5)
Hugh, VII, 203
James, VII, 183, 185,
  188; XIII, 95; XV,
  223
John, VI, 402; VII, 605;
  VIII, 670; X, 192(2),
  193; XII, 205
ALEXANDER, John, Junior,
  VII, 605
  John Stewart, XIII, 580
    (3), 581
  Mark, XIV, 241
  Richard, XV, 179
  Robert, VI, 399, 400(3),
    401(3); XIII, 99(3),
    100; XV, 347(2)
  William, VIII, 625, 627;
    XI, 164; XII, 207;
    XIII, 137, 580; XIV,
    270; XV, 43
  William Thornton, XII,
    580, 581; XII, 481
ALFORD, Elizabeth, II, 161
  (4)
  John, II, 160, 161(3)
ALPORT, Thomas, VII, 215
ALGIER, Magis, VII, 186
ALINGTON, Richard George
  W., II, 511
ALISON, Ann, XIV, 163(4)
ALLEN, III, 568; VIII, 283,
  285
  Arthur, III, 41, 554
  Benjamin, XV, 30
  Charles, XI, 273; VIII,
    556; XV, 390, 425;
    XV, 353, 354
  Charles, Junior, VII,
    228
  Hannah, IV, 539(2),
    540(5)
  Hugh, VII, 190, 191
  James, VII, 190; XI,
    273; XII, 676; XIV,
    425
  James, Junior, VII, 190
  John, I, 87; IV, 539, 540

(5); VI, 242; VII, 216
  (2); XVI, 157(2)
John H., XVI, 406(2)
Jonathan, IV, 78
Joseph, IV, 539(3), 540
Julius, XII, 383
Mary, XV, 353, 354
Malcolm, VII, 203
Robert, VII, 196, 199;
  XII, 607
Robert, Junior, VII, 196
Samuel, XIV, 269, 311,
  328, 390; XV, 30, 99
Thomas, I, 86; VII, 216;
  XI, 57; XII, 631, 672
William, I, 138; IV, 539
  (2); VII, 568; VIII,
  67, 290; XIII, 316
  (2); XIV, 419; XV,
  339, 354(4)
ALLERTON, Isaac, II, 433
ALLGOOD, John, XVI, 419(3)
ALLISON, Charles, VII, 196
  John, XVI, 434
ALLYN, William, XIV, 322
ALLYNE, Samuel, XIII, 219,
  220
ALMON, William, XVI, 57
  (3)
ALMOND, Edmund, XIII, 223
ALSBURY, Thomas, XV, 379
ALSTON, John, VII, 204
ALTEPER, John, XVI, 29
ALTMAN, Thomas, V, 74

AMAN, Mathias, XV, 359
AMBLER, Edward, VII, 138
  Jaquelin, XI, 496, 511;
    XV, 71
  John, XVI, 52, 100
  John (widow of), XVI,
    52
  Richard, V, 371
AMIES, Thomas, III, 564
AMON, Matthias, XVI, 49
AMOX, James, VIII, 129

ANDERSON, V, 66; VI, 14;
  VII, 127; XIV, 156
  Andrew, XVI, 405
  Cecilia, XIII, 624(2),

1
2

625; XIV, 332(2)*,
  417(3)
Charles, XIII, 609(3)
Cuthbert, XV, 291
David, IV, 113; XVI,
  149, 212, 318
Francis, XIV, 390; XV,
  30
George, VII, 185, 195;
  XII, 583
Henry, VII, 201
Jacob, VII, 205
James, VII, 179, 180,
  187, 188; VIII, 405;
  XIII, 275
James, Junior, XVI, 173
Jasper, XVI, 149
John, VII, 194, 208, 214;
  X, 193(3), 194; XII,
  375, 404; XIII, 73,
  544; XIV, 158; XV,
  363; XVI, 223
Mary (Gist), XI, 54(4)
Matthew, XV, 67
Mead(e), X, 193(3),
  194; XIII, 193
Meade(t), XV, 114(3),
  120, 257(2); XVI,
  346
Meadis, XIII, 278
ANDERSON, Nathaniel, XIII,
  599; XIV, 425
  Paulin, IV, 142
  Peter, XV, 379
  Pouncey, VIII, 457
  Reynold, III, 479(2)
  Richard, VIII, 457
  Richard Clough, XII,
    395, 456; XVI, 377
    (2)
  Robert, VII, 187; XVI,
    221
  Rowland, II, 308(3)
  Samuel, XV, 30
  Thomas, VII, 126(2);
    IX, 334(2); XI, 29;
    XIII, 315, 316; XIV,
    156(2), 425; XVI,
    171(3)
  William, VI, 242; VII,
    190, 195, 209, 224;
    XI, 54(2); XII, 83,

673(3), 674; XIII, 73,
  623, 624(3); XIV,
  155, 269, 332(2); 417
  (2); XV, 70(2)
ANDREWES, William, I, 549
  (4)
ANDREWS, IV, 268
  James, IV, 462
  John, I, 85
  John, Junior, I, 36
  Nicholas, I, 84
  Richard, VII, 206, 209
  Robert, IX, 314, 328; X,
    521, 524, 528, 530,
    531(2), 532, 533(2),
    534(2), 535; XI, 554
    (2), 555, 556; XII,
    492; XIII, 145; XIV,
    308; XVI, 50
  William, I, 384; II, 197,
    198, 205
ANDROS, Edmund, III, 8(2),
  125, 136, 165
ANDRUS, Richard, V, 369
ANGLIN, Samuel, XIII, 565
  William, XIII, 565; XV,
    425
ANNANDALE, William, V,
  196
ANNE OF DENMARK, III, 423
ANNE, QUEEN, III, 176, 218,
  224, 227, 229, 231,
  235, 237(2), 238(2),
  240, 241(2), 242(2),
  247, 248, 253, 308,
  310, 311, 327, 355,
  397, 440, 442, 454,
  481, 482(2), 486, 493
  (2), 497, 499, 501,
  502, 503, 504, 505,
  506(2), 509; IV, 9,
  30, 31, 57(2), 46, 55,
  57, 81, 93, 115, 125,
  151, 152, 168, 179,
  222, 420, 429, 548,
  554, 555, 561, 565; V,
  69, 245, 272, 304, 432;
  VI, 53, 101, 151, 481;
  VII, 56
ANON, James, VII, 191
ANTHONY, V, 66; VI, 15;
  VII, 127; XIII, 166

Charles, I, 83
John, VII, 206, 207;
  VIII, 585
Joseph, XIII, 297; XIV,
  316; XV, 210
ANTROBUS, George, II, 583

APPERCHANKING, V, 297(4),
  298(4), 299
APPLING, John, VII, 201

ARBAUGH, Joseph, XIV, 322
ARBUCKLE, James, VII, 194,
  635; VIII, 129
  Charles, XV, 53, 173
  John, VIII, 129
  Matthew, VIII, 129
ARCHER, VIII, 556(2), 562
  (2); XIV, 155; XV,
  263, 350
  Abraham, XIV, 308
  Edward, VII, 437; XV,
    23, 447
  Gabriel, I, 83
  John, VI, 277; XII, 591;
    XIII, 153(2), 293;
    XIV, 390; XV, 259
  Peter Field,* XIII, 293;
    XIV, 390; XV, 188,
    259
  Sampson, VII, 179, 180,
    183, 104(3)†
  William, VII, 592; XVI,
    409
ABELL, Christiana, XV, 65
  (2)
  David,† XV, 65(3)
  Richard, XV, 65(2)
  Samuel, XV, 65(3)
ARGALL, I, 3
ARCENBRIGHT, George, XIV,
  322
ARISS, John, VIII, 624
ARLINGTON, II, vi, 427, 511,
  516(2), 519(5), 520
  (2), 521(4), 522(2),
  563, 569(2), 570, 571,
  572(2), 573(3), 574
  (2), 575(5), 576(4),
  577(6), 578(3), 579,
  580(2), 581(2), 582
  (5), 583(3)

ARMESTEAD,§ Anthony, II,
  530, 545
ARMISTEAD, Anna, VI, 243
  Anna (Lee), IV, 443
    (2), 444, 445(4)
  Bowles, VIII, 487, 667,
    668(2), 669(3)
  Dun, VI, 242
  Henry, VIII, 487, 668
  John, III, 560(2), 565
    (2); VI, 243, 405(5),
    406(7), 407, 443(3),
    444(10), 445(2);
    VIII, 446, 487(2), 488
    (4), 489(2), 580, 667,
    668(3); XIV, 331
  Judith (Dray Ingles),
    VI, 413, 415(4), 416
    (2)
  Lucy, XIV, 331(2), 332
    (2)
  Mary, VIII, 446
  Robert, XII, 375, 534,
    732; XVI, 427
  Robert B., XVI, 427
  Susanna, IV, 444(2)
  Susanna (Meriwether)
    VI, 405, 406
  Theoderick, XV, 437;
    XVI, 40, 58, 100, 136
    413, 415(6), 416(2),
    443, 444(2); VIII,
    487(5), 488(5), 489
    (4), 490, 667(4), 668
    (5), 669(4); XII,
    380, 361, 420
ARMONTROUT, Christopher,
  VII, 187
ARMSTEAD, XIV, 155
  Anthoney, III, 181, 202
ARMSTRONG, James, XII,
  262; XIII, 582
  John, VII, 187, 199;
    VIII, 127; XV, 228
  Lantey, VIII, 127
  Maxwell, XIII, 292;
    XV, 249
  Robert, VII, 191, 192
  Thomas, VII, 190
  William, VII, 189, 199

3
4

*See Abrell.   †Sylvester.
*Cleaty.   †Mead.
*Peterfield.   †Samson.   ‡Arel.   §Armestead.

ARNOLD, III, 569; X, 576;
XVI, 176
Anthony, II, 370, 461,
560
George, XIII, 292
James, VII, 201; XIII,
292
Stephen, XII, 631
ARNOTT, Thomas, V, 119,
120(2)
ARRENTON, Samuel, VII, 205
ARRENTROT, John, VII, 194
ARTHINGTON, Jeptha, VII,
211
ARTHUR, Barnabas, VII, 206
Barnabas, Junior, VII,
206
James, VI, 275, 288
John, XV, 233, 234
William, VII, 206, 207;
XVI, 129
ARUNDELL, John,* I, 170,
187, 203
ARVIN, Mary, XII, 363(5)

ASBERRY, John, XV, 270
Joseph,† XV, 245(2),
274, 291(3)
ASHBY, V, 208, 300; XV,
110, 298, 299 (2);
XVI, 51
ASNELEY, II, 511
ASHER, William, VII, 220
ASHLEY, XII, 524
John, I, 83
William, VII, 225
ASHLY, Anthony, I, 81
ASHMORE, William, VII, 631,
632, 633
ASHTON, Henry, VIII, 640,
641; XIV, 152
John, II, 156, 157(2)
Peter, I, 414, 422, 530;
II, 16
Roger, I, 82
ASHWORTH, Isaac, VII, 223
John, VII, 223; VIII,
132
Samuel, VII, 223
ASKEW, James, I, 84
ASKINS, John, XII, 363(4)
AST, William Frederick,

XIV, 308(3), 309,
413, 414
ASTON, Walter, I, 147, 154,
168, 178, 186, 202,
239
ATCHISON, Thomas, VI, 281
ATHER, John, VII, 225
ATKINS, Edward, VII, 224
Frass, VII, 24
ATKINS, John, I, 149
Richard, II, 328
Thomas, IV, 532; VI,
20; XIV, 156
ATKINSON, John, XV, 124
Roger, VI, 277, 294;
VII, 569, 602; XVI,
62
Roger, Junior, XIII, 570
Thomas, XV, 213
William, I, 84; VIII,
226(2)
ATWELL, Thomas, VII, 229

AUBREY, XIV, 153
Thomas, VIII, 369
AUCHER, Anthony, I, 82, 83
AUSTIN, XIV, 158
James, II, 330
John, VII, 225
Joseph, VII, 227
Moses, XIII, 541
Peter, II, 154(2)
Thomas, XV, 353
Walter, I, 262
& Company, XIV, 158
AVERA, Alexander, VI, 508
(2), 509(2)
AVERY, Billy Haley, XII, 364
AVERY, George D., XVI, 209
John, VII, 201; XVI,
346
William H., XV, 265
AVEY, Christian, VII, 181

AWBREY, Francis, V, 66;
VII, 218

AYERS, James, XVI, 38
John, XVI, 38
AYLETT,‡ IV, 267, 335, 383,

385, 387, 481; V, 137,
142, 144; VI, 169,
173, 176; VIII, 78, 98,
100, 324; IX, 154,
160, 488, 510, 513; X,
273, 356, 475; XI,
211, 235, 237; XII,
404; XIII, 479, 503,
677, 678(2); XV,
156(2), 274(2)

B

BABB, James, IV, 529
BACHE, George, I, 86
William, XV, 271
BACHELIER, Thomas, II, 583
(2)
BACON, Francis, I, 82, 90
Langston, XVI, 403
Liddal,* VII, 226; VIII,
645
Nathaniel, I, 422, 499,
506, 512(2); II, 31,
147, 159, 320, 330,
342(4), 544(2), 545
(2), 546, 547, 548,
549, 551(2), 553, 554,
557, 560, 563, 568,
569; III, 8(2), 562,
557, 570(2)
Nathaniel, Junior, II,
iv(4), vi, 349(5),
367, 368, 370, 373
(3), 374(4), 375(6),
376(3), 377, 380, 391
(2), 395, 404(2), 405,
423(2), 424(2), 425,
426(2), 428, 429(2),
440, 458, 459(2), 460
(5), 461(2), 509, 528,
531, 543(5), 544(3),
545(3), 548, 555, 556,
569; III, 541, 542, 567
(2); XV, 471, 410
BADGER, John, I, 85
BAGGE, James,† I, 67 ,77
BAGNALL, James, I, 322, 386
BAGWELL, Charles, IX, 310;
XII, 636(5)

Anne, VIII, 283, 284
(2), 265(2)
John, VIII, 283(4), 284
(3)
Philip, XII, 404(2);
XIV, 164, 266(2),
267; XVI, 223(2)
William, VIII, 284, 580
AYRES, John, X, 325
AYRES, Nathan, XIV, 328

Henry, I, 149, 179
John, II, 371, 379, 557
Thomas, I, 138, 381
BAILEY, III, 472
Anselm, VI, 240
Anselm,‡ Junior, VI,
240
BAILEY, Charles, XI, 185
James C., XVI, 140, 346
Jeremiah Garland, VII,
531(3)
John, XI, 335, 336
Nathaniel, VII, 215
Peter, VII, 215
Thomas, XII, 402
BAINE, Robert, K, 452(8)
BAIRD, XII, 676
Adam, XVI, 280(2)
David, XII, 718, 719
(3); XIII, 42
James, XII, 676, 719
John, VII, 609; XI, 57
BAKER, Abraham, XIV, 322
Benjamin, VIII, 660;
IX, 400, 488
Humphrey, VIII, 129
James, V, 271; VI, 275,
288; XIII, 297
Jerman, VIII, 302
John, I, 85; XIII, 224
(2); XVI, 423
Laur(ence), II, 249
Lawrence, VI, 288;
XIV, 431
Martin, II, 38, 158
Michael, XIII, 216
Richard, VI, 451; VIII,

462; XVI, 226
Thomas, ‖I, 555(2),
VII, 210, 214
William, V, 200(2); VI,
508; VII, 213; XII,
393
BALDRY, Robert, I, 530
BALDWIN, Abraham, I, 23
Cornelius, XIV, 334;
XVI, 52
John, VII, 201
BALENTINE,* Hugh, XVI, 72,
398
BALFOUR, James, V, 370
BALL, II, 257; IV, 363; VI,
18; XIV, 154
Burgess, X, 469, 470
(5); XV, 214
Hannah, III, 60
Henry, I, 323
James, IV, 452, 453(2);
X, 469, 470
James, Junior, XII, 215
James Wallace, XII, 215
BALL, Jesse, V, 250
Joseph, VII, 52
Spencer, XVI, 395
William, II, 329
BALLAH, Augusta, XVI, 224
BALLARD, Edmond, VII, 202
John, V, 370
Francis, XIII, 267;
XIV, 169; XV, 309
Servant, IV, 440
Thomas, II, 225, 226,
249, 254, 320, 488,
545, 546, 547, 548,
551, 560; III, 428; V,
60
William, XI, 185
BALLENDINE, John, XI, 462
BALLENGER, XIII, 42, 481
Henry, XVI, 429
John, VII, 213
BALLENTINE, Hugh, XV, 63;
XVI, 172
BALLER, John, XIV, 266
BALLINGER, XIV, 425(2)
BALTICE, Leonard, VII, 475
BALTIMORE, I, 425, 552; II,
183, 184(5), 200, 426;
VIII, 368; X, 526(3)

BANDFORD, VII, 515
BANDY, Richard, X, 325
BANGER, John, VII, 214
BANISTER, II, 382; XII, 593;
XIII, 569; XIV, 390
John, I, 46; VI, 485;
VIII, 494, 606
John Monroe, XVI, 376
Richard, I, 83
BANKS, Alexander, XIII, 314
Henry, XII, 282, 639,
725, 726; XV, 49, 419;
XVI, 354
John, I, 83
Judith, IX, 574, 575(3)
Miles, I, 86
Ralph, V, 214(3), 215,
216, 306, 307; VII,
293(4), 295
Robert, VI, 243
Tunstel, VII, 293, 294
(4), 295(6); VIII,
478(2)
William, V, 214(4),
215(5), 216(3), 306
(5), 307(6), 308(2);
VII, 293(3), 294(3),
295(2), 296; XIII,
582; XIV, 241; XV,
210, 309; XVI, 182
William B., XVI, 268
BANKSON, Benjamin, Junior,
XI, 575
BANNISTER, John, VIII, 602
BAPTISTA, John, II, 370, 375
(2), 377, 547(2)
BARBER, IV, 479; V, 15; VI,
428, 429(2), 430
John, I, 548
Richard, VIII, 57
Thomas, I, 83
BARBOUR, James, XIII, 142
(2), 143(5), 144;
XV, 271
Mordecai, XV, 176
Philip, XI, 470
BARCLAY, Robert, XV, 223
BARDIN, James, VII, 223
BARDWELL, William, I, 84
BARE, Jacob, XV, 377
BARHAM, Anthony, I, 148

Charles, IV, 377; VI,
239
BARKER, II, 424, 533, 567
Edmonds, VII, 212
Lewis, VII, 212
Robert, I, 85
BARKLEY, George, VII, 198
William, XIII, 151;
XIV, 242
BARKLY, William, XIII, 292
BARKSDALE, XVI, 27
Beverley, XIII, 275
Nathaniel, VII, 588
Peter, XV, 380
William, XII, 792; XIII,
41, 42(3), 481(2),
504, 599
BARKSHIRE, Ralph, XVI, 235
BARLER, Adam, VII, 23
Christopher, VII, 23
BARLOW, John, XVI, 432
Kitty, XVI, 432
BARNARD, Allan, XV, 355(3)
John, XIV, 269
BARNARS, Anthony, I, 83
BARNES, Edward, I, 84
Lancelott, I, 149
Leonard, XIII, 217
Richard, IV, 378
Thomas, XVI, 224
William, I, 83
BARNET, Alexander, XVI,
193(2)
James, XII, 202
John, VII, 212
Joseph, XII, 676
Robert, VII, 204
BARNETT, XV, 346
James, XIII, 87, 585
John, XIV, 260(2),
261, 267(2); XV, 342
(4); XVI, 136, 346
Thomas, I, 179; XV,
342(2); XVI, 217
William, I, 372
BARNHART, Daniel, XIII, 585
BARON, Christopher, I, 85
BARR, John, IX, 320(4), 321
(2)
Robert, XIII, 231
William, VII, 24
Zachariah, IX, 320

BARRAUD, Philip, XVI, 68
BARRET, Charles, IV, 372,
373, 374; XII, 375
Hancock, X, 124
John, XIII, 316
William, VI, 383(2);
XIII, 204
William E., XVI, 246
(2)
BARRETT, XIV, 155
Charles, XV, 121
William,* I, 289, 322,
358
BARRINGTON, I, 142
Robert, I, 148
BARRON, James, XI, 195;
XII, 299
Robert, XV, 309
BARROW, Thomas, VII, 185
BARRY, John, VI, 396, 397
BARTER, Ardree, XIII, 223
BARTILEY,† Morrice, I, 78
BARTLETT, John, XIII, 607
Josiah, I, 36, 46
BARTLEY, Joshua, XIV, 336
BARTON, Richard, II, 370
(2), 379(2)
Valentine, VII, 25
BASCOMB,† Benjamin, VI,
375(2); XIV, 155
BASKERFIELD, John, VII, 248
(2), 453, 454; VIII,
460
BASKERVILLE, William, XIII,
296
BASKINE, John, VII, 187
Thomas, VII, 187
BASS, Nathaniel, I, 129
BASSE,§ Nathaniel, I, 129,
139, 140, 153, 169
BASSET,‖ V, 143; VI, 173;
VIII, 79
Burwell, VIII, 149, 302;
XVI, 50, 197
Richard, I, 22
William, II, 220(2); V,
279, 282
BASYE, James, XV, 121
Joseph, XV, 121
BATEMAN, Robert, I, 85
BATES, David, XV, 48(2),
67, 120

Joseph, VIII, 128
Thomas Fleming, XII, 682
BATHURST, V, 559
Thomas, I, 85
Timothy, I, 86
BATSON, Margery, XII, 294
Samuel, VII, 24
BATT, Henry, IV, 363
William, I, 386
BATTAILE, Hay, XV, 157
Lawrence, VI, 495; XII, 698; XVI, 157
BATTE, Henry, VI, 13, 14; X, 365; XII, 404; XIV, 155
Thomas, X, 365(2); XII, 405(6)
William, I, 506
BATTERSBY, VI, 21
William, V, 365
BATTSON, Nathaniel, I, 385
BAUGH, John, I, 289
Peter, V, 66; VI, 15; XIV, 155
BAXTER, Alexander, VII, 23
Edmund, XIII, 218
BAYARD, John, X, 534
BAYLESS, Charles, XII, 299
BAYLEY, Anselm, Junior, VI, 240
Edward, III, 565, 566 (2); V, 368
Jeremiah Garland, VIII, 79
Richard, III, 564
Thomas, I, 86
BAYLEYS. Charles, XIV, 169
BAYLIS, John, VII, 24, 427, 472(2); VIII, 158
William, VII, 24, 25; VIII, 133
BAYLOR, Gregory, VIII, 633; X, 103
John, V, 289; VI, 394; VII, 64, 485, 568; VIII, 477, 489; XII, 698; XIII, 287, 676
John, Junior, VIII, 580
Walker, XII, 396
BAYLY, III, 220
Arthur, I, 239

Pierce, XV, 223
BAYNHAM, Richard, XV,·67
BAYNHAM, Alexander, I, 387
BAYTOP, James, XIII, 137; XV, 67
Thomas, XV, 67
BEACHAM, Rebecca, VII, 52

BEADLES, John, XIV, 322
BEAKER, Abraham, XIV, 312
BEAL, John, XIII, 171
BEALL, Samuel, XII, 496
Walter, XII, 580(3), 581, 631(2), 632, 676, 155, 348
BEALE, Charles, XVI, 46, 72, 155, 348
Edward, I, 86
John, VIII, 201; XV, 46(2), 167(3)
Taverner, VIII, 624
Thomas, II, 320, 406, 421, 544
719
BEAMONT, Samuel, XIV, 428
BEARD, Adam, VII, 207
John, VI, 381, 506; XV, 49
Stephen, XV, 228
William, VII, 193, 194
BEASLEY, John, XIII, 607
BEATTY, Henry, XV, 260
BEAUCHAMP, John, I, 546
BEAUMARCNAIS, Caron de, XIII, 339(2); XVI, 22
BEAUMONT. Samuel, XV, 176
BEAZLEY, Job, I, 414
BECKLEY, Charles, XV, 30
John, I, 29, 31; IX, 176; X, 520(2), 536, 537, 538(3), 639, 541, 543, 544, 545, 559, 567(2), 568, 569, 570; XI, 611, 545, 552, 553; XII, 690; XIII, 629
BECKNEL, William, VII, 203
BECKWITH, Marmaduke, V, 148, 145; VI, 177, 224; VIII, 79, 98, 323; IX, 154, 161, 488, 511

Marmaduke B., XVI, 177
BEDFORD, I, 101; V, 559; VII, 437; XI, 557
Benjamin, XII, 603
Gunning, Junior, I, 22
Thomas, VII, 307; XIV, 422(4)
BEDINGER, Daniel, XVI, 130
Solomon, XVI, 100
BEEDEL, Gabriel, I, 84
John, I, 84
BEELOR, George, XIV, 410
BEEMAN, Edmond, II, 158
BEEN, John, VII, 204
BEESON, Jacob, XVI, 209
BEIMER, Frederick, XVI, 31
BEIRNE, Andrew, XVI, 398
BELCHE, Robert, VII, 186
BELCHES, William, XII, 608
BELFIELD, John, V, 285(4), 286(6), 287
Mary, V, 285(2), 286 (2), 287
Thomas Wright, V, 285
BELL, Benjamin, XII, 631
David, VII, 187; VIII, 412(2); XII, 657*; 661; XIII, 316(2), 587
George, VII, 215
Henry, XII, 657*; XIII, 315, 316; XIV, 269
Humphrey, VII, 130
James, VII, 181, 190, 191; VIII, 625
John, VII, 191; XVI, 100
John M., XIII, 143, 144 (2)
Joseph, VII, 190; XIII, 554; XV, 291
Mary, VIII, 472
Moore, XIV, 337(4)
Nathaniel, VII, 214
Samuel, VII, 191
Thomas, VII, 225, 420, 421; XIII, 159; XVI, 308, 330
William, VII, 192; VIII, 131, 472
BELSCHES, James, XII, 364

BENDER,† Elliott, VII, 325
John Weldrick, VIII, 130
BENGER, Elliot, VII, 446; VIII, 28
BENIGAR, Henry, VII, 184
BENN, George, VII, 226; XIII, 300
James, VI, 375(2); XIV, 155
BENNET, I, 425; IV, 528; VI, 375; XIV, 155
George, I, 85; VII, 215
Richard, I, 187, 235, 288, 297(2); VIII, 287(2), 288(4), 289
William, I, 86; XII, 386 (3); XIII, 288, 289
BENNETT, I, 288(4), 427; XVI, 110, 135, 140, 185, 345, 433
Jacob, XV, 223, 224
Philip, I, 289
Richard, I, 5(4), 139, 140, 169, 238, 322, 365, 367, 368, 371, 377, 383, 385, 388, 392, 407(2), 408(2), 431, 432, 604, 526, 529; II, 225, 226, 320; VII, 304, 305
Thomas, I, 179; XV, 49
William, XVI, 100
BENNING, John, VII, 305
Joseph, VII, 205
BENNINGHAM, Henry, VII, 179
BENSON, X, 315
Nicholas, I, 85
Peter, I, 85
BENTLEY, Efford, XV, 30
Peter E, XVI, 402
Thomas, XI, 437
William, I, 130; XIII, 293; XIV, 319; XV, 425; XVI, 184(3), 188(5), 409
William A, XVI, 402
BENTLY, John, IV, 535; VIII, 131
BENTON, Epaphraditus, IV, 528
BENTS, Alexander, I, 84

BERET, Dimnick, VII, 191
BERKELEY, II, 559
Edmund, VI, 407
Edward, I, 86
Frances (Stephens), II, 321, 323(7), 324(4), 326(2), 568(4), 559 (6)
George, I, 84
BERKELEY, John, I, 111, 116; IV, 616(2), 616(2), 617, 618(3)
Morrice, I, 78
Maurice, I, 81, 90
Nelson, XIV, 243, 268; XV, 155
Norbonne,* VIII, 5(3)
William, I, v, xiii, xiv, xx, 4(3), 5(6), 84, 86, 235, 267†(2), 282, 284, 286, 309, 321, 322, 338, 339, 356, 357(2), 366(2), 375, 364(2), 407(3), 408, 427, 526(2), 527, 528 (6), 529(5), 530, 543(4), 544(4), 545, 546(2), 547(2), 649, 550(3); II, vi(2), vii (2), 9, 10(4), 13, 17 (2), 31(2), 32, 33, 99, 147, 148(2), 152 (2), 163, 165, 172, 176, 179, 195, 196, 200, 204, 213, 218, 223, 228, 248, 251, 252, 254, 263, 276, 285, 292, 302, 310, 314, 315(2), 319(5), 320(6), 321(6), 323 (5), 324(4), 325(3), 340, 359, 365, 366, 368, 374, 401, 414, 423, 424(3), 429(2), 461(3), 509, 511(2), 516, 517(3), 519, 531, 643(2), 545(2), 547, 548(2), 549, 551, 553, 554, 655, 556, 558(6), 659(2), 560(2), 564 (3), 665, 566, 567; III, 642(2), 543, 667

(2), 568(4), 569(2); XIV, 166; XV, 267
BERKENHEAD, II, 204(2)
BERKLEY, John, VII, 21
William, II, 249
BERNARD, Allen, XV, 31
Joseph, XV, 31
Richard, VI, 175; VIII, 79
Robert, IV, 458(6)
Thomas, I, 236, 283, 289
William, I, 239, 288, 322, 339, 408, 432, 499, 505, 508, 516, 526; IV, 457, 468(3), 459; VII, 569
BERRY, Benjamin, XV, 121
James, VIII, 129
John, II, 548, 649, 555; VII, 213; XI, 363; XVI, 161
Joseph, VI, 17; XIII, 151; XV, 163
Richard, VII, 224
Thomas, XI, 363; XIII, 544
William, VII, 24
BERRISFORD, Robert, I, 86
BERRYMAN, John, XII, 216; XV, 184
BEST, VI, 174
BETTS, Charles, VII, 51(2), 53
BEVANS, Thomas, VII, 131
William, VII, 64
BEVERLEY, III, 9, 222, 650; IV, 59
Carter, XV, 61(4), 62
Christopher,† VIII, 228
Harry, IV, 74, 235; VI, 403; VIII, 166(5), 167(3), 168, 280(4), 281(6), 282(2); XII, 219(2)
John, VIII, 228(2)
Peter,‡ II, 162; III, 97, 106, 107(3), 117, 118 (2), 125(3), 136, 165, 167(3), 181, 203, 216, 217, 223, 226, 228, 495(2), 496, 550; IV, 29, 50, 67, 74, 136,

137(4), 138(4); VIII 228(2)
Robert,* I, vi, xiii, 119, 121, 146, 513, 526; II, 309, 371, 380, 401, 406, 420(2), 423; 424, 426, 428, 432, 454, 457(4), 470, 488 (2), 489, 545, 552(3), 557, 561(2); III, 9, 39(5), 41, 181, 202, 542(3), 543(7), 544 (4), 545(4), 546(5), 547(5), 548(3), 549 (2), 550(2), 551(3), 552(5), 553(6), 554 (4), 555(4), 556(8), 557(4), 559, 560(4), 561(2), 562(7), 563, 564(3), 565(7), 566 (6), 567(7), 568(5), 559(5), 570(5); VI, 243; VII, 620, 637; VIII, 165(2), 168(3), 169, 227(2), 228(5), 229(6), 280, 281, 282 (3)
Robert, Junior, XIV, 244, 245(2)
Robert Gaines, XII, 219 (4)
Thomas, VIII, 228(2)
William, IV, 116; V, 289(2), 321, 402(2), 403; VII, 473, 474; VIII, 228(2); XII, 601
BEVIL, VIII, 604
BEWTOOLE, Gasper, VII, 216
BIBB, XVI, 184
John, XIV, 156
William, XII, 665; XIII, 655; XV, 182(3), 183
BICKLEY, Humphrey, VII, 222
BIERS, William, VIII, 302
BIGGE, Richard, I, 129
BIGGERMAN, XI, 366
BIGGS, Benjamin, XIII, 297
Joseph, XIV, 418(2); XV, 463

RIGS. John, VII, 204
DILBERRY, Benjamin, X, 372 (2)
BILLING, Thomas, VIII, 130
BILLINGSLEY, I, 385
John, II, 162
Elizabeth, II, 162(2)
John, II, 162
BILLIOTT, Widow, I, 409
BILLUPS, Richard, XIII, 137
BINGAMAN, Christian, VII, 186
John, VII, 186
BINGHAM, John, I, 82
Roscow Cole, XII, 693 (4)
Stephen, XII, 693(2)
BINNS, V, 370
Charles, VI, 240
BIRCHETT, Robert, XVI, 62, 100, 376
XIV, 419
BIRD, Abraham, XI, 57; XIV, 419
Robert Armistead, V, 364; VI, 17
William, II, 434(3), 448, 453(2), 454(2), 470(2)
BIRK, Elizabeth VII, 202
BISCOE, Henry L, XV, 374
William, XV, 348(3);
BISKOP, Edward, I, 85
XVI, 30(2)
BISHOPP, John, I, 283
BIST, Abraham, VII, 199
BLACK, IX, 259; XIV, 156
Anthony, VII, 190
David, XVI, 417(3)
John, VII, 170, 180, 190, 191; XV, 133, 233, 234, 359
Joseph, IX, 555
Matthew, VII, 181, 184, 186
Robert, VII, 186, 188
Samuel, XVI, 149, 179
Thomas, VII, 190
William, VII, 181; VIII, 45; XV, 419; XVI, 155, 186, XV, 192(2), 133
BLACKBOURNE, Benjamin, XIII, 616

BLACKBURN, Andrew, VII, 216, 217
Benjamin, VII, 216
John, VII, 217
Samuel, VII, 217; XVI, 94, 100
Thomas, IX, 61; XII, 372; XIII, 680
William, VII, 216
BLACKBURNE, B e n j a m i n, XIV, 278 (5); XV, 182(2)
Thomas, VIII, 494, 627; XII, 604; XVI, 395
BLACKE, William, I, 512
BLACKEMORE, Joseph, XIV, 322
BLACKMORE, George, XV, 121
Thomas, VII, 230
BLACKSTONE, III, 171
BLACKWELL, VI, 16(2); VII, 466, 487; VIII, 641; XIV, 154
Armistead, XV, 120
James, VIII, 641(2), 642(5), 643(3)
John, VIII, 642(2); XII, 217; XV, 120
John, Junior, XIII, 92
Joseph, XV, 223, 282
Josiah, VIII, 642
Samuel, VII, 51(3), 52 (6); XV, 223
BLACKWOOD, William, VII, 179, 180, 190
BLACKY, William, I, 431
BLAGG, John, VII, 493
BLAIN, David, XVI, 403
BLAIN, William, XVI, 231
BLAIR, Archibald, III, 431; IV, 115(3); XI, 552
James, VIII, 171(2); XV, 216
John, I, 22; V, 321; VI, 197, 227, 230; VII, 164, 195(2), 214, 288, 568, 647(2); VIII, 5, 209, 346, 378, 501, 578, 649(2), 662; IX, 103; XI, 548
John, Junior, VII, 568;

VIII, 213, 365, 378
John D. XVI, 335
BLAKE, James H., XVI, 337, 379
John, II, 249, 250
BLAMIRE, James, XVI, 188
BLANCHARD, Aaron, IV, 528
Thomas, XV, 447; XVI, 40, 58
BLANCHETT, Robert, VII, 201
BLANCKEVILE, Charles, II, 654(3)
BLAND, II, 518, 519(3), 520 (7), 521(8), 622, 523, 525, 527(3), 529, 531 (2), 533, 545, 549, 555(2), 561; III, 30, 543, 546(2), 548(2), 550(3), 551; IV, 266; V, 143
Edward, VI, 303(3), 304(3), 305, 306; XVI, 410
Giles,* II, 370, 461, 550
John, II, 199(3); VI, 303(5), 304(2), 306
John, Junior, VII, 24
Margaret, VI, 304(3)
Peter, XVI, 410
Peter Randolph, VII, 609
Richard, I, 3, 223, 224, 230, 370, 551; II, vii, 13, 249, 509; III, 8; IV, 5; V, 66; VI, 14, 418, 437, 485, 507, 524; VII, 13, 39(2), 76, 116, 120, 127, 229, 276, 288, 354, 568, 637, 647; VIII, 67, 115, 169, 175, 367, 494, 578, 606; IX, 49, 95, 230; XV, 161, 266
Richard, Junior, VII, 229, 568
BLAND, Sarah, VI, 303(4), 304(2), 305, 307(2), 308
Theodorick,† I, 527(2), 543(2), 549(2); II, 199(3); VII, 570,

613; XII, 792; XV, 128
Theodorus, II, 15
BLANE, Alexander, XII, 396
BLANKENBECKER, J o n a s, XV, 223
BLANKENSHIP, S t e p h e n, VIII, 128
BLANKS, Richard, VII, 300
William, VII, 223
BLANTON, XIV, 156
James, VII, 588; XIII, 296, 298, 574, 575
BLANY, Edward, I, 129
BLATT, John, XIII, 108(4)
BLEDSOE, Anthony, VII, 127
Peachy, XIV, 281
BLEVINS, James, VII, 220
John, VII, 220(2)
William, VII, 220
William, Junior, VII, 220
BLINCOE, John, IV, 116
BLOODWORTH, VII, 256(2)
BLOR, John, VII, 183
BLOUNT, Richard A, XV, 338
Samuel, XVI, 346
William, I, 22
BLOW, Henry, XVI, 346
John, VIII, 589
John Thomas, XI, 159 (2); XII, 386; XIII, 289, 549
Richard, XIII, 159, 175; XV, 23, 365, 437, 447; XVI, 100
Richard, Junior, V, 271
William, XVI, 346
BLUDDER, Thomas, I, 82
BLUE, John, Junior, VIII, 275
BLUNDELL, John, I, 82
BLUNT, Benjamin, XIII, 173, 297
John, I, 86
Thomas, VIII, 589
BLYTH, Joseph, XV, 55

BOARD, James, VII, 207, 209
William, VII, 209
BOATE, Nicholas, II, 16
BOBINGTON, Ma., II, 583

BOGGESS, Vincent, VII, 21
BOGGS, John, XII, 614
BOISE,* Chene, I, 138, 147, 178
BOLDIN, Thomas, VII, 224
BOLIN, Garrel, VII, 22
BOLLARD, Thomas, III, 570
BOLLING, V, 143, 233(2), 234; VI, 14, 173, 177, 224, 226, 293, 352(2), 473, 485(2), 486(2); VII, 46(2), 48(2); 128, 334; VIII, 78, 97, 100(4), 101(3); IX, 154, 159, 160, 488, 510, 513(2), 514; X, 273, 356, 475; XI, 210, 235, 237(2), 238 (2); XIII, 479, 502; XIV, 155
Alexander, IV, 363; VI, 14; VIII, 290; X, 365; XII, 404
David, VIII, 131
John, IV, 266, 331(2), 382(2), 387; V, 136, 143, 145, 233(3), 234; VI, 172, 176, 226, 277, 293, 294, 352, 473; VII, 24, 532, 533, VIII, 78, 98, 100(4), 101(6), 236.322, 412; IX, 154, 159, 160, 488, 510, 513(3), 514; X, 273, 356, 475; XI, 210, 235, 237, 238(3); XII, 65; XIII, 479, 503
Lennaeus, I, v
Powhatan, XIII, 296; XV, 99
Robert, VII, 294, 351; VII, 531(2), 533(2), 592, 602, 608; VIII, 78, 101(2), 236, 291, 292(2), 293, 508, 509 (5), 510, 606; X, 565; XI, 382, XII, 64(2); XIII, 599; XV, 155; XV, 66, 207(4), 218, 297, 351; XVI, 62, 268, 434

Robert, Junior, VIII, 35, 62, 149; XII, 792; XIII, 42, 174, 481
Thomas, VIII, 149
William, VII, 25; XVI, 330
BOLLS, George, I, 83
BOLTON, IV, 363; VI, 19; XIV, 156
BOMMAN, VIII, 44
BOND, George, XI, 570
Hance, XIII, 216
John, I, 386, 431, 506, 528; II, 39
BOND, Martin, I, 84
Thomas, VIII, 132
BOODLE, III, 569
BOOKER, VII, 126; XV, 97 (2)
Edward, VIII, 554; XIII, 626(7), 627; XIV, 156
George, XII, 635
James, XIII, 137
Richard, VII, 201; XIII, 273(3), 481(3), 505
William, XI, 273
BOON, XI, 580, 581
Daniel, X, 135
Jacob, XIII, 585
BOONE, Daniel, XII, 361, 633
Jacob, XII, 633
Levi, XV, 425(2)
BOOT, Nicholas, II, 34
BOOTH, David, VII, 214
Elizabeth, VIII, 640(4), 641(2)
George, XV, 67
Henry, I, 146
Robert, I, 379, 387
William, VIII, 391, 640 (6), 641
BORELAND, James, VII, 182, 192, 199
BORELANE, James, VII, 196
BORNE, Robert, I, 431
BOSHER, Charles, XVI, 408 (5)
BOSWELL, XI, 310
John, VIII, 131, 457
Joseph, VI, 446, 447
Machen, XIII, 137

William C., XVI, 309(2)
BOTETOURT, VII, 192
BOTT, Joel, XV, 31, 55
John, XIV, 416(2)
BOTTERS, Jacob, VII, 196
BOTTS, Alexander, L, IX, li; X, li(3); XI, li(3)
Benjamin, XVI, 236
BOUCHER, Daniel, I, 379
BOUDINOT, Elias, XI, 551
BOULDEN, Thomas, VII, 307
BOULDIN, Joseph, XIII, 297
BOURAN, William, XIII, 560
BOURNE, David, I, 84
BOUSH, VI, 176; XI, 318
Arthur, VIII, 454
Caleb, XIV, 308; XV, 23
Goodrich, VII, 435, 437; VIII, 269; XIII, 207; XV, 60
John, XIII, 226(4)
Mary, XIII, 207(4); XV, 60(3)
Philip, VII, 236
Samuel, v, 142, .144; VI, 173, 227; VII, 435, 437; VIII, 78, 269; XVI, 58
Samuel, Junior, VI, 227; XVI, 58
BOUSMAN, James, IX, 234
BOUVIIS, Jacob, VIII, 131
BOWDOIN, John, VIII, 494; XIV, 162; XV, 125, 166
Peter, XII, 496; XIII, 290
BOWEN, Henry, VII, 214
John, VII, 192
John, Junior, VII, 195
Moses, VII, 195
Thomas, VII, 187
BOWENS, Thomas, VII, 184
BOWIE, James, VII, 318(2);
James, Junior, XIV, 154
Sarah, XV, 363
BOWIN, Henry, VII, 195
John, VII, 195
John, Junior, VII, 195
Moses, VII, 195

Reice, VII, 195
William, VII, 195
BOWKER, Achilles, VI, 403
Martha, VI, 403
BOWLER, III, 220(2), 472, 473; IV, 267, 335, 382, 479; V, 142, 144; VI, 169, 176; VIII, 78, 97; IX, 332, 468, 510; X, 355, 475; XI, 210, 235; XII, 581; XIII, 479, 502
BOWLING, John, VI, 169; XIV, 282
Robert, VII, 213
William, VII, 218; XIV, 282(2)
BOWMAN, Edward, II, 16
Isaac, XV, 99
Jacob, VIII, 475
John, VII, 23; VIII, 415; XI, 283
BOWNESS, John, XIII, 82(2)
BOWORN, William, VII, 22
BOWYER, Henry, XII, 202, 675; XIII, 83, 171; XIV, 275(2), 308; XV, 44, 55; XVI, 53
John, VIII, 332; XI, 164, 341
Robert, I, 83
William, VIII, 549; XIII, 174, 553
BOYCE, James, XVI, 324
BOYD, IV, 336, 384, 386; V, 143, 145; VI, 18, 174, 176, 493; VII, 584; VIII, 79, 98; IX, 154, 159, 161, 488(2), 510, XII, 513(3); X, 273 (2), 356(2), 475(2); XI, 188, 211(2), 235 (2), 237(2), 238(3); XII, 301, 581; XIII, 480, 503(2), 553, 570(2); XIV, 153, 156, 172; XV, 157, 312; XVI, 182
Alexander, VII, 493, 569; XVI, 136, 346
Andrew, VIII, 554; XIV, 156; XVI, 167

David, VII, 54
Elisha, XV, 99, 110; XVI, 423
George, VIII, 130
John, IX, 233; XIV, 157
Margaret, VII, 299(2); XIV, 156
Patrick, IX, 233; XIV, 157
Robert, VII, 180; XV, 114; XVI, 427
Walter, VIII, 320(3), 322, 324
William, VII, 207; XV, 114
BOYENS, John, VII, 192
BOYER, John, VII, 192
Peter, XVI, 246
BOYKIN, Francis, XIII, 173, 300;* XV, 205(7), 349(2)
BOYNE, Thomas, VII, 183
BOYS,† John, XIII, 174
BOYSE, Christopher I, 375
Luke, I, 129
BRABSTONE, William, XV, 137(3)
BRACEWELL, Robert, I, 378
BRACKEN, John, XVI, 50, 107(5), 388(2)
BRACKENRIDGE, Alexander, XII, 337
George, VIII, 203
Robert, VII, 195, 475; 397
BRADDOCK, IX, 263
BRADFORD, John, XV, 223
BRADLEY, Edward A., V, 135
James, XV, 426
John, VII, 195, 214
Joseph, VII, 218
William, VII, 435, 437; VIII, 269; XI, 36(3), 37(3)
BRADSHAW, James, VII, 185
Thomas, VII, 194
BRADY, William, XII, 76
BRAKE, Jacob, VIII, 275
BRAMHAM, John, Junior, VII, 300

BRAMLETT, Ambrose, VII, 209(3)
Amhus, VII, 205
BRANCH, IV, 532; VI, 20; XIV, 156
Benjamin, XIV, 277; XVI, 275(4), 343(4)
Edward, XV, 240; XVI, 275(4), 343(2)
John, I, 239
BRANDER, John, XVI, 48: 237(3), 238
BRANDON, David, IX, 233; XIV, 157
Jonathan, XVI, 330
BRANHAM, Nimrod, XVI, 149(2)
BRANNER, Thomas, VII, 189
BRANSON, Lionel, XVI, 51
BRASHIERS, Marahem, X, 293
BRASSFIELD, John, VII, 201
BRATCHY, William, VII, 203
BRATTON, James, XVI, 194
Robert, VII, 183
William, VII, 181
BRAUNOUGH, Francis, VII, 230
BRAXTON, Carter, I, 36; VII, 485, 489; VII, 163 (2), 284, 434(2), 477, 642(5); IX, 49, 328; XII, 406; XVI, 223
George, VII, 260(3), 361(3), 568; VIII, 49, 474(2), 475(2)
George, Junior, V, 215 (6), 216, 303(2), 306 (2), 307(2), 396; VII, 294(2); VIII, 216(2)
BRAY, V, 14, 142, 143, 144; VI, 173, 176, 278; VII, 432; VIII, 78, 98, 101, 323; IX, 154, 160, 332
Angelica, IV, 371, 373 (2), 374
Ann,* IV, 371; VI, 413 (2)
David, III, 431; IV, 370 (2), 371, 372(4), 373 (2), 374(2), 375(2).

376(2); V, 278, 279, 280; VI, 412, 413(5)
David, Junior, IV, 371 (5), 372(2), 373(2), 374
Elizabeth, V, 278, 280; VI, 413, 414(8), 415 (2); VII, 247(7), 248 (2), 452(4), 453(5); VIII, 461(10), 462, 463(2)
James, II, 544, 546, 548; III, 210; IV, 371(2), 372(2); VI, 413(3)
John, VII, 226
Judith, VI, 413, 415(4), 416(2)
Thomas, IV, 370, 372 (7), 373(8), 374(7), 375(9); VI, 413, 414, 416; VII, 247, 452; VIII, 461, 462, 463
BREARLEY, James, I, 83
BREARLY, David. I, 22
BRECKENRIDGE, Alexander, XII, 225
John, XIII, 175, 316(2)
James, XIII, 83, 171; XIV, 275(2); XV, 44, 55, 66; XVI, 53
BREDIN, John, XV, 373
Scott, XV, 373(3)
Thomas, XV, 373(2)
BREEDEN, William, XVI, 323 (3)
BREEDLOVE, William, XV, 411
BREE, John. I, 35
BREMAN, Thomas, I, 386
BRENT, XI, 310
Charles, Junior, XVI, 379
Daniel C., XIII, 585
George, III, 25, 39; XIII, 585, 586
GILES, II, 149, 150(4), 151(2), 155, 403†(2)
Richard, XVI, 236
Robert, IV, 268, 331 (3); IX, 305; XIII, 585

William, V, 292(3), 293 (6); VIII, 670; XV, 120
William, Junior, V, 292, 293(6)
BRENTON, Henry, VII, 203
BRERETON, Thomas, I, 407, 408, 545(3); II, 329
BRETT, George, VII, 126
BREWER, VIII, 602
George, VII, 212
John, I, 148, 169, 187, 202, 431, 548
BREWSTER, Ebenezer, XVI, 194
Edward, I, 86
Richard, I. 138, 148, 203
William, I, 83, 86
BRIANS, William, XIII, 228
BRIDGER, James, VI, 450, 451
Joseph, I, 431; II, 197, 198(2), 205, 225, 226, 249, 254, 320, 330, 544, 548, 551, 557, 560, 663, 568, 569; III, 557, 570; VI, 275, 288, 448(2), 449(3), 450(10), 451(3), 452; VII, 515; IX, 240
Samuel, VI, 449(3), 450 (2)
William, V, 74; VI, 449 (3), 450(3)
BRIDGES, David, VII, 23
BRIDGMAN, John, III, 39
Orl, II, 511
BRIDGWATER, II, 528
BRIDIE, Charles, XVI, 136
BRIGGS, Benjamin, XI, 599
David, VIII, 497
George, V, 368(2), 369
John Howell, XII, 364, 635*
Samuel, VII, 181; IX, 555
Thomas, VII, 211
BRIGHT, Charles, VII, 207 (2), 210(2), 211
Edward, VII, 207, 210 (2)
Lydia, XVI, 26(7)

BRINCKLEY, John, IV, 529
BRINSLEY, I, 82
BRISCOE, John, XIV, 241
Philip, XVI, 408(2)
BRISTOE, XV, 333
BRISTOW, II, 510
Robert, II, 428; XIV, 237
BRIT, Richard, IV, 331(2)
BRITAIN, Thomas, I, 85
BRITTAIN, George, XVI, 225
BRITTON, Anderson, XIV, 155
George, XVI, 379
Isham, XV, 380
William, XVI, 310(2)
BROACH, VI, 16(2)
BROADDUS,† Robert, XVI, 432
Thomas, XV, 121
Warner H., XV, 464
BROADHURST, Walter, I, 379
BROADWATER, IV, 268, 331 (2)
Charles, VII, 21
BROCAS, William, I, 282, 322, 339
BROCK, XVI, 51, 56(2)
Elias, VIII, 131
John, XV, 31
Joseph, X, 370
BROCKENBROUGH, John, XVI, 34, 90, 100, 335(2)
William, XVI, 223(2)
BROCKETT, Thomas, I, 86
BROCKMAN, Samuel, XVI, 149
BROLL, Jacob, VII, 214
BROKENBOROUGH, Newman, IV, 267; XIV, 399
BROKENBROUGH, V, 143: VI, — 174: VIII, 79, 98
BROMFIELD, BRIDGET, I, 405
—John, I, 405
BRONAUGH, Benjamin, XV, 120
John, XVI, 236
William, VI, 528; XII, 605; XVI, 51, 168
BROOK, VI, 18; XIV, 153, 154

BROOKE, III, 471; VI, 14, 18; XV, 420
Calisthenes, I, 81
Christopher, I, 90
Edmund, XV, 179, 242
Elizabeth, VIII, 474(3)
Francis T., XII, 661; XV, 242; XVI, 47
George, VII, 402(2); VIII, 474(3), 475(6), 580, 633; X, 103; XIV, 154
Humphrey, XII, 217, 685
John, I, 82; XV, 359 (2), 360
Reuben, XIV, 339
Richard, I, 83; VIII, 601; XVI, 31(2)
Robert, V, 305; XV, 69
Sarah, V, 250; VI, 212 (2), 278*; VII, 432
Thomas, XIV, 339
BROOKER, Hugh, I, 83
BROOKES, VIII, 45
Joseph, VI, 242
BROOKHART, Jacob, XII, 595
BROOKS, Charles, XII, 398
John, XV, 258(4)
Thomas, XII, 633
William, XV, 121; XVI, 194
BROOM, Jacob, I, 22
BROTHERS, John, V, 73(2), 74
John, Junior, V, 73(2)
Richard, V, 74
BROTTON, Robert, XII, 601
BOUCHER, A., II, 511
BROUGH, John, XVI, 231
Robert, XIII, 106; XV, 23, 447; XVI, 40, 58
BROWDER, WM, XII, 308(2)
BROWN, IV, 19
Aaron, XV, 52
Abraham, VII, 194
Alexander, XVI, 316
Bazaleel, XVI, 149
Baziel, XIV, 330
Benjamin, VII, 130; XVI, 60
Bennet, XV, 259

Berryman, XIII, 221
Billy, XV, 418(8)
Brightberry, XV, 227
Burnard, XV, 227
Campbell, XVI, 38(2)
Charles, XVI, 157(2)
Coleman, XVI, 395
Cornelius, XIII, 283; XIV, 158
Daniel, VII, 326, 447
Edward, VII, 214; XV, 444
Francis, VII, 213
Henry, I, 235; VII, 615
Isaac, VII, 206, 209
Jacob, VII, 203; VIII, 128
James, XIV, 426; XVI, 79
Jesse, VII, 211, 623(2), 624
John, I, vii; VII, 190, 191, 205, 206, 475 (2); XII, 223; XIII, 174; XIV, 336, 360; XV, 166, 447; XVI, 161
Mary, VI, 239(2), 240
Matthew, I, 84
Oliver, XV, 119(2); XVI, 159, 412
Preston, XV, 266
Robert, VII, 191; VIII, 656; XV, 418(2)
Sally, XV, 418(3)
Samuel, IV, 363; VII, 207, 210(2); VIII, 660(3); XI, 139; XII, 72, 581; XIII, 297
Thomas, XI, 185, 332; XII, 299
William, I, 81, 85; V, 368; VII, 22, 23(2); VIII, 618; XI, 57, 105(4); XII, 393; XIII, 94, 175; XV, 30, 139; XVI, 100
William, Junior, XI, 57
BROWNE, I, 551; XIV, 166
Devoraux, II, 197, 198
Henry, I, 238, 282, 288.

822, 339, 516(2); II, 319
John, II, 371; XVI, 94
Mary Burnet, XVI, 57 (3), 58(2)
William, I, 527; II, 319
William Burnet, XVI, 57(6), 58(3)
BROWNFIELD, Robert, XV, 55
BROWNING, Charles, XV, 30
Francis, VIII, 128
Jacob, VII, 22
James, VII, 213
John, I, 139, 148; VII, 22
BROWNINGE, John, I, 179
BRUA, XIV, 156
BRUAS, VII, 300
BRUCE, Alexander, VII, 437
Jacob, IX, 146(2)
James, XV, 380
Richard, XV, 204(3)
BAUDENELL, Edmond, I, 84
BRUISTER, James, VII, 194
BRUMLEY, Samuel, VII, 50
William, IV, 242
BRUNDICK, Timothy, XIV, 394; XV, 37; XVI, 174
BRYAN, IV, 371, 373(2), 374
Ambrose, VII, 207
George, X, 521, 524, 528, 530, 531(2), 532, 533(2), 534(2), 535
James, VII, 205; VIII, 128
Jesse, VII, 206
John, VII, 203
William, VII, 211
BRYANS, David, VII, 196
James, VII, 191
BRYANT, Ambrose, VII, 204
John, VII, 126
BRYCE, Archibald, VIII, 656
BRYDGES, Grey, I, 81, 90
BUCHANAN, VI, 242; VIII, 423
Anne, XI, 155(3)
Alexander, VII, 196(2); XIII, 175

Andrew, VII, 196, 198; XV, 43
Archibald, VII, 196(2); VIII, 543
David, XIII, 599
James, VII, 196; VIII, 423, 497, 656; X, 318; XI, 155(4), 156, 450; XII, 280
John, V, 188(4), 189 (2), 292, 293(2); VII, 182, 189, 192, 193, 194, 197(6), 402; XIV, 156; XVI, 335
Nell, XIII, 570
Sarah, XIII, 301(6), 302(5)
William, VII, 24, 196; XIII, 48; XIV, 183; XV, 121, 339
Cornelius, XV, 374
Elizabeth, I, 406
John, XIV, 416
Richard, I, 405(2)
Thomas, XII, 672; XIII, 48; XIV, 158
BUCKELLS, James, XIII, 297
BUCKLES, William, XIII, 174
BUCKNER, Horace, XIV, 246
John, II, 518; III, 553, 554, 566; VII, 202; VIII, 601
Mordecai, VII, 493
Richard, XI, 369
Robert, IV, 234, 235(2), 236(2); V, 197(2), 198(2)
Samuel, V, 399; VI, 411(3)
Thomas, IV, 113, 439
William, III, 181, 202; XI, 539(5)
BUCKSTON, James, VI, 375 (2)
BUCKUS, Robert, VII, 216
BUFFINGTON,* Thomas, XV, 425; XVI, 158, 228 (2)
William, VII, 25(6); VIII, 275; XV, 463

BUFORD, XV, 187, 188(2), 236
  Henry, XIV, 418; XV, 419
  James, XI, 172
  John, XIII, 81
BULLET, Thomas, VII, 493
BULLIT,* Alexander Scott, XII, 395; XIII, 91
  Cuthbert, IX, 328; XII, 382, 512, 603, 604, 684, 695(2); XIII, 480(2), 504; XV, 153; XV, 67
  William, XII, 87; XV, 274
BULLOCK, David, XV, 121
  Francis, I, 247(2)
  Hannah, XIII, 105
  James, XIII, 104(2), 105(4)
  John, I, 83
  Rees, XIII, 285
  Rice, XII, 702
BULLOCKE, Richard, I, 202
BUMCARNER, Rudulph, XII, 625
BUMPASS, William, VII, 204
BUNCH, James, VII, 130
BUNTON, James, VII, 198
BURBAGE, I, 406(2)
  Thomas, I, 405(4)
  William, I, 405
BURCHINAL, Thomas, XVI, 330
BURFORD, III, 220, 472
  Luke, VI, 318
  Sarah (Smith), VI, 318
BURG,† William, II, 162(4); VII, 202
BURGE, Drury, XV, 345(4)
  William, XV, 345(3)
BURGES, Charles, IV, 451 (2), 452, 453(3)
  Frances, IV, 452, 453 (2)
  Thomas, I, 149
BURGESS, Edward, XVI, 196 (3)
  Joseph, VII, 201
BURGOYNE, Peter, I, 85
  Robert, I, 85

  Thomas, I, 85
BURK, James, VII, 183
  John, I, xiii, 3, 76(2), 123, 146, 428, 429, 507, 513,‡ 528(2); II, 618, 519(3), 520 (8), 621(4), 523, 525, 527(3), 528(2), 531 (2), 533, 543, 545, 548, 549, 555(2); III, 542(2); XI, 530, 531(2); XV, 270
  Richard, VII, 22
BURKE, John, XV, 259
  Samuel, XI, 530
BURKEM, Solomon, VII, 215
BURKHART, Peter, XIII, 174
BURKS, Boling, VII, 210(2)
  John Patrick, VII, 210
  Richard, VII, 210
  Richard, Junior, VII, 210
  William, VII, 210(2)
BURLACIE, John, I, 82
BURLEY, Francis, I, 85
BURNDRAGER, Andrew, XV, 31
BURNETT, William, VII, 189
BURNHAM, John, II, 329, 564 (2)
  Rowland, I, 283, 359
  Samuel, I, 86
BURNLEY, HARDEN, VII, 129 (2)
  Zachariah, VII, 206; XIV, 323
BURNSIDES, James, VII, 198
BURRAY, I, 82
BURROUGHS,§ Christopher, I, 289
BURROWERS, Charles, I, 370, 373
  John, I, 406
BURRUS, Joseph, XIV, 322; XV, 419
BURSON, Joseph, VII, 21
BURTON, Alexander, XVI, 308(3)
  Caleb, VII, 203
  George, I, 84
  Jesse, XII, 398; XVI, 308

  John, VIII, 494
  Martin, XV, 353
  May, Junior, XIV, 322
  Peter, VII, 201
  Robert, XVI, 79, 308(2)
  William, XVI, 308(2)
BURWELL, XI, 258; XIV, 153
  Armistead, VI, 230; VII, 128
  Carter, V, 300(2), 402, 403(2); VI, 18, 197, 212, 298, 418, 437, 454, 524, 528; VII, 13; VIII, 448(3), 449
  Edward, I, 84
  Frances (Thacker), VI, 314(3), 315(2); VII, 343(2), 344(5)
  James, VIII, 459, 481 (6), 482(3), 483
  John, IX, 239
  Lewis, II, 564; III, 425, 428; IV, 534(3), 535 (5), 536(10), 537 (2); V, 300, 371; VI, 7, 13, 314(2), 315 (2); VII, 128, 288, 343(2), 344(7), 353, 466, 468, 566, 647 (2); VIII, 146, 213, 365, 376, 448, 459, 463, 482, 663(4), 664 (7); X, 121; XV, 67
  Mary (Willis), VIII, 663(2)
  Nathaniel, VIII, 448, 449(4); IX, 239; XI, 310; XII, 495; XIII, 287; XIV, 266
  Nathaniel, Junior, VIII, 482
  Nathaniel Bacon, V, 371; VIII, 481(2)
  Robert, V, 300(2); VI, 275, 288, 451; VIII, 216(2), 462(2), 448 (5), 449(6), 464(2), 664; XIV, 334(2)
  William A., XVI, 45, 136, 346
BUSBY, Ralph, I, 86
BUSELL, Matthew, VII, 52

BUSH, XI, 367
  Edward, VII, 214
  James, VII, 60
  John, VII, 211
BUSHOPP, John, I, 369, 379
BUSKRIDGE, John, I, 85
BUSIIROD, Richard, I, 545(2)
  Thomas, I, 506
BUSTARD, Claudius, XV, 270
BUTLER, VI, 175; VIII, 79
  Beckwith, XI, 526; XI, 110
  Demsey, XI, 152(3)
  George, I, 87
  John, XIII, 297
  Percival, XIII, 231
  Pierce, I, 23; IV, 142
  Thomas, XII, 83; XIV, 157
  William, I, 236, 379, 430
BUTT, Benjamin, Junior, XVI, 26(7)
  Lydia (Bright), XVI, 26(7),
  Robert, XV, 228
  Wilson, XV, 24
BUTTERWORTH,* Isaac, VII, 205, 206
BUTTON, Thomas, I, 83
BUTTS, Eleanor, XV, 464(2), 465
  Josiah, XIII, 175
  Judith, V, 297; VII, 488 (2)
  Peter, VII, 230
BUXON, Thomas, I, 87
BUXTON, James, XIV, 155; XV, 444
BUYERS, William, VII, 195
BYNAM, William, XIV, 336
BYNE, Edmund, XIII, 182
BYNUM, Turner, XV, 176
BYRD, VI, 17(2), 226, 362; VII, 149, 632, 533 (3); VIII, 78, 98, 100 (5), 101, 236, 322, 324, 493, 495(2), 497 (4); IX, 154, 159, 160, 332, 488, 510, 513(5); X, 273, 474,

*Bullitt   †Burgh   ‡Burke   §X'pher

21

*Buterworth

22

475; XI, 210, 235, 237(4), 238(4); XII, 66, 67, 258, 280, 281 (3), 455, 582(2), 667 (2), 787; XIII, 179 (3), 479, 503, 571, 572, 573(2), 579(2); XIV, 154
  Andrew, XV, 31
  Evelyn, VI, 319
  James, IX, 420
  Lucy (Parke), VI, 319
  Richard W., XVI, 140, 346
  Wilhelmina, VI, 319
  William, I, 76(2); II, 328, 554(2), 563; III,

218, 431, 470, 557; IV, 266, 302(3); V, 191(2), 192(3), 358, 378; VI, 14, 174, 223 (2), 224, 281, 307, 501(4); VII, 493; VIII, 115, 149, 271, 421, 422, 539, 578, 656; IX, 237; X, 446 (6); XV, 31
BYRNE, James, XVI, 62, 232, 434
  Richard, VII, 24
BYRNSIDE, John, XV, 223
BYWATERS, Thomas, XV, 120

C

CADELL,* George, XVI, 210 (2)
  John, VIII, 44; XII, 661; XIV, 156
  Joseph, VIII, 35, 62, 193, 271; XI, 29; XII, 702; XIII, 315, 316
  Joseph, Junior, XII, 661; XIII, 316(2)
  Landon, XV, 419
  Nicholas, XII, 665(2), 666(3); XIII, 315, 316, 481; XIV, 156; XV, 44, 182
  Samuel Jordan, XII, 229, 665; XIII, 296, 316(2); XV, 182, 419
  William, V, 190, 364 (3); VI, 15, 16(2); VII, 55, 126, 202, 402 (2); VIII, 10, 124, 149, 193, 271, 300 (3); IX, 49, 61, 95; XI, 272, 341, 450; XII, 665, 702; XIII, 315, 316, 572, 573(2), XIV, 322; XV, 182 (3), 419
  William, Junior, VII, 202, 232, 568; VII,

300, 301; XII, 665; XIII, 315, 316; XV, 44, 182
  William H., XV, 442; XVI, 335(2)
CACKLEY, Ellis, XV, 274
CADON, Thomas, VII, 197
CADOWGAN,† William, V, 73; VI, 266, 267, 268
CAESAR, Julius, I, 393, 394
CAFFEE, William, XIII, 583, 590
CAGE, Edward, I, 85
CAGHEY, James, VII, 191
CAIN, John, VII, 198
CALDER, John, XIII, 103(3), 104; XV, 381(5); XVI, 41(6)
CALDWELL, David, VII, 226 (2), 227, 307
  George, VII, 206
  James, VIII, 224; XIII, 282; XIV, 158
  John, VII, 224, 226; XII, 514, 661, 676, 719
  Joseph, XV, 386(3), 387; XVI, 31
  Robert, VII, 224, 226, 227; XV, 119(2)

Thomas, VIII, 129
  William, VII, 223, 307
CALL, John, XIV, 267
CALLAND, Samuel, XII, 659; XIV, 316; XV, 160, 334; XVI, 52
CALLAWAY,* Charles, XV, 49, 97
  Henry T., XVI, 136, 346
  James, VII, 204, 207, 210(3), 211, 475; VIII, 585; X, 109(2); XI, 134, 135, 250; XII, 70, 732; XIII, 81, 429; XIV, 422; XV, 49, 137(2); XVI, 43, 45
  James, Junior, XV, 60
  John, XI, 61; XII, 398, 732; XIII, 81, 429
  Richard, VII, 204, 207 (2), 475; IX, 317(2); X, 135, 143(2), 144 (3), 196
  Thomas, VII, 219(2)
  William, VII, 203, 211 (2), 473; XI, 171; XIV, 422; XV, 137
CALLIS, James, XV, 447
  William O., XV, 240
CALMEES, Marquis, VIII, 624
CALMES, Fielding, XIII, 171
CALTHROPE,‡ Christopher, I, 373, 379, 530
CALTON, John, VII, 212
CALVERT,‡ Charles, III, 200
  Cornelius, VII, 437, 569
  George, I, 83
  John, XV, 30
  Joseph, VIII, 208(3), 209
  Maximilian, XI, 167
  Philip, II, 201
  Thomas, XV, 329
CALVIN, William, VII, 217
CAMBDEN, John, XV, 444
CAMBLE, James, VII, 183, 185, 197(3)
  John, VII, 191
  Matthew, VII, 196
CAMDEN, XVI, 417(2)

CAMERON, Charles, XIV, 266; XVI, 161
  John, XVI, 493
CAMMACK, William, XV, 447
CAMP, Henry, XV, 175, 210
  James, VII, 217; XV, 336
  John, VII, 221; XV, 122
CAMPBELL, Aeneas, VII, 222, 236
  Alexander, XI, 164
  Ann (Alison), XVI, 163(5)
  Archibald, VII, 205, 208, 435, 437; VIII, 269; XIII, 170
  Arthur, VIII, 129; XI, 164
  Charles, XIV, 266, 110
  David, Junior, XVI, 32
  Donald, XIII, 599
  Hugh, VII, 181
  Hugh R., XVI, 226
  Jacob, VII, 193
  James, I, 86; VII, 187, 200, 201, XI, 792; XIII, 590, 599; XIV, 275(2), 322; XV, 66, 111, 218, 351, 364, 365; XVI, 48, 62, 388 (2)
  John, VII, 187, 193, 195; VIII, 33; IX, 330; X, 293, 295(2); XI, 276, 277(4), 283, 321(2), 322(5), 335, 336, 345, 346(2), 474(6), 475 (5); XII, 84, 225, 282, 396(3), 396; XIII, 310(3), 311(5); XIV, 276(2); XV, 429
  Mary(—) (Spotswood), VII, 451
  Matthew, VII, 195(2)
  Michael, XII, 719
  Niel, VIII, 469; IX, 335
  Patrick, VII, 194
  Robert, VII, 192, 198; XV, 426; XVI, 163(5)

*Cabel, Cabbell, Cabball   †Cadawgon

23

*Calaway, Calloway   ‖Callthrop, Calthropp   ‡See Baltimore

24

7

Samuel, VIII, 126
Samuel L., XVI, 403
Thomas, VII, 200; XV, 419
William, IX, 555; X, 195(3); XIII, 171; XV, 30
CAMPDEN, William, XV, 32 (3)
CAMPE, Lawrence, I, 85
CANEFAX, John, XIII, 151; XIV, 157
CANNAIRD, Andrew, VII, 24
CANNING, Paul, I, 86
William, I, 86
CANNON, IX, 659; XVI, 70
John, XII, 684
Thomas, I, 86
William, VII, 201; IX, 234; XII, 657*, 661; XIV, 269(4), 260, 269(3), 321
CANT, David, I, 630; II, 156
CANTERBURY, I, 101
CANTLEY, John, VII, 198
CANTON, Simon, XII, 580, 633(2)
CANTREL, William, I, 84
CAPERTON, Hugh, XIII, 95; XVI, 38, 244
CAPITO, Daniel, XVI, 56
CAPLINER, George, VII, 184
CAPPER, John, VII, 216
CAR, John, VII, 218
Mary, VII, 192
William, VIII, 159
CARBERRY, II, 528
CARE, John, VII, 214
CARELES, Thomas, I, 84
CAREW, Edward, I, 85
George, I, 81, 90
CAREY, Elizabeth (Williams) XIII, 610
Henry, I, 81, 90
John, XIII, 610
Robert, I, 82
CARGILL, XIV, 156
Cornelius, Junior, VII, 223
Daniel, VII, 223; VIII, 369

John, VII, 223, 227(2)
John, Junior, VII, 223
CARGON, Patrick, VII, 197
CARLILE, John, VII, 212
Robert, VII, 192
CARLIN, Daniel, XV, 185(3), 186
CARLOCK, Conrad, VII, 200
CARLYLE, VII, 22
James, VII, 189
John, VII, 189, 190; VIII, 55, 56
Robert, VII, 190; VIII, 126
William, XVI, 334
CARMICHAEL, William, X, 553
CARNAL, Abraham, Junior, V, 75(2)
Catharine (Edwards), V, 75(2)
Isaac, V, 75
CARNS, Michael, XII, 297
CARPENTER, Andrew, VII, 23
David, XVI, 181(3)
Joseph, VIII, 126
Joseph, Junior, VIII, 127
Nicholas, XII, 209, 295, 639
Thomas, I, 83
William, I, 86, XV, 223
Zopher, VIII, 126
CARPER, Nicholas, XIII, 228; XIV, 375
CARPINTER, George, XIII, 297
Nathaniel, III, 167
CARR, Dabney, XV, 427; XVI, 149, 318, 379
Henry, VII, 182, 184
John, VII, 199; XV, 427; XVI, 149, 318
Joseph, XVI, 51
Margaret, XIII, 616, 617
Peter, XV, 427; XVI, 149, 379
Richard, VII, 199
Samuel, VII, 195

William, VII, 424, 425 (2), 426(2), 427; XII, 372, 684
CARRINGTON, Clement, XIII, 193
Edward, XIII, 293, 318; XV, 66; XVI, 34, 100, 335
George, VI, 291; VII, 570; VIII, 10, 124, 412(2), 603; XIII, 104, 173, 193, 278, 553; XV, 48(6), 69, 172(2), 173, 380
Joseph, XII, 583, 611, 657*; XIII, 171
Mayo, XI, 310; XII, 583, 657*; XIII, 171
Paul, VII, 307; VIII, 141; IX, 49, 95; XI, 250, 272; XII, 611, 770; XVI, 299
CARRIL, John, I, 85
CARROL, Benjamin, V, 370 (2); VI, 240
Joseph, VII, 216
CARROLL, Charles, I, 36
Daniel, I, 46
Dempsey P., XVI, 52 (3)
CARSON, Elizabeth, VIII, 130, 172, 173(2)
James, VII, 208
William, VII, 173; VIII, 208
CARTER, I, 514; II, 10, 14 (2); VI, 17; VII, 630; VIII, 45; IX, 563; XIII, 155, 171 (2), 481; XIV, 154
Anne, VII, 455(5), 456
Charles, IV, 454, 455 (3), 456(2), 531; V, 194(2), 259, 289(2), 302(2), 303(2), 370; VI, 282, 418, 437, 454, 524; VII, 13, 76, 120, 222, 276, 288, 455, 568, 647; VIII, 25(5), 26(6), 152, 214(2), 215(2), 216(2), 218 (8), 219(5), 220(3), 221(4), 436(2), 437

(4), 438, 464, 465(2), 466(5), 467(7), 576; IX, 305; X, 446(2); XI, 55(4), 204; XIII, 616; XV, 176; XVI, 182, 193(3)
Charles, Junior, VI, 282; VII, 120, 431; VIII, 214; XIII, 316 (2)
Charles Landon, IX, 574(2), 575(2), 576
Charles of Caroloman, IX, 574
Charles of Ludlow, IX, 574(2), 575
Edmund, VIII, 149
Edward, I, 430, 506, 512(2), 526; II, 473; XIII, 87, 315, 316; XV, 121, 179
Elizabeth, IV, 454(2), 455, 456(3), 467(2); VII, 478; VIII, 466
George, V, 300(4), 302 (3), 303(3); VII, 455; VIII, 215(3), 216(3), 217(2), 487, 667; IX, 574; XII, 215; XIV, 334(3)
James, VII, 231, 670
Jeduthan, XVI, 338
Job, XIV, 409(4)
John, I, 239, 359, 386, 389(2), 431, 432, 501, 504, 505, 506, 612, 514, 515, 530; II, 155, 201, 329; IV, 454, 455(3), 456(2), 457; V, 143, 301, 302; VI, 174, 510; VII, 24, 568; VIII, 167(2), 214, 215(3), 218(2), 219, 220(2), 221(2), 281, 282, 437(3), 464, 465(5), 466, 467(2); XVI, 325, 326(2), 390
John Hill, IX, 574
Joseph, XV, 334; XVI, 52, 338

Judith, XIII, 616(2), 617
Landon, V, 300(2), 302; VI, 18, 454, 524; VII, 13, 76, 276, 288, 455, 568, 647; VIII, 214 (2), 215(3), 218(2), 219, 220(2), 221(2), 370, 437(6), 438; X, 365; XII, 217(3); XIV, 153, 154; XV, 116(4)
Landon, Junior, VIII, 494, 664
Merry, VII, 206, 225
Nicholas, V, 300
Peter, VIII, 128-
Priscilla, IV, 454(2), 455, 456(2), 457(2); VII, 478
Randel, I, 84
Robert, I, 3; III, 165, 198(4); IV, 5(3), 49, 376, 454(2), 455; V, 250(2), 300, 301; VI, 16(2); VII, 455(4), 456, 457(3), 478(8), 479(5), 568, 647(2); VIII, 25(3), 26(2), 27(2), 218(2), 378, 445(2), 446, 447(2), 464(3), 465(4), 466, 467(2); XV, 223, 267; XVI, 68
Robert, Junior, IV, 454 (7), 455(8), 456(4), 457(3); V, 300; VII, 478(2)
Samuel, XIV, 390, 425; XVI, 268
Solomon, VII, 203
Walker, Randolph, IX, 574(2), 575(2), 576
William, XII, 383; XIII, 582; XV, 129(3)
CARTHREY,* XV, 356
John, Junior, XV, 227, 359, 360; XVI, 211
CARTIE, William, VII, 204
CARTMELL, John, XII, 674
CARTMILL, James, VII, 197
John, VII, 193, 198

CARTWRIGHT, XIII, 41
Abraham, I, 85
Caleb, XV, 379(2)
Thomas, VII, 21, 218
CARUTHERS, James, XV, 66, 442; XVI, 403
John, XIV, 308; XV, 44, 216
William, XV, 66, 442; XVI, 403, 429
CARVER, William, II, 250, 370, 375(2), 377
CARVIN, William, VII, 190, 199(2); VIII, 127
Edward, VIII, 127
CARY, IX, 154, 159, 160, 488, 510, 513(4); X, 273
Ann, VI, 243
Archibald, VII, 39, 40, 116, 120, 212, 313, 354, 408, 440, 443(2), 444(8), 456, 568; VIII, 35, 62, 115, 124, 149, 174, 271, 412(2), 422, 494, 578, 604, 654(2); IX, 61, 70, 213; X, 318; XI, 393; XIII, 541
Harwood, VIII, 34(3), 62(3)
Henry, III, 226, 286(2), 287(3), 485(5); IV, 95, 307, 362; VI, 14 (2); VII, 127(2), 440, 441(8), 442(4), 443(2)
John, IX, 466
Margaret, VIII, 34(2)
Martha, VIII, 62(2)
Miles, I, 512, 529, 648; II, 31; III, 111, 202; VII, 441, 442, 443; VIII, 177
Richard, X, 101; XII, 769
Richard, Junior, III, 97
Robert, VIII, 464; XIII, 316(2); XV, 269
Samuel, XIII, 137, XV, 67
Thomas, II, 330
William, VIII, 34(7),

35(6), 61(2), 62(6), 63(3); XI, 473; XIV, 308
Wilson, VII, 441(4); XII, 97; XIII, 324(2)
Wilson Miles, VIII, 302, 653
CASEY, John, VII, 205
Nicholas, XIII, 90; XIV, 389
Peter, XII, 223
CASH, Stephen, VII, 203
CASHADAY, Thomas, VII, 191
CASNIAH, Sandiver, VII, 206
CASON, Edward, VIII, 131 (2)
John, I, 85
Larkin, VIII, 131(2)
CASSEN, Allen, I, 85
CASSON, Thomas, VIII, 19 (2), 20
CASTLE, Valentine, VII, 183
CASWELL, Richard, I, 83
CATCHMAIE, George, I, 528
CATER, William, I, 85
CATLETT, John, V, 288(2); XV, 67
Kemp, XVI, 212
CAUDLE, Charles, XVI, 434
CAUFIELD, Robert, VII, 514 (3), 515(5), 516(2)
William, VII, 514
CAULTER, John, XV, 442
CAULTROPP,* Christopher, I, 283, 289
CAUSEY, Nathaniel, I, 129
CAVADY, John, I, 86
CAVAN, Patrick, XII, 600
CAVE, V, 143, 145; VI, 174, 177; VII, 79, 98, 324, 160; IX, 154, 161, 235, 489, 511; X, 182
Belfield, XIII, 609, 610; XV, 30
John, VII, 23
William, XIII, 170
CAVENAUGH, Philemon, IV, 363; VI, 17
CAVENDISH, William H., XIV, 275(2); XV, 44
CAVERLEY, Peter, XV, 66(2)

CAWFIELD,† William, I, 430, 506, 527
CECIL, Edward, I, 81, 90
Robert, I, 81
Thomas, I, 81, 90
William, XV, 270
CEELY, Thomas, I, 130, 140, 148
CENEY, Henry, I, 178, 203
CENNEY, Edward, VII, 196
CENY, Henry, I, 148
CHADWELL, David, XIV, 322; XV, 164
CHAFFIN,† John, XV, 129
Joshua, VII, 226; XIV, 390; XV, 140, 259
CHALLONER,§ James, I, 78, 81, 90
CHALMERS, I, xiii, 526
James, XV, 380
CHALMOR, William, VII, 208
CHALMORE, William, VII, 205
CHAMBERLAYNE, IV, 335, 381; VI, 16(2); XIV, 153, 154
Abraham, I, 81
Anne Kidley, V, 118, 119(2), 120(3)
Edward Pie, V, 118, 120; VII, 126
Elizabeth, V, 118, 120
Elizabeth (———), V, 118(4), 119, 120(3)
James, VII, 21
Mary, V, 118, 120
Richard, I, 83; V, 118, 120
Roger, VII, 126
Thomas, V, 118, 120; VI, 319(2), 320(6)
Wilhelmina (Parke), VI, 319, 320(3)
William, V, 117, 118(4), 119, 120(5); XVI, 427
CHAMBERS, David, XII, 639, 702; XIII, 618; XIV, 157
William, XIII, 174
CHAMP, John, XV, 64

8

CHAMPAIN, John, VII, 216
CHAMPAINE, James, III, 228
CRAMPE, John, VI, 282; VII, 120, 327, 427, 449, 569; VIII, 30
  William, VIII, 626
CHAMPION, Richard, I, 84
CHANDLER, Abraham, VII, 205
  George, I, 86
  John, I, 339
  Thomas, XIV, 339
  Thomas, Junior, XIV, 339
  Timothy, XIV, 268
CHAPLAIN, Moses, XIII, 321
CHAPLAINE, Abraham, XII, 223
CHAPLIN, Abraham, XI, 335, 336
  Isaack, I, 129
  William, XVI, 315(3)
CHAPLINE,* Moses, XII, 599, 639; XV, 169
CHAPMAN, VII, 311, X, 363
  Benjamin, XV, 30
  Isaac, XVI, 403
  Richard, V, 114, 115 (2), 116(8)
  Thomas, XIV, 394; XV, 37
  William, XVI, 158
CHARLES I., I, iv, xiv, 4, 129, 132, 133, 187, 260(2), 558, 527; II, 11, 24, 319
CHARLES II., I, xiii, xiv, xx, xxi(2), 368, 513, 527 (2), 528(2), 529(2), 644; II, iii(2), vi, vii, viii(3), 9(2), 11(3), 41, 163, 168, 180, 182, 208, 214(2), 224(2), 226, 229(2), 255, 264 (2), 265, 270(2), 271, 272(2), 278, 286(2), 287, 291, 293(2), 294, 303, 304, 311, 312, 320, 326(3), 327, 339, 341(2), 366(3), 367, 391(2), 401, 407(2), 409, 421, 423, 424,

426, 428, 432, 433, 434, 455, 458(3), 459, 488, 490, 491, 521(2), 523, 528, 532, 560, 564(5), 569, 578; III, 9, 10, 288, 315, 429, 505, 514; IV, 557; V, 304; VI, 92, 132, 198
CHARLTON, James, XIII, 585; XVI, 217
  Stephen, I, 289, 340, 374
CHASE, Samuel, I, 36; XII, 50
CHATFIELD, James, I, 83
CHEATHAM, James, VII, 201
  Matthew, XI, 393; XIII, 314; XIV, 265
  William, XIV, 281
CHEEKE, Hatton, I, 82
CHEESMAN, Edmund, II, 370, 374, 375(3), 377
  John, I, 372
CRENING, Robert, I, 87
CHENOWETH,† John, XII, 701, 702; XIII, 151; XIV, 153(2)
CHERRYSTONE, IV, 266, 336, 382, 384, 386; V, 142, 145, 146; VI, 173, 177(2), 443(2), 445; IX, 154, 161, 488, 489, 511, 513; X, 273, 356, 475; XI, 211(2), 235, 237; XIII, 503
CHESHIRE, John, XIII, 216 (2)
CRESMAN, John, I, 239
CHESTER, VIII, 598; XII, 375, 376, 526, 527, 672; XV, 339
  Sarah, VII, 23
CHETWOOD, VI, 17
  Thomas, IV, 113; V, 88
CHEVALIER, Anthony, XIII, 217
CHEVALLIE, John A., XIII, 323(3); XVI, 204
CHEVIS, David, XII, 226(2), 227
CREW, Coleby, XV, 49
  John, I, 138, 239, 283; XVI, 47

Larkin, VII, 493; VIII, 167, 281(2)
  Margaret, VI, 403
  Mary (Perrot), VI, 403 (4), 404(2)
  Robert, VI, 402, 403(5), 404(4); XVI, 47
CHEWNING, Christopher, XIV, 336
CHICHESTER, Daniel McCarty, XVI, 177
CHICKLEY,* Henry, I,414; II, vii(3), viii(6), 320, 454, 458, 544, 554, 561, 568, 569; III, 544, 548, 561(2), 562 (4), 570
CHICK, George, XII, 672, 673
CHICKELEY, Clement, I, 86
CHILDE, II, 578
CHILDERS, XIV, 321
  John, VII, 219
CHILDRE, XV, 346(2)
  William, VII, 201
CHILES, Alexander, I, 84
  Henry, V, 276, VI, 411
  John, XIII, 73; XIV 268
  Math., I, 236
  Walter, I, 239, 262, 322, 359, 377(2), 378(2), 379, 382(2), 383(4), 506; II, 31, 197(2), 198(2), 211
CHILTON, VII, 472(2)
  Charles, VIII, 625
  Edward, III, 549, 552, 553, 554, 555, 556, 557, 560, 561(4), 562(4); V, 111(2)
  Francis, V, 111
  Mark, VII, 21
  Thomas, VIII, 391
CHINN, Charles, VIII, 64
  Joseph, VII, 58
CHINWORTH,† John, XIII, 297; XV, 274
CHIPOAK, V, 78
CHISUM, John, VII, 214
CHISWELL, John, IX, 237
  Elizabeth, VIII, 350(2)
  John, VI, 291, 418, 437, 524, 528, 529; VII,

13, 39(2), 76; VIII, 115, 132, 270(2), 271(2)
CHOAT, Augustine, VII, 207
  Edward, VII, 207
CHOLMONDELEY, V, 559
CHOWNING, II, 473; III, 472
  John, XI, 370; XIV, 164; XVI, 334
CHRISMAN, Gabriel, XV, 166
  Isaac, XIII, 557
CHRISTIAN, Archibald, XVI, 427
  Gilbert, VII, 181
  Israel, VII, 475(2); VIII, 129(2), 616
  John, V, 188(3), 189(2)
  John H., XVI, 427
  Michael, VIII, 661
  Robert, XVI, 427
  William, VII, 190, 192, 194, 475; X, 288; XI, 164, 283; XII, 223, 383
CHUKE, William, X, 325
CHUMLEY, John, VII, 201
CHURCH, Thomas, I, 85
CHURCHILL, XVI, 333
  Armistead, VII, 157, 158(6), 159
  Elizabeth, VII, 158(2)
  Priscilla, VII, 158(2)
  William, VII, 157, 158 (4), 159; VIII, 486
CLACK, Sterling, XIII, 608
CLAGG, Alexander, XIV, 418 (2)
CLAIBORN, V, 278
CLAIBORNE, VI, 426(2), 427; VII, 480(2), 481, 482 (2), XIV, 154
  Augustine, VI, 277, 298; VII, 568
  Buller, XIV, 390
  Elizabeth (Dandridge), VII, 295(2), 297(7), 486(4), 487(5); VIII, 224, 225
  Herbert, XVI, 57(2), 58(2)
  Mary Burnet (Browne),

XVI, 57(3), 58(2)
  Philip, XV, 338; XVI, 60, 346
  Philip Whitehead, VII, 296(2), 297(8), 486 (5), 487(4), 489; VIII, 224, 225, 286, 463
  Richard. VIII, 645
  Thomas, VI, 17(2); VIII, 434(2), XIII, 625(4); XIV, 154
  William, I, 282, 288 (3), 365, 367, 368, 432, 495, 499, 500, 501, 503(2), 504(3), 508, 512, 523, 526, 547; II, 10, 39, 197, 545, 547
  William, Junior, II, 328
  William Dandridge, XII, 407; XIV, 266; XVI, 223(2)
CLANBICKARD, I, 101
CLAPHAM, John, I,85
  Jœias, VII, 126, 217, 236; IX, 62, 586; XI, 605; XIII, 171
  Samuel, XV, 214
CLARE, George, XVI, 194
CLARK, XI, 310; XII, 118(2)
  Abraham, I, 36
  Benjamin, IV, 528
  Christopher, XIII, 105; XV, 44
  David, XIII, 553
  Edward, IV, 528
  George, VII, 199
  James, VII, 190, 192, 201; XII, 595; XV, 95, 160
  John, VII, 192
  Robert, XIII, 105
  Samuel, XIII, 582; XIV, 241
  Thomas M., XVI, 379
  William, VII, 129, 181; XIII, 87, 175; XV, 207, 297(3), 334; XVI, 62
CLARKE, I, 82
  Benajah, XIV, 139

George* Rogers,† X, 26, 161, 389, 505; XI, 283, 310, 327, 335(2), 336, 561, 562(2), 568, 573; XII, 232(2); XIII, 211; XV, 70
  James, VII, 569; XII, 293; XIV, 319, 422
  John, XII, 395, 398; XIV, 339(2); XV, 380
  Jonathan, XII,376, XIV, 421(2)
  Robert, XI, 61, 172
  Samuel, XVI, 31(3)
  Thomas, XIV, 422
  Thomas M., XVI, 338
  Watson, XV, 31(2)
  William, VIII, 375; XI, 335, 336; XII, 662; XV, 62
CLARKSON, William, XVI, 149(2)
CLAUDAY, William, I, 85
CLAUSE, Phettiplace‡, I, 139, 179
CLAXSONN, John, I, 381(2)
CLAY, Charles, XIII, 81
  Green, XII, 282, 603; XIII, 87
  Henry, VII, 202
  Matthew, XIII, 193, 275; XIV, 267; XV, 70
CLAYBORNE,§ I, 137, 142
  Thomas, V, 190
  William, I, 116, 153, 170, 178, 187, 202, 286, 371, 377, 380, 383, 385, 407, 408(2), 549; II, 249, 347
CLAYPOLE, Jacob, XVI, 51
  Joshua, VII, 218
CLAYPOOLE, Abraham, XII, 661
CLAYTER, John, XVI, 38
CLAYTON, VII, 326(2), 447
  George, IV, 241
  John, IV, 49, 115(2); VI, 242(2);
  Philip, VII, 306

Thomas, VII, 569; XIV, 322
CLEAVE, Christopher, I, 82
CLEEKE, Matthias, VII, 196
CLELAND, James, XII, 512, 514; XIV, 157
CLEMENT, Adam, XII, 398
  Benjamin, VII, 226
  Christian, VII, 181
CLEMENTS, XV, 32
  Charles, XV, 32
  Isham, XV, 30, 32(2), 458(3)
CLEMONS, James, VIII, 132
CLENDINEN, George, XI, 341, 450; XII, 72, 282, 725, 726; XIV, 312, 321 (2), 322(2)
  William, XII, 671, 725, 726(2); XIV, 312, 322; XVI, 48(3), 246
CLENDININ, Arabel, VIII, 198
  John, VII, 198
CLENE, Richard, I, 87
CLERK, Anthony Gavin, V, 268
  John, VII, 107
  Joseph, VII, 191
  William, XV, 120
CLIFFORD, T., II, 511
CLIFTON, William, V, 364; VI, 19; XV, 158
CLINCH, Joseph, V, 368
  Philip, VI, 297, 298(2), 299
  Rebecca (Edloe), VI, 297(2)
  William, V, 367; VI, 230(2), 240(2), 297 (3), 298(3), 299(2)
CLINE, George, XVI, 56
CLINGAN, William, I, 46
CLINTON, Henry, I, 87
CLITHEROE, Christopher, I, 86
CLOUD, Daniel, VII, 187
CLOUGH, George, XII, 374
CLOWDER, Jeremiah, IV, 236
CLOYD, XVI, 54
  David, VII, 180, 182, 225; XV, 124
  Gordon, XVI, 217

James, VII, 199
  John, VII, 229
  Joseph, XIII, 595
  Michael, VII, 199; XV, 31
CLUVERIUS, Benjamin, VII, 569
CLYMER, George, I, 23, 36
COAGHILL, Daniel, XIV, 336
COALTER, John, XV, 44; XVI, 94, 100, 405
COAN, VIII, 98; IX, 154, 161, 488, 511; X, 273, 475; XI, 235, 392; XIII, 480, 503
COHN, Robin, XV, 359
COBBS, VII, 420
  Charles, XII, 605
  John, X, 288
  John C., XIII, 626, 627
  Joseph, I, 279(2)
  Robert, VII, 402
  Samuel, VIII, 412
COBHAM, V, 569
COBURN, James, XII, 297
  John, XII, 369; XV, 234
  Jonathan, IX, 265
COCHRAN, Peter, VII, 197
COCK, Nicholas, II, 302(2); III, 479(2)
  Richard, I, 386
  Robert, I, 86
  Thomas, VI, 285, 286
COCKE, V, 370
  Abraham, IV, 95
  Allen, VIII, 618
  Anderson, XV, 30
  Benjamin, V, 250(2), 268(2), 378(2); VI, 15(2), 451; VIII, 67
  Bowler, VII, 390
  VIII, 466
  Bowler, Junior, VI, 281, 307; VIII, 149
  Catesby, VIII, 449
  Charles, XIV, 314; XV, 164
  Collin, XV, 408
  Elizabeth, (Carter), VIII, 466

Hartwell, VII, 515, 570, 618
James, VII, 75, 173, 233, 234, 257, 349, 359, 371, 382, 465, 502, 568; IX, 96, 122; XV, 265
James Powell, XIII, 588
John, VII, 456(4)
John Hartwell, XI, 57
John P., XV, 265
Richard, I, 283, VII, 569; XI, 57; XIV, 321
Thomas, IV, 460; XV, 122, 265
Thomas W., XV, 343(4)
William, I, 322; VII, 230, 493
COCKERAIN,* William, II, 197, 205
COCKETT, V, 190(2); VI, 15(2)
COCKFIELD, XIV, 155
COCKRAN, James, XV, 270
  Samuel, XV, 233, 234
COCKS, William, VIII, 415
CODD, St. Leger, II, 329, 433
COFFEE, Osborne, XIII, 607
COFFEE, Francis, XVI, 177
  James, XII, 201
  John, XVI, 49
COFFIELD, VI, 14
  Willis, VIII, 553
COFFMAN, John, XV, 49
COGGAN, III, 470
COGGIN, VI, 13; VIII, 174, 175(3); XIV, 155; XV, 50
COGH, Phely, VII, 196
COIEFIELD, III, 471
COITMORE, Rowland, I, 87
COKE, Sohn, I, 82
  William, I, 82
COKER, Bryan, VII, 223
  Joseph, VII, 223
COLBURN, William, XVI, 38 (3)
COLDWELL, George, VII, 204
COLE, I, 361; XIV, 156
  James, II, 39
  John, X, 112
  Thomas, XV, 411

Walter King, X, 300(6), 301; XI, 35(3)
William, I, 139; II, 329 (6), 324(5), 330, 544, 548, 549, 551(2), 563, 554, 587, 560, 568, 569; III, 557, 570; XV, 111, 207, 213, 265, 297(3), 364; XVI, 229(2), 230
COLEMAN, I, vii
  Ambrose, VII, 420
  Daniel, XVI, 52, 338
  Henry, I, 223; XIII, 553; XV, 380
  Henry E., XIII, 104, 173, 193; XV, 69; XVI 403
  John, VII, 226; XI, 250, 333; XIII, 104, 173, 315
  Nathaniel, XV, 54
  Richard, IV, 378; XVI, 177
  Robert, VII, 306, 307 (3), 326†, 447; XV, 419
  Robert Spilsbee, V, 305 (3)
  Samuel, XIII, 607, 608; XV, 190(3)
  Stephen, XIII, 276
  Thomas, X, 210
  William, XIV, 339
COLES, Henry, VII, 186
COLES, Isaac, XI, 250, 333; XIII, 173
  Isaac H., XV, 380; XVI, 136, 268, 346, 403
  John, XIII, 315, 316; XIV, 425; XVI, 68
  John, Junior, XVI, 68
  Walter, VII, 402; VIII, 554, 555; XV, 223
COLLCLOUGH, George, I, 507, 509, 512
COLLEY, Christopher, VII, 185
  John, VII, 185
  William, XV, 269(5)
COLLIER, Alexander, VIII, 129

Daniel, VII, 212
John, V, 370; VI, 239 (2); XII, 580(2), 581
Thomas, V, 369(2)
Vines, VII, 211
COLLIN, William, VII, 214
COLLINGS, Ann, VI, 242
COLLINS, Henry, I, 84; X, 288(2); XL 283
  James, XVI, 54
  John, I, 46; XIII, 284; XIV, 158; XVI, 431 (3)
  Luke, VIII, 129
COLMES, Hugh, XV, 387
COLQUHOUN, Robert, XVI, 100
COLSON, Charles, VII, 215 (2)
  John, VII, 225
COLSTON, Charles, VII, 636; VIII, 169
  Frances, VII, 636; VIII, 169(2)
  John, VII, 216
  Mary, VII, 636, 637; VIII, 169(2)
  Rawleigh, XV, 121; XVI, 423
  William, VII, 636(3), 637(2), 638(2); VIII, 168, 169(4), 170(2)
COLTER, James, VII, 196(2)
COLTHURST, Henry, I, 86
COLVERT, Samuel, XV, 365
COLVIN, Stephen, XIII, 90
COLWELL, Robert, XVI, 348 (2)
COMBS, Gilbert, XIV, 277(2)
  Josiah, VII, 216
COMER, William, VII, 226
COMOCK, I, 83
COMPTON, Reuben, XIII, 132, 214(4)
  William, I, 81

CONNAL, John, XIII, 297
CONNALLY, Thomas, VII, 212
CONNELL, James, X, 372, 373 (4)
  John, XV, 119(2)*, 160; XVI, 246, 412
CONNELLY, George, XVI, 407
CONNER, John, XIII, 48
  Lewis, XVI, 225
CONNOLLY, John, X, 293(2); XI, 276, 277(3), 321 (4), 322(4), 474(5), 475(3); XII, 395, 396; XIII, 310(2), 311
CONNOR, Charles XIV, 333 (3)
  John, XIV, 157
  Lewis, XV, 121
CONOWAY, Christopher, XI, 514(3)
  Sarah (Withers), VI, 514, 515(2)
CONRAD, Jacob, XIV, 322
CONROD, Edward, XV, 459
  Henry, XVI, 29
  Stephen, XV, 377
CONSOLVER, John, XV, 134 (2), 187(2)
CONSTANCE, IV, 266, 382, 385; V, 14, 142, 145, 199, 242; VI, 173, 177; VII, 532; VIII, 79, 98, 323
CONSTEMAN, Lawrence, VII, 200
CONWAY, IV, 336, 383, 386, 387; V, 14, 137, 142, 144, 233; VI, 169, 172, 175; VII, 77, 97, 101, 323; IX, 153, 160, 486, 510, 513(3); XIV, 154
  Darby,† VII, 179, 180
  Edward, I, 81, 90; IV, 452, 453; XII, 215
  Edwin, XIV, 408, 409
  Francis, IV, 268; IX, 234; X, 197; XI, 363 (3), 364; XIV, 154
  Miles Withers, XII, 361, 608; XIII, 163

Peter, XIV, 409
Richard, XIII, 94, 175, 312, 592; XIV, 387; XV, 89
Sarah, VIII, 19
Thomas, I, 83
Withers, VII, 231
CONYERS, John, XV, 43
COOK, XIV, 268
  Benjamin, XV, 50, 160, 233, 234
  Elizabeth, VIII, 193
  Harmon, XII, 659(2), 660
  John, VII, 216, 217, 220
  Stephen, XIII, 592
COOKCAS, Henry, XV; 139
COOKE, Benjamin, XV, 95; XVI, 45
  Harman, XV, 160
  John, VII, 201, XIII, 595, 611
  Shem, VII, 201
  William, VII, 212
COOKSON, William, II, 370, 375(2), 377, 547
COONES, Joseph, XV, 178(3)
COONROD, Wooley, VII, 179, 180, 182
COOPER, III, 415
  Edward, XII, 299; XIV, 169; XV, 309
  Francis, VII, 22
  Isles, V, 294(5), 295(4), 296(6)
  James, VII, 224
  Jeremiah, VII, 184
  John, I, 85; VII, 216, 217; XVI, 420(2)
  Leonard, VII, 216; XIV, 312, 322
  Lewis, XVI, 231
  Mary, ___ (Lutz), XIII, 303(4)
  Matthew, I, 87
  Nathan, XVI, 334
  Richard, I, 85
  Robert, I, 85
  Susannah, V, 296(5)
  Susannah (Sanders), V, 294(6), 295(8)
  Thomas, VII, 204

William, XIII, 303(2)
COPE, Anthony, I, 81
  Walter, I, 67, 77, 82, 90
COPELAND, Henry, V, 74
COPLIN, Benjamin, XIII, 292; XIV, 242
COPLINGER, George, VII, 182; VIII, 126
COPPACK, Moses, VII, 25
COPPEDGE, Charles, VII, 52
COPPIN, George, I, 82, 90
COPSEY, John, XV, 379
CORBEN, Henry, I, 506
CORBIN, V, 250; VI, 18
  Coventon,* VII, 64, 131
  Francis, XII, 698; XIII, 287
  Gawin, V, 66; VII, 458
  Gawin (of King and Queen), VII, 458
  Gawin (of Westmoreland), VII, 458(4), 459(3), 460(7), 461
  George, XII, 364; XIII, 233(2)
  Hannah, VII, 458, 459, 460, 461
  Henry, I, 512(2), 530; II, 156, 320
  Johanna, VII, 459
  John, VII, 458, 459; VIII, 128; XV, 121
  John Tayloe, VIII, 456, 633; X, 103
  Martha, VII, 458(2), 459, 461
  Richard, VI, 394; VII, 459(2), 460, 461, 481; VIII, 159, 160, 161 (4), 370, 580
CORBYN, Henry, II, 201
CORD, William, VII, 131
CORDER, James, VII, 214
COREHAM, John, VII, 24
CORKER, John, I, 178, 196 (2), 203, 222, 289, 371, 377, 383
  William, I, 430
CORNECK, Lemuel, XI, 58
CORNELIUS, John, I, 84
CORNET, Martin, VII, 180

CORNHILL, John, XIV, 415
  Mary, XIV, 415(3)
CORNICK, Joel, XI, 270
  Lemuel, XI, 270
CORNWALL, John, XV, 24,228
CORNWALLIS, X, 572, 574
CORNWELL, John, VII, 24
CORREE, James, VII, 208
CORWINE, Richard, XIII, 183
COSBY, Anne, VII, 160
  John, VII, 179, 180
COTRELL, Thomas, VII, 203
COTTEN, John, V, 74
COTTERELL, Moses, XIV, 322
COTTOW, Rowland, I, 82
COTTRELL, Thomas, VII, 52
COTTRILL, William, VII, 218
COUCH, Daniel, XVI, 404
  James, XIII, 657*
  John, XIII, 149
  Samuel, XIII, 70(2)
  Tetrarch, VIII, 186
COUDEN, James, VII, 195
COULSTON, Lyonell, I, 133
COULTER, John, XVI, 348(2)
COULTHARD, Thomas, VII, 22
COUN, Gerrard T., XV, 426
COUNCIL, Michael, XII, 105 (3), 106
COUPLAND, David, XII, 661; XIII, 101(5), 102, 149, 315, 316; XIV, 269
  James, XIII, 101(3)
COURSEY, Henry, II, 201
COURTNEY, Philip, XV, 411
  William, I, 82; XIII, 210(2), 211(2)
COUTT, VIII, 423; XII, 221 (2)
COUTTS, VII, 221; XII, 385
  Patrick, VIII, 656; XII, 385(2); XIII, 228(3), 229(5)
  Reuben, XII, 385(5), 386(2); XIV, 155
  William, XIII, 228, 229; XIV, 272
COVEL, Francis, I, 83
COVENTON, Richard, VII, 230
COVENTRY, Henry, II, 430, 528, 565

COVINGTON, Francis, XIII, 221
  Richard, VII, 213
  Thomas, VII, 227
COWAN, Andrew, XVI, 331 (2)
  James, VII, 192
  John, X, 288; XI, 283; XII, 322, 466
  Robert, XIII, 61
  William, XVI, 183
COWDOWN, James, VII, 198
COWDREY, Savage, VIII, 469
  Mary, VIII, 469
COWEN, John, VII, 203
COWLE, VI, 14(2)
COWFER, Andrew, XII, 595
  Edward, XI, 185
  John, XII, 479, 492; XIII, 175
  John, Junior, XIII, 159
  Robert, XII, 211
  Wells, XII, 211, 479
  William, IX, 466
  Wills, VIII, 543; XIII, 175, 232(3)
COX, Abner, XVI, 196(2)
  Charles, VII, 208; XIII, 544; XVI, 355
  David, VIII, 129
  Edward, XV, 50
  Fleet, XI, 363
  Gabriel, XII, 719
  George, XII, 721; XIII, 297; XIV, 157
  Isaac, XI, 283, 470; XII, 282, 631
  John, V, 367; VII, 201, 213, 214; VIII, 129; XI, 29, 30; XIII, 96 (2), 99(3), 541, 614 (2); XV, 239(6)
  Josiah, VII, 220
  Mary, XVI, 196(2)
  Richard, I, 83
  William, IV, 539; VII, 220
COXE, Richard, I, 178
COYLE, George, VIII, 127
COYBE, William, I, 83
CRABELL, Jonas, XVI, 47

CRABTREE, William, VII, 208
CRADDOCK, Richard, VII, 201
CRAFFORD, David, V, 257, 258(2), 259(2); VII, 130
CRAFURD, John, VII, 192
CRAGHEAD, George, XVI, 346
William, XV, 353
CRAIG, XII, 580
Adam, IX, 145, 146(2)
Alexander, VII, 160(2), 187, 188, 195
David, XV, 446; XVI, 407(2)
Elijah, XIII, 170
Hiram, XVI, 269, 270
James, VI, 528; XIII, 77, 585; XIV, 321; XVI, 194, 217
John, XI, 283; XII, 83; XIII, 183(2)
Robert, VII, 195; IX, 555; XV, 426
Robert, Junior, XV, 446
Toliver, XIII, 170
CRAIGEN, John, XVI, 51
CRALLE, John, XV, 121
CRAMER, Ambrose, XV, 276 (3)
CRAMPE, Thomas, I, 154
CRAMPTON, I, 142
CRANE, James, XII, 371
CRANSHAW, Thomas, III, 471
CRASHAW, Relegh, I, 84
William, I, 83
CRAVEN, II, 528
CRAVENS, William, VII, 180, 183, 187(2)
CRAWFORD, VI, 14(3)
Anne, XVI, 425(3)
Charles, VII, 204
Carter, XIII, 607(2)
David, VI, 300, 301, 302(2)
John, VII, 127
Nathan, XIII, 316(2)
Nelson, XV, 343
Reuben, XVI, 425(3)
William, VI, 265, 266; VII, 207, 208; XIII, 106; XV, 215, 445, 456(2); XVI, 188

William S., XIII, 316 (2); XIV, 322; XV, 419
CRAWLEY, James, III, 118
CRAWSON, James, XVI, 188 (3)
CRAY, Alexander, XI, 242
CREAMER, George, XIV, 270
CREEL, George, Junior, XVI, 246
CRENSHAW, Thomas, VI, 16
William, VIII, 55, 56
CRESAP, XII, 259, 456
Thomas, XII, 61(2), 62 (3); XIII, 480(2), 504
CREVENS, John, VII, 188
CKEW, Anthony, I, 83
Randall,* I, 239, 283, 323, 340
CREWDSON, James, XV, 31
CREWES, James, II, 370, 375 (2), 377, 547(7)
CREWS, David, XII, 603
CRIGLER, Lewis, XV, 223
CRIPPS, Zachary,† I, 139, 169, 187, 203
CRIPS, Zachary, VIII, 453(4)
CRITE, Hamon, VII, 219; VIII, 130(2)
CRITTENDEN, Elinor, XIII, 616, 617
John, XI, 283
CROCKET, Hugh, VII, 210; XIII, 585
James, VII, 25
John, VII, 189, 191, 193
Joseph, VII, 194, 208; XII, 282, 370, 391, 400
Walter, X, 195(3) ;XIII, 583, 590
CROCKETT, Andrew, XVI, 174(4)
James, XVI, 174(4)
John, XV, 270
CROFORD, George, VII, 191
CROFT, Robert, I, 78
CROFTE, Herbert, I, 82
CROGHAN, George, X, 139(2) 140

William, XII, 397; XIII, 299
CROLEY, Benjamin, VII, 220
CROMWELL, Henry, I, 85
Oliver, I, xiii(2), 5, 78, 81, 90, 280, 358, 509, 513, 527(6), 528; II, 391(2), 517
Richard, I, xiv, 358, 509(2), 511, 527, 528, 544
CROPPER, John, XII, 496; XIII, 233(2)
John, Junior, XII, 364, 402
Robert, VII, 216
CROSBY, Henry, VII, 131
John, VII, 185
John, Junior, VII, 184
William, I, 83
CROSHAW, Joseph, II, 161
Rauleigh, I, 129
CROSS, William, VII, 215
CROSSE, VII, 221
CROUCH, William, VII, 25
CROUCHE, III, 470; VI, 14; VIII, 263(4), 370(2), 555
CROUDSON, John, XV, 260
Samuel, XV, 65, 383
CROW, XII, 61(2), 259, 456; XIII, 163
John, XI, 285
William, VII, 552, 554; XII, 62(2), 83, 675 (3); XIII, 480(3), 504; XIV, 155, 156, 375
CROWS, III, 569
CROWSHAW, Joseph, I, 506, 512, 530
CRUES, Nicholas, XIV, 266
CRUCER, William, XIV, 277
CRUMLEY, James, VII, 214
William, VIII, 415
CRUMP, Charles, VII, 228
Edward, VII, 198
Goodrich, XIV, 319
John, XV, 223
Richard, XII, 591; XIII, 293; XIV, 319
William, VII, 21

CRUMPE, Elizabeth, I, 405(2)
Thomas, I, 178, 203
CRUPPER, Gilbert, VII, 24
CRUROTHERS, William, VII, 196
CRUTCHFIELD, IV, 335, 383; V, 142, 326(2); VI, 169, 172(2), 176, 224, 473; VII, 64(3), 65 (3), 127(2), 128, 129 (2), 532, 533; VIII, 78, 98, 100(5), 236*, 321, 322, 390, 407; IX, 154, 159, 160, 488, 510, 513(4); X, 273, 356, 475, 476; XIII, 271(2), 479, 503
Stapleton, XII, 729
CRUTE, John L., XV, 31
CRYER, George, VII, 239
CUGLEY, Daniel, I, 146
CULBERSON, VIII, 600
CULDERTSON, Joseph, XV, 390, 392
CULL, James, VII, 191
CULLER, Thomas, I, 86
CULLINS, John, XV, 182(4), 188(4)
CULPEPER,† John, I, 84; IV, 515(2), 516, 520; VII, 201
Thomas, I, 84; II, vi, viii(10), 427, 458(3), 464, 466, 488, 508(2), 517, 518(3), 519(3), 520(2), 521(5), 522 (2), 523, 529, 560, 561, 563, 564(3), 565 (6), 566(6), 567(2), 568, 569(3), 570(3), 571, 572(2), 573(3), 574, 575(6), 576(4), 577(5), 578(4), 579, 580(4), 581, 582(7), 583; III, 25, 546, 550, 555(2), 557, 561, 563, 664, 570(2); IV, 515 (2), 516, 520(2), 521 (4), 522
CULTLETT, John, II, 184
CULTON, James, VII, 196

CUMPTON, Ambrose, VII, 202
CUNLIFFE, John, XV, 374
CUNINGHAM, Jacob, VII, 191
William, VII, 191
CUNNINGHAM, VII, 191
Andrew, VII, 180
Andrew, Junior, VII, 179
James, VII, 214; XIII, 267; XIV, 169; XV, 309
John, VII, 179(2), 180, 184; XVI, 66
John, Junior, VII, 180, 185
Robert, VII, 181(2), 185, 188, 214
Sarah, VII, 197
Walter, VII, 183, 193, 195, 493
William, VII, 179, 180, 181(2), 185, 222*, 223; XII, 672, 673
CUNROD, John, VII, 184
Walter, VII, 185
Willry, VII, 187
CUPPY, John, XV, 49
CURD, John, XII, 400(3), 401 (2); XIII, 296; XVI, 530

CURETON, James, XIV, 320; XV, 66, 218, 265, 351
CURL, VI, 224
CURLE, Nicholas Wilson, VIII, 264
Priscilla, VI, 242
Wilson, VI, 223; VIII, 78
Roscow Wilson, X, 102
CURRELL, Nicholas, XV, 129 (3)
CURREY, William, VII, 192
CURRIE, James, XVI, 95
CURRY, Barnaby, VII, 21
CURTIS, Christopher, VII, 227
Edmund, I, 365, 367, 368
John, I, 530
Thomas, XII, 402
CUSTIS, Daniel Parke, V, 117
Edmund, XII, 496
Eleanor, XIII, 99(3)
Frances, (Parke), IV, 29; VI, 319
Henry, IX, 310
John, I, 499; II, 428, 552, 557, 569; III, 546 (3), 570; IV, 29
John Parke, XIII, 99(5)
Thomas, VII, 200
William, I, 499

William, XII, 227
DAMERON, Bartholomew, VII, 52 (4), 53
DAMOUYEL, Samuel, IV, 549 (3)
DANA, Francis, I, 46
DANBY, Henry, I, 83
DANCEY, XIV, 155
DANDRIDGE, Bartholomew, VIII, 284; IX, 68
Dorothea, VIII, 224, 225, 226
Elizabeth, VII, 296(2), 297(7), 486(4), 487 (5)
Julius B., XIII, 318
Martha, VIII, 224, 225 (2), 226
Nathaniel West, VI, 322(3), 323(3), 428, 429, 430(3), 431(5); VIII, 224(5), 225(6), 226(3), 227, 284, 638, 639(6)
Stephen, XVI, 423
Unity, VII, 296, 297(3), 486(2), 487(4); VIII, 224(4), 225, 227(3), 639
Unity (West), VI, 322 (2), 323(2), 428, 429 (7), 430
William, VI, 322(4), 323(7), 428, 429(5), 430(3); VIII, 286; XIII, 621
DANDY, Thomas, VII, 223
DANGERFIELD, William, VII, 493; VIII, 149
DANIEL, Henry, XIV, 334
Joshua, XII, 600
Peter V., I, ii(4); X, ii; XI, ii(3)
Robert, XII, 602
Travers, Junior, XIII, 585
Walker, XI, 283, 335, 336; XI, 601, 602; XIII, 68(2)
William, XV, 259
DANNAR, Jacob, XIV, 323
DANSIE, VI, 492; VII, 583

Thomas, VI, 211, 426, 426(5), 427(5)
DANTIGNAC, John, XIII, 97 (2), 98(2)
DARBY, Edward, VII, 223
DARDEN, Jacob, VIII, 552, 553
DARKE, William, XII, 371
DARNELL, Henry, VIII, 132
DARNS, William, VII, 218
DARRACOTT, Richard, XIV, 243
William, XIII, 73
DASBY, Jacob, XVI, 79
DAUGHERTY, James, XII, 213
Thomas, VII, 223
DAUGLOSS,* Adam, XVI, 52
DAULTON, James, VII, 225
DAUNN, John, VII, 208
DAVENPORT, XIV, 156
Birkett,† XI, 36; XIII, 143; XIV, 245
Catherine, VIII, 406
George, VIII, 83, 176, 260, 351, 361
Matthew, IX, 68
Thomas, VIII, 658
DAVICE, John, VII, 192
Samuel, VII, 196
DAVIDSON, Christopher, I, 111
Daniel, XIV, 334
Isaac, XIV, 242
Nathaniel, XV, 267
Samuel, VII, 192
William, XV, 383; XVI, 100, 232
DAVIES, Abraham, I, 86
Benjamin, XVI, 191; XII, 297
Jane, II, 559
Jonathan, XV, 67
Nicholas, VIII, 555(2); IX, 233; XI, 341(2); XIV, 155
Tamerlane William, Whiting, VII, 333
Thomas, I, 516
DAVIS, I, vii, 516(2); IV, 267, 332, 336, 383, 385; V, 142, 144; VI, 173, 175; VIII, 78,

D

DABNEY, XI, 170(2), 310; XIV, 154
Charles, XV, 223
Francis, XVI, 338
George, IV, 113; VI, 17; XV, 323
Isham E., XVI, 419(2)
James, VIII, 457
John, XVI, 338
William, VI, 291
DACKER, William, I, 236
DA COSTA, XIII, 323(3)
DADE, Baldwin, VII, 605; XV, 49(2)
Horatia, VIII, 626
Townshend, XI, 110

William Alexander, XVI, 236
DAIC, VI, 19
DAILEY, James, XVI, 162
John, VII, 202
DAINGERFIELD, Henry, XVI, 232
Robinson, VIII, 634
William, VIII, 290, 302; X, 470
DALE, Thomas, I, 3(2)
DALTON, VII, 22
Charlotte, XII, 226(3), 227(3)
Samuel, XII, 226(2), 227(2)

98, 509(2); IX, 154
(2), 159, 161(2), 488,
511(2), 513(2), 514
(2); X, 273(2), 356
(2), 475(2); XI, 211
(2), 235(2), 237(2),
238(4), 391; XII,
581; XIII, 480(2),
503(2); XVI, 182,
334
Augustine, XV, 118, 419
Benjamin, VII, 192, 213,
306, 307(6); XII, 614
Charles, XIII, 296; XVI,
404
David, VII, 203
Edward, VII, 21, 208;
XIII, 296
Henry L., XV, 167(2),
168
Hezekiah, XIII, 151
Hugh, I, 146
Isaac, XIII, 175; XIV,
322
Isaac, Junior, XIV, 330
Isham, VII, 203
Jacob, XIV, 322
James, VII, 191; XIV,
322
John, I, 85; VII, 181,
185, 194, 198, 208,
218, 224; VIII, 658;
XIII, 583; XIV, 272,
322
Joseph W., XVI, 185
Lancelot, I, 87
Micajah, XIV, 266, 267
Nicholas, VI, 375; VII,
202; VIII, 44; IX, 585
(2)
Nicholas C., XV, 343(5)
Robert, I, 284; VII, 202
Rowland,* III, 557
Samuel, I, 279; XIII,
169, 174, 175; XVI,
309
Sarah, VIII, 130, 172,
173(2)
Thomas, I, 431; II, 15;
V, 74; XIV, 322
Walter, XIII, 554
William, I, 239, 339;

VII, 208; XIII, 296;
XIV, 322; XV, 242;
XVI, 309
William, Junior, XVI,
266
DAVISON, Daniel, XII, 295,
661
George, VII, 196
Hezekiah, XII, 295, 661.
XIV, 158
James, VII, 196
John, VII, 191(2)
William, XV, 274; XVI,
52
DAVISSON, John, XII, 209
DAWBER, Edmund, I, 375,
376(3)
DAWE, Philip, XIV, 394; XV,
37
DAWEN, Daniel, II, 12
DAWKES, Henry, I, 84
DAWLEY, James, XV, 40
DAWS, Thomas, VII, 209
DAWSON, Elizabeth (Church-
ill), VII, 158
John, VII, 21
Lewis, XV, 343
Martin, XVI, 318
Pleasant, XVI, 68
DAY, Benjamin, XII, 420;
XIII, 100; XV, 58
Samuel, XV, 155
William, VII, 214
DAYMES, William, I, 376
DAYTON, Jonathan, I, 22

DEAN, Adam, VII, 193
John, VII, 182; VIII,
130
Joseph, XVI, 337
Richard, I, 83
DEANE, Francis, XV, 30, 32
(2), 268(3)
James, XIII, 171; XV,
30, 32
Joseph, XVI, 379
Thomas, XV, 30, 32
DEANS, James, VII, 408
DEARBORN, XVI, 130(2)
DEARING, Henry, XII, 661
John, XV, 30

DEATH, Charles, II, 371
Richard, I, 239, 283
DECKER, XIV, 157
John, VII, 25
Sarah, VII, 25
DEEKER, XVI, 44
D'EEM, Adam XVI, 245
DEERING, Henry, XIV, 242,
272; XV, 249
DEGELL, Edward, VII, 216
DEGRANCH, John Abraham,
VII, 224
DELANEY, Daniel, VII, 23
DELAWAR,* I, 3; V, 559
DELLINGER, George, XVI, 29
DELONEY, XIV, 155
DELONY, Henry, X, 372(2)
Lewis, VI, 376(2)
DEMOVIL, Sampson, VII, 21
DENEAL, James, XIV, 394;
XV, 37
DENEALE, James, XVI, 174
DENEALLE, William, XV, 282
DENISTON, Daniel, VII, 190
DENNEY, William, VII, 52
DENNIS, Edward, II, 161, 162
Nathaniel, XVI, 333(2),
334
Thomas, I, 82
DENNISON, William, XV, 338
DENNY, Benjamin, VIII, 128
Edmund, XIV, 395
Walter, XV, 124
DENSON, William, I, 528
DENTON, Thomas, VII, 212
William, VII, 212
DEFRIEST, John, VII, 204;
XV, 95, 160
Langsdon, VII, 204
DEQUESTER, Matthew, I, 85
DERBY, VIII, 301, 302(2),
303
DE RICHBOURG, Claude Phil-
ip, III, 228
DERING, Henry, XVI, 334
DETTOR, John, XVI, 179
DEVINNISH, Robert, XVI,
223
DEVORE, James, IX, 546
DEW, Robert, VII, 195
Thomas,† I, 236, 370,
373, 379, 384, 386,

408, 422(3), 432, 505,
608, 526
DEWEY, Stephen, VI, 485
DEWHURST, I, 82
DEWIT, Ezekiel, IX, 265
DEXTER, I, 82

DIAL, XII, 83; XIV, 153
DICE, Matthias, VII, 187
DICK, I, vii; XII, 118, 400(2)
Charles, IX, 72
DICKENSON, Henry, VII, 222
John, VII, 182
DICKERSON, Robert, XVI,
410
DICKIE, Michael, VII, 181
DICKINSON, Adam, VII, 191
John, I, 22, 46
DICKSON, Benjamin, VIII,
130
John, VII, 216
DICKY, Matthew, XV, 30
DICTOM,‡ Joseph, VII, 188
(2)
DIER, John, VII, 201
DIEUGUID, William, XIII, 587
DIGBY, John, I, 82; II, 370,
375(2), 377, 547
DIGGES, Dudley, I, 82, 90; VI,
415, 416, 418, 437,
524; VII, 13, 39, 40,
76, 84, 136, 288, 647
(2); IX, 49, 95; X,
209; XII, 496
Dudley, Junior, VIII,
365, 378, 482
Edward,§ I, 5(4), 388,
403, 408, 426(2), 428
(2), 431, 529; II, 320;
V, 366, 371, 402, 403
(2); VI, 197; XII,
685; XIII, 92
Elizabeth (Wormeley),
VII, 452(2)
Thomas, XII, 685; XIII,
92
William, VII, 418, 437,
524; VII, 13, 76, 288,
568; VIII, 452(2),
453(3)
DIGGS, Cole, XVI, 223
DIKE, John, I, 86

DIXTON, Joseph, VII, 185
DILKE, Clement, I, 129
Roger, I, 203
DILLARD, James, VII,219(5),
XV, 419
John, XIV, 316; XV,
176, 419
Mary, XIII, 516
Thomas, Junior, VIII,
208
DILLIARD, James, XIII, 587
DILLINCHAM, Vachel, VII,
226
William, VII, 220, 226*
DIMER, V, 142, 145
DINGLEY, John, I, 84
DINWIDDIE, Robert, V, 567,
568; VI, 7, 324, 454,
560; VII, 7, 75, 561,
662; X, 36
DIPNALL, Thomas, I, 386
DITCHFIELD, Edward, I, 84
DIVER, Charles, VII, 180
Hugh, VII, 180(2)
DIVERS, George, XIII, 169,
175; XV, 271, 427;
XVI, 149, 318
DIX, XIV, 156
James, XIV, 267
John, VIII, 193; IX, 334,
335; XV, 166
William, XIV, 261(4),
262
DIXON, VI, 226; VIII, 100
(2), 236, 322(3), 323,
493, 495(2), 506; IX,
146(2), 154, 159, 161,
489, 510, 513(2); X,
273, 356, 475; XI, 211,
236, 237, 238(2);
XIII, 480, 504; XIV,
264; XV, 257(2), 268
Edward, VI, 318(2)
Elizabeth, XIII, 136,
137
Haidenby, III, 420
Henry, XV, 426
Henry St. John, XVI,
110, 167(2), 181
James, XIV, 335(2),
336
John, V, 371;VI, 223,

224; VII, 23; VIII,
78, 98, 497; XIII, 136
(5), 137(4), 138, 139
(2), 140(5), 141(10),
144; XIV, 335; XV,
110
Lucy, XIV, 335
Michael, VII, 226
Nancy, XIV, 336
Patsey, XIV, 335
Roger, VI, 282; VII, 22,
23(2), 327, 449; VIII,
30, 33, 485, 494; X,
121
Sarah, XIV, 335
Thomas, XIII, 136, 137
William, VII, 223
DIXTON, John, VII, 209

DOAKE, Robert, XVI, 94
DOBBINS, Richard, VII, 212
DOBSON, William, I, 83
DODD, Zachariah, VII, 225
DODDERIDGE, John, I, 67, 77
DODDRIDGE, Joseph, XV,
169; XVI, 169
Philip, XV, 169; XVI,
159
DODINGTON, George, V, 559
DOE, Thomas, I, 138
DOEG, V, 104; XIV, 153
DOGGETT, Richard, VII, 213
DOHERTY, James, VII, 224
DOLBY, John, II, 199
DONALD, George, VIII, 656
James, XVI, 308
Robert, VII, 129, 130;
XVI, 308
DONALDSON, John, VII, 211
DONALLY, Andrew, XVI, 157
Andrew, Junior, XVI,
194
DONIPHAN, Anderson, VI,
495
DONLAP, Nathaniel, VII, 190
DONNALLY, Andrew, XIV,
321, 322
Charles, XV, 362
DONNE, Samuel, VI, 282
DONNELLEY, Andrew, XI, 139
DONNELLY, Andrew, XI,841;
XII, 72; XVI, 29(2)

John, VIII, 128
DONNOLLY, Andrew, XI, 450
DOODES, Minor, II, 308(2);
VII, 499
DOOE, John, VII, 236
DOOLEY, Abraham, VIII, 129
Henry, VIII, 129
James, VIII, 129
Thomas, VII, 211
DORREL, V, 259
DOSWELL, James, XIV, 243,
268; XV, 165
DOUGHERTY, Michael, VII,
190
William, VII, 200
DOUGHTIE, Edward, IV, 528
(2)
James, IV, 528
DOUGLAS, Adam,* XIV, 378;
XV, 99, 250, 274
Edward, I, 283, 323
James, VII, 316(2), 426
(2), 427
John, IV, 308
DOUGLASS, Achilles, XII, 398
Adam, XVI, 100
George, XVI, 408(2)
John, XV, 30
Jonathan, XII, 194
Judy, XVI, 408(2)
Margaret, XVI, 408
William, XII, 383
DOUTHAT, Robert, XIII, 174
DOWDALL, John, XIV, 376
DOWDAS, Minor, I, 499
DOWELL, John, VII, 24
DOWLAND, Thomas, VIII, 552
DOWNES, George, I, 164, 170,
179, 187
DOWNING, Thomas D., XV,
121(2)
William, XI, 171
DOWNMAN,† John, I, 133,139
Joseph Ball, XII, 215
DOWNS, Henry, VII, 188
DOWNTUS,‡ John, I, 111
DOYLE, Thomas, VII, 24

DRANSFIELD, Avern, I, 86
DRAPER, Thomas, I, 84
DRAYTON, William II., I, 46
DREW, John, VIII, 553

Perez, XIII, 90
Thomas, IV, 363; VI,
19; XIV, 156
William, X, 536, 537,
538(2), 539, 541, 543,
544, 545, 567(2), 568,
569, 570; XI, 546,
552, 553
DRINANE, John, XV, 445
DRINKARD, William, XV, 411
William, Junior, XV,411
DRIVER, Charles, VII, 179
John, IX, 466; XII, 211;
XIV, 308
DRODDY, William, XVI, 44
DROMGOOLE, Edward, XV, 52
DROMOND, William, I, 649(2)
II, 158(2)
DROUT, Richard, III, 95
DRUERDENT, Philip, I, 86
DRUITT, Jonathan, VIII, 607;
VIII..171
DRUM, William, II, 253
DRUMER, III, 568, 569
DRUMMON, Aaron, VII, 224
DRUMMOND, II, 558(6); III,
471; V, 191; VII, 614;
XII, 488
Richard, XII, 402(2)
Thomas, XIV, 261(2)
William,§ II, 226(2),
370, 375(2), 377, 546,
558(3)
DRUNN, Lewis, XV, 249
DRURY, Drue, I, 81
Robert, I, 81, 90
DRYSDALE, Hugh, I, 3; IV, 5,
142, 181

DUANE, James, I, 46
DUCKETT, J., X, 552, 556
DUCKWORTH, John, VII, 217
DUDGEON, John, VII, 226
Richard, VII, 223, 226
William, VII, 223
DUDLEY, V, 16(4); XIV,
164(2)
Ambrose, VIII, 149
George, VI, 242
DUDLY, III, 220(2)
DUEK, William, I, 46
DUFF, William, XIV, 420

DUKE, V, 269
Henry, III, 181, 202
DULANY, Anthony, XIV, 336
Benjamin, XII, 393
Joseph, XIV, 336
William H.,* XV, 99;
XVI, 29
DULING, Edward, XIII, 283
(2); XIV, 157, 158
DULY, James, VII, 210
Thomas, VII, 210
DUN, Daniel, I, 82
William, I, 85
DUNBAR, Richard, VI, 243
Robert, XIV, 245, 308
William, X, 139, 140(2)
DUNCAN, VI, 256
Alexander, XVI, 100
Charles, XI, 282
Howson, XV, 120
James, XIII, 88, 176(2)
John, VII, 214, 230
Joseph, VII, 214
William, VII, 23
DUNCANSON, James, XI, 36
DUNCKLEBERRY, Abraham,
VII, 191
DUNDAS, John, XIII, 94, 174;
XIV, 263(3), 404
DUNKLE, George, VII, 185,
187
John,† VII, 182, 185,
187
DUNLAP, IX, 263; XIII, 166;
XIV, 426; XV, 345,
466; XVI, 172, 422
DUNLEVY, Anthony, VII, 217
DUNLOP, Adam, VII, 179,
180, 195
Archibald, X, 477; XII,
364
James, VI, 275, 288;
VII, 197
John, VII, 196
Robert, VIII, 126
DUNMORE, VIII, 5(4); IX,
75, 93, 320; X, 558;
XIII, 50, 205

DUNN, James, XV, 31
Lewis, X, 211(2)
Waters, VIII, 131(2)
William, I, 86
DUNNEVANT, Daniel, XIII,
608
DUNSCOMB, Andrew, XIV,
308
DUNSTON, John, I, 358
DUNWIDDIE, XV, 53
DUPPA, James, I, 87
Jeffry, I, 84
DUPREE, Lewis, XV, 338;
XVI, 60
DUPUY, James, XVI, 410
DURBIN, Daniel, VII, 220
DURELL, XV, 111
James, XV, 263
William, XI, 382
DURETTE, Philip, I, 84
DURRETT, James, XVI, 179
DURTIN, Philip, XV, 63
DUVAL,‡ XVI, 94
Claiborne, XII, 222(2)
Daniel, IX, 573
Philip, XIII, 587
Samuel, VI, 281; VIII,
656; X, 318; XII, 222
(4), 223(3); XIII,
28; XV, 50
William, XII, 222(2);
XIII, 229, XVI, 79, 95
DUVALL, John Pearce, XII,
639
DYER, XI, 557(2)
James, XIV, 322; XVI,
56
John, VIII, 131
Roger, VII, 182, 185
Samuel, XIV, 420
William, VII, 182, 184,
185
DYMER, VII, 173, 175; VIII,
78, 98, 323; IX, 164,
161, 488, 511; XI, 391
(3), 392; XIII, 480,
503; XV, 166(2)

E

EARHART,* Abraham, VII,
183
Michael, VII, 180, 182,
183, 184, 190
EARHEART, Martin, XIII, 297
EARL, Samuel, XIV, 153
EARLE, Samuel, VII, 588
EARLY,† Jeremiah, VII, 207,
210(2), 211, 475; X,
109(2)
John, VII, 186; XIII,
193, 585
Jubul,XIII, 586
EARSKIN, Michael, XV, 223
EARSOM, Jacob, XII, 403;
XIII, 171, XIV, 153
EASLEY, James, XIV, 322
EASON, John, XV, 365
Samuel, XIII, 685
EAST, John, VII, 223
Talton, VII, 223
Thomas, XV, 166, 210
William, VII, 223
EASTER, John, XV, 52
EASTHAM, James, XVI, 403
William, VII, 23
EASTIS, William, VII, 224
EATON, Francis, VII, 21
Thomas, IV, 306, VII,
317(2), 318, 319, 320;
XV, 164, 165
EBERMAN, Jacob, VII, 185
John, VII, 185
Michael, VII, 184, 185
ECHOLLS,‡ Jacob, XVI, 324
Joseph, XII, 512; XIV,
157, 257; XV, 125
EDDINGTON, Joseph, XII,238
EDMESTON, Samuel, VII, 198
William, VII, 198
EDGAR, David, XV, 345
Thomas, XI, 139; XIV,
375; XV, 63
EDGENTON, George, XV, 167
EDIE, John, XVI, 64
EDLOE, XIV, 155(3); XV,
272(2)

Anne, VI, 312
John, V, 111; VI, 312,
376(2)
Philip, VI, 297(3), 298
(2), 299(2)
Rebecca, VI, 297(4)
William, VI, 312
EDLOW, I, 249, 278
EDLOWE, Matthew, I, 136,606
EDMISON, Robert, XV, 360
EDMISTON, David, VII, 196
Moses,§ VII, 196(2)
Samuel, XVI, 32
EDMONDS, Anne, V, 196(2)
Elias, VIII, 625; IX,
577; XII, 685; XIII,
92; XVI, 322(3)
Elizabeth (Miller), IX,
577
John, XVI, 379
William, XII, 685; XIII,
92
William, Junior, XV,242
EDMONDSON, Henry, XVI,
194, 217
James, XV, 99
James Powell, XIII, 609
John, XIII, 607
Thomas, XI, 158(2)
William, IX, 555
EDMUNDS, Howell, VII, 44;
VIII, 177
John, VII, 515
Thomas, XI, 159(2);
XIII, 289, 549
EDMUNDSON, James, IX, 247
William, XIII, 216, 217
EDWARD, II, 563
EDWARDS, Abraham, V, 75
Benjamin, IV, 460; VI,
285, 286; VII, 24;
XIII, 283; XIV, 153
Catherine, V, 75
David, VII, 25
Frederick, VIII, 131
Henry, VII, 51
John, VII, 26, 220; XI,
283, 335, 336; XIII,
88, 176(2)
Joseph, VII, 25(3)

Nathaniel, Junior, VIII,
459
Richard, VII, 206
Thomas, V, 367; VII,
219; VIII, 64
William, I, 373,379,430;
IV, 78; VII, 204, 206,
212, 213, 219; VIII,
555; XI, 57, XV, 134
(2)
EDZAR, James, XIII, 96, 97
James, Junior, XIII, 96
(4)
Willison, XIII, 96
EFFINGHAM, Francis,* III,
8(3), 25, 40, 41(2),
548, 550
EGGLESTON, George, XV, 31
Joseph, XIII, 293; XIV,
390; XVI, 410
EIB, Jacob, XVI, 334
EISTER, Frederick, VII, 187
ELAM, Joel, VII, 223
Joseph, XIII, 98
ELAN, Alexander, XIII, 608
ELATE, William, VII, 197
ELAY, Lancelett,† I, 342, 362
ELDER, Thomas, XV, 64(5)
ELDRED, John, I, 67, 77, 83,
90
ELDRIDGE, Rolfe, XIII, 316
(2)
Thomas, XVI, 330
ELEY, Robert, XV, 205
ELIZABETH, Queen, III, 504;
IV, 478
ELKIN, James, VII, 220
ELLERY, William, I, 36, 46
ELLICOTT, Andrew, XI, 555,
556
Nathaniel, XIV, 429(5);
XVI, 48
ELLICOOD, Jacob, VI, 227
ELLINGTON, Nathan, XV, 30
ELLIOT, Thomas, XV, 194(2)
ELLIOTT, Anthony,‡ I, 316,
339, 356, 431, 432,
606, 615

John, VI, 242
Robert, VI, 243
William,§ VI, 242; VII,
181, 191
ELLIS, Charles, VI, 375(2);
VII, 202(2), 203, 204;
XIV, 155
James, VII, 226
John, I, 86; XII, 118;
XV, 343
John Woodson, XIII,
213(3)
Nathan, VII, 226
Thomas, I, 407, 408
ELLISON, Francis, VII, 203
Robert,|| I, 422, 503,
527; II, 31, 161, 197,
198(2), 205, 211
ELLZEY, X, 56
Lewis, VII, 21(2)
Thomazon, XV, 282
William, VII, 569; IX,
247; XV, 223
ELMORE, Thomas, XV, 30
ELZY, William, VI, 396, 397

EMBERS, John, VII, 230
EMERSON, James, VII, 215
William, I, 202
EMMEN, XV, 226, 227
EMORIE, Stephen, VIII, 132
EMPEROUR, Francis, II, 158

ENGLIS, XIII, 184
ENGLISH, Stephen, VII, 207
William, I, 139, 140, 170,
179, 187, 203
ENNESS, Hugh, VIII, 208
ENOCHS, Henry, VII, 18

EPES, Archibald, XV, 265
Francis, I, 154, 168, 186,
372; II, 330; XVI, 410
Freeman, XVI, 410
John, XVI, 410
Richard, XVI, 410
Thomas, XVI, 410
EPPERSON, Anthony, X, 325
John, XIV, 390; XV,
117(3), 120
EPPES, Archibald, XVI, 325
(3)

Francis, VIII, 442, 443
(3), 450(5), 451(5);
XIII, 570; XIV, 390
Isham, VI, 485
Mary, XVI, 325(3)
Peter, IX, 230(2)
Richard, VI, 227, 294;
VII, 408, 509, 592,
VIII, 370
William, IV, 266
EPS, John, II, 161

ERICKSON, Benjamin, XIII,
91
ERIES, Benedict, XIV, 314
ERVIN, Edward, VII, 187(3)
ERVING, William, XIV, 314
ERWIN, John, XVI, 56

ESKRIDGE, Charles, XIII, 530
Elizabeth (Scott), XII,
220(3)
George, V, 392(2), 393
(8), 394(4); XV, 224
William, V, 392(3), 393
(3), 394; XII, 220(2)
ESSEX, II, 528
ESTAVE, Andrew, VIII, 364,
365(3), 366
ESTES, Triplet T., XVI, 212
ESTILE, Wallace, VIII, 127
ESTILL, Isaac, XV, 223
John, XIII, 87, 88; XV,
30
Samuel, XIII, 87, 88;
XV, 270
ESTIS, John, VII, 201
Moses, VII, 201
Thomas, VII, 231
William, VII, 201
ESTRE, James, X, 135

ETHERIDGE, Amos, VII, 653
George, I, 85

EVANS, IV, 528; XV, 442
Anna, XV, 64(2)
Daniel, VII, 183, 184*
Dudley, XII, 702; XIII,
284, 285; XIV, 158,
410; XV, 274; XVI,
273(2), 330

Evan, VII, 193
Hugh, I, 83
James, XIV, 399
Jesse, XIII, 583, 590
John, VIII, 426(2); XII,
212, 639
John, Junior, XV, 31, 49
Nathaniel, VII, 189, 195
Philip, XIII, 321
Rhoda, VII, 180, 182
Richard, I, 83
Thomas, I, vii; VII, 64;
XII, 83, 364, 402;
XIV, 157, 399; XVI,
31, 44
Thomas R., XV, 420
William, I, 83; XV, 99
EVELYN, Robert, I, 83
EVENARD, Michael, I, 83
Thomas, VII, 75, 173,
233, 234, 257, 349,
359, 371, 382, 465,
502, 568; VIII, 378;
IX, 70, 96, 122, 201;
X, 572
EVERITT, Charles, XV, 427
John, VIII, 660
EVRICK, Francis, XIV, 302
EVINS, Daniel, VII, 187

*EWELL, Bertrand, VII, 424,
425(4), 426(2), 472
(5)
Charles, XVI, 225
Jesse, XII, 604; XIV,
264(2), 394; XV, 37,
135(6)
EWENS, Ralph, I, 83
EWING, XIII, 559
Baker, XII, 83
George, XIV, 315(2)
James, VIII, 127, 546
John, X, 521, 524, 528,
530, 531(2), 532, 533
(2), 534(2), 535; XI,
555, 556
Robert, VII, 208; XI, 61
William, XIV, 322; XV,
164
EWINGS, Joshua, VII, 215
Samuel, VII, 229
EWRE, Ralph, VII, 81

EXETER, I, 90
EXTON, Nicholas. I, 86
EXUM, Elizabeth, VI, 283(3), 284
EYRE, Littleton. VI, 19, 227.

F

FACIT, Edward, I, 85
FACKLER, John, XVI, 94, 100
FAIR, Edmund, VII, 210(2)
James, VII, 207, 210(2)
FAIRCLAUGH, Robert, XIII, 213(2)
FAIRFAX, Bryan, VIII, 650; IX, 247; XIII, 171, 312
Denny, XV, 22(2), 23 (7), 267
Ferdinando, XV, 110, 127(4), 186
George William, XII, 404; XIV, 153
John, XV, 274
Thomas, IV, 451(3), 514, 522(2); VI, 198, 199(4), 269, 377, 454, 522; VII, 10, 77, 86, 236, 262, 264(2), 315, 688; VIII, 189, 220; IX, 247, 248(2), 361; X, 124, 528; XI, 160 (3); XII, 112; XIII, 531; XIV, 153(2), 420; XV, 22(3),23(3)
William, VI, 18(2); XIV, 153
FALKNER, I, 279
FALLIN, Charles, IV, 479
FALLING, William, VIII, 131
FALLOWES, Thomas, I, 236
FANN, John, VII, 226
FANSHAW, Henry, I, 82, 90
FANTLEROY, V, 143, 146; VI, 177
Moore,* I, 289, 340, 379, 422, 427, 506, 507(3), 512, 530; II, 14(3), 36(3), 152(2); VI,

444, 445(6), 496; VIII, 263; XII, 364
Severo, VIII, 365, 494, 539, 570
EYRES, Robert, I, 323

406, 444(2); VII, 230
406,444(2); VII, 230; VIII, 194
Susanna (Armistead), VI, 444(2)
Susanna (Meriwether) (Armistead), VI, 406
William, IV, 267
FARELEY, Thomas, I, 148
FARGUSON, Bryan, VII, 201
Edward, VII, 201
Richard, VII, 201
Thomas, VII, 201
William, VII, 201; XV, 178
FARGUSSON, John, XIV, 277 (2)
FARLEY, George, VII, 201
John James, VII, 201
FARLOE, George, II, 370, 375 (2), 377
FARLOWE, Thomas, I, 154
FARMAR, Richard, II, 550
FARMER, George, I, 86
John, I, 83
Lodowick, VIII, 444, 645
Richard, II, 370; III, 561(3), 562
Samuel, VII, 437
Thomas, I, 147
FARRAR, I, 145, 147
Abel, VIII, 128
George, VIII, 128
John, III, 21(2)
John Sutton, IV, 307
Nicholas, I, 85
Thomas, IV, 240
William, I, 137, 140, 153, 168(2), 178, 186, 202, 527; II, 330; IV, 240; VII, 225

FARRARS, I, 154
FARRELL, Hubert, II, 330
John, VII, 183
FARRINGTON, Richard, I, 86
FARRIS, John, XVI, 56(2)
William, XVI, 311(2)
FARROW, Abraham, VII, 631, 632, 633
John, VIII, 554
William, VII, 24
FARSES, Edward, VII, 191
FARTHING, Richard, IX, 242
FAUCETT, Joseph, XV,389(3)
FAUCETTE, Benjamin B., XIV, 419
FAUCONBERG, II, 528
FAULCON, Jacob, VIII, 618; XI, 57
Nicholas, V, 367(7); VI, 239
Nicholas, Junior, VIII, 618; XI, 57
FAULKNER, Jacob, XV, 48 (2), 67, 173; XVI, 411 (3)
John, XV, 48(2), 67, 173
William, XVI, 411(3)
FAUNTLEROY, XIV, 164, 408
Moore, VIII, 46, 47(2); XV, 363
Samuel, XIV, 268
Thomas, XIV, 399
FAUQUIER, Francis, VII, 7, 173, 568; VIII, 5
FAURE, Peter, III, 228
FAUSTER, James, VII,224(2)
John, VII, 202
Richard, VII, 201
Robert, VII, 201
FAVER, John, Junior, VII,214
FAVERS, John, VII, 326, 447
FAWCETT, Thomas, I, 139
FAWDOWNE, George, I, 322
FEARN, George, X, 124
FEARNE, Thomas, XIV, 241, 267
FEAZLE, Jacob, X, 325
FELGATE, II, 13
Robert, I, 148, 150, 187
William, I, 84

FELLCATE, I, 138
FELTY, John, XIII, 91
FENDALL, Philip R., XIII,592
FENLY, James, V, 190; VI, 16; VII, 56
FENN, Thomas, XIII, 204
FENNELL, John, V, 369
Nicholas, VII, 211
FENT, Joseph, VII, 493
FENTRESS, David, XV, 228
Grace, XIII, 304
Hillary, XIII, 303, 304 (3)
James, XIII, 304(4)
John, XIII, 303(2), 304 (3)
Sophia, XIII, 304(2)
FERGUSON, Benjamin, XV, 120
Henry, VII, 207, 209
James B., XVI, 330
Robert, XIII, 210(4)
Samuel, XV, 120, 270
FERN, Thomas, VII, 220
FERRAR,* William, II, 196, 205, 249
FERREL, John, VII, 186
FERRILL, Gabriel, VII,224(2)
FEW, William, I, 23

FHARES, John, VII, 184

FIE, Charles, VII, 186
FIELD, IV, 113; XIV, 156
Charles G., XV, 268
Henry, VIII, 669
James, VII, 602
John, VII, 22(2), 213; XV, 223; XVI, 149(2)
Theophilus, VII, 128
William, I, 84
FIELDER, William, VII, 24
FIELL, William, VII, 126
FIERER, Charles, XIV282(3)
FILBRICK, Henry, VIII, 129
FILCHETT, William, XVI, 333
FILMER, Henry, I, 239
FINCH, Henry, I, 153, 202
FINK, Henry, XII, 661
FINLEY, Andrew, XIV, 266
John, VII, 190, 191

John, Junior, VII, 190, 191
Robert, VII, 195
Samuel, XV, 270
FINN, Thomas, XIII, 617
FINNEY, Christopher, VII, 192
John, XIV, 390
FISHBACK, John, VII, 24; XV, 178; XVI, 329
Martin, XVI, 329
FISHER, Adam, XVI, 51
Anne, VIII, 440
Daniel, IX, 314, 328; XV, 338
Frederick, XIII, 319(5)
George, XVI, 388(2)
Jacob, XV, 274
John, VIII, 440(2); XV, 176, 338
Lewis, VII, 23
Maddox, VIII, 440
Philip, VIII, 440,441(3)
Robert H., XVI, 110, 135, 185(2)
Tamar, VIII, 440
Thomas, VII, 624; VIII, 440(3), 441(3)
FISHPAOL, Mary, V, 196(2)
FISK, Moses, XV, 435, 436
FITCH, John, XII, 616(3), 617(4)
FITZGERALD, Edmund, XV, 334
Francis, XV, 161; XVI, 410
Francis, Junior, XVI, 410
James H., XVI, 410
John, XII, 393; XIII,94; XVI, 410
Robert, XV, 161; XVI, 410
Thomas, XVI, 410
William, XV, 161; XVI, 410
FITZHUGH, IV, 112, 439
George, XI, 363; XII, 217
Henry, V, 292, 293; VIII, 449; XII, 511; XIV, 154

John, VI, 282; VIII, 627
John T., XV, 241
Nicholas, XV, 465
Richard, XVI, 177
Thomas, XV, 43
William, III, 473, 547, 552; IV, 268; VI, 18; VIII, 494; IX, 72,305; X, 470; XI, 204; XII, 210, 511; XIII, 79; XIV, 154; XV, 43
William, of Marmion, VIII, 220, 221(2)
William, of Somerset, VIII, 220, 221(2)
FITZJARREL, William, VIII, 127
FITZPATRICK, Andrew, VII, 196
John, VII, 211
Fitz RANDOLPH, Samuel, XIV, 322
FITZSIMMONS, Thomas, I, 23
FLACK, James,XV, 270(2)
FLAGG, Thomas, XVI, 185
FLEET, IV, 480; V, 128; VIII, 72; IX, 485; XI, 208; XVI, 48
Anne, VI, 494(2)
Henry, I, 318(2), 319 (2), 374, 377, 390
FLEETE, John, II, 267
FLEETWOOD, Edward, I, 84
FLEMIN, William, VII, 185
FLEMING, Gardner, VIII, 543
John,* IV, 190; VI, 15; VII, 408, 570; VIII, 35, 62, 115, 124, 149; XIII, 541, 621(2)
Joseph, VII, 216
Tarlton, VII, 19; VI, 15
William, VII, 408, 493, 569; VIII,503; IX,61; X, 288, 667(4); XI, 283, 335, 336; XIII, 202,770; XIII, 293(2)
William R., XIII, 290; XVI, 330
FLESHMAN, Peter, VII, 214
FLETCHER, Benjamin, IV, 377

George, I, 370*, 374, 378, 379, 383, 384
James, XVI, 410
John, I, 83; XV, 178
Nathan, XVI, 136, 346
Thomas C., XVI, 60,149, 318
FLET, Benjamin, XIII, 300
FLIN, James, VII, 223
John, VII, 223; XIII, 48; XIV, 156
FLINT, I, 140
Thomas, I, 139,148,239, 340
FLOID, Henry, VII, 24
FLOOD, Henry, XIII, 587; XV, 120
John, II, 138
Thomas, II, 138
William, VIII, 17, 18 (2)
FLOUD, John, I, 325, 328
FLOUBNOY, Samuel, VIII,606
FLOWER, VI, 283
FLOWERE, Daniel, XV, 30
FLOYD, VII, 153
Ebenezer, V, 189; VI, 19
John, I, 348; X, 288, 293; XI, 100
William, I, 36; VII, 202; XIII, 215, 216
FLUDD, John, I, 154, 178, 239, 370, 380
FLYNT, Thomas, I, 154, 169, 179, 187, 203
FOARD, Thomas, VII, 24
FOLK, Lodowick,† VII, 182, 184
FOLLAS, William, VIII, 131
FOLLY, XII, 435
FONTAINE, John, XIII, 297
FONTAINE, James Maury, VIII, 435
Patrick H., XVI, 136, 346
Peter, VI, 253
Peter, Junior, VI, 382
FONTLEROY,I VI, 177
Moore, I, 283
FOOLAM, Benjamin, VII, 215
FORBES, James, X, 553

John, XV, 233, 234
FORD, VIII, 474
Boaz, XIV, 240, 328
Christopher, XV, 140
John, XIV, 331(2)
Richard, I, 343, 627
Samuel, VII, 191; XV, 30
Thomas, VII, 191
William, VII, 201
FOREMAN, XVI, 153
Benjamin, VIII, 368
Reuben, XII, 598,599(2)
FOREST, Thomas, I, 84
FORGARSON, John, XIII, 586
FORMAN, John, VII, 25
FORREST, Anthony, I, 82
George, VI, 242
FORSTER, Elizabeth, VI, 403
Thomas, VI, 403
William, VII, 201
FORT, Joshua, XVI, 140, 346
FORTH, John, II, 370, 374, 377, 461
FORTUNE, Vincent, XVI, 167 (2)
FOSSETT, Thomas, I, 148
FOSTER, VIII, 642(2)
Arthur, XV, 254(2), 255
Charles, XIII, 582; XIV, 241, 316; XV, 95, 210; XVI, 136, 346
James, XV, 241
John, XVI, 95
Peregrine, XIV, 242,272
Richard, I, 414; XI, 273
William, XII, 211
FOULKE, Thomas, I, 506, 530
FOULKS, John A., XV, 380
FOUNDLING, John, XV, 459
FOUNTAIN, Patrick, XV, 210
FOUSHEE, XIV, 156
John, VIII, 369
John H., XV, 259; XVI, 34, 335
William, XI, 399; XIII, 316, 318, 599; XVI, 34, 335(2)
FOWDEN, George, I, 379
FOWKE, Gerard, I, 512; II,

14

150(7), 151, 154, 197, 198, 205
FOWLER, Bartholomew, III, 182
Elias, VII, 212
Francis, I, 236
James, VII, 25, 179, 180, 181(2), 186, 188
John, Junior, XII, 391
Joshua, VII, 203
Thomas, XII, 376
William, VIII, 128
Fox, V, 250; VIII, 645; XIV, 154, 156
Anne, XIII, 136(2), 137 (2), 139(3), 140(4), 141
Anne (West), VI, 321, 428
Arthur, XII, 361, 633; XIII, 182, 183
Henry, VI, 321, 428
John, IV, 141; VIII, 285 (2), 423(2); V, 121 (4), 365; XIII, 137
Nathaniel, XIII, 585; XVI, 176(3), 406(3), 421, 422
Richard, VII, 588
Thomas, I, 86; VI, 494 (2)
FRAIZER, John, VII, 186
FRAME, Matthew, XV, 383; XVI, 185
FRANCES, Rawleigh, II, 197
FRANCIS, Enoch, XIV, 430 (3), 431(2)
Giles, I, 85
Thomas, I, 422, 430
FRANCISCO, Jacob, XVI, 310
Peter, XIII,220(3), 221
FRANK, Graham, VII, 569
Nicholas, VII, 182, 183
FRANKLIN, Benjamin, I, 23, 36
Elijah, XVI, 339(3)
Ferdinand, I, 236
James, XIV, 322; XV, 419
Joel, XV, 419, 444
FRANKLYN, John, I, 85

FRASER, William, VIII,49(4)
FRAVELL, Henry, XI, 57
FRAZER,* IX, 488, 510; X, 273, 366, 475; XI, 211, 235; XIII, 479, 503; XV, 420
Alexander, XIV, 320
James, XIII, 554
John, IV, 308
FRAZIER,* V, 104, 364; VI, 16(2); 19(2); XIV, 153(2), 154; XV, 156 (2)
Alexander, VII, 214
Patrick, VII, 194
William, VII, 402(2); XIV, 154
FREAKE, Thomas, I, 78, 82
FREALE,† Thomas, I, 78
FREELAND, James, XI, 65(5)
Mace, XI, 65(4)
Mary (Williams), XI, 65(2)
Spice, XI, 65(3)
FREEMAN, Anne (Robins), IV, 463(5), 464(2)
Bridges, I, 148, 178, 339, 342, 372, 408
Edward, VII, 212
John, VII, 203
Martin, I, 84
Nathaniel, VII, 24
Peter, VII, 212
Ralph, I, 84
Robert, IV, 463(6), 464; XV, 178
Thomas, XV, 178
William, VII, 435, 437; VIII, 269
FREES, Michael, VII, 184
FREEZE, Michael, VII, 182
FRENCH, Daniel, VII, 121
David, XVI, 403
George, XIII, 100; XV, 58; XVI, 100
James, XIII, 87
FREZIER, Joseph, XIII, 182
FRIEND, Jonas, VII, 179, 180, 181; VIII, 126; XIII, 48; XIV, 411
Joseph, XVI, 41(2)
FRISBY, Nathaniel, XV, 30

FRISTOE, John, XVI, 233
FRITH, Richard, I, 85
FROGG, John, VII, 24; VIII, 549
FRONT, William, VIII, 471
FRY, XV, 267
Henry, VII, 60, 149; XII, 87, 625
Joseph, VII, 21
Joshua, V, 378(2); VIII, 270; IX, 562,564; XII, 566; XIV, 269
Reuben, XV, 223; XVI, 42(2)
FRYER, I, 82
FRYETT, Edward, XIII, 297
John, XIII, 297
FUDGE, Jacob,VII, 186
FULGHAM, VI, 351; VIII, 78, 98; IX, 154, 159, 160, 488, 510, 513; XI, 97 (2); 210, 235, 237(2); XIII, 479, 503

Charles, VI, 289(2); XIII, 567; XIV, 165
FULKERSON, James, XIII,544 John, XV, 360
Peter, XIV, 322
FULL, Andrew, VII, 184, 185
FULLER, Henry, VII, 203
William, IV, 372, 373
FULLOM, Benjamin, VII, 216
FULSE, John, VII, 187
FULTON, Andrew, XIII, 554; XV, 270; XVI, 405
Hugh, XV, 234
John, XV, 218
Rebecca, XVI, 26(2)
FUNK, Jacob, XVI, 47
John, VII,475; VIII,415
FUQUA, John, VIII,554; XIV, 156(3)
Joseph, VII,554; XI,171
Ralph, VII, 207
William, VII, 205, 207, 220, 402; VIII, 128, 555
FURBER, Chrisley, XVI, 233

*Frazier †See Freake

G

GAINES,* VII, 326, 447
Daniel, IX, 668
Harry, VII, 298,402,568
Henry, VII, 23; IX, 235
Philip, XIV, 315
William F., XV, 70
GAINS, Bernard, VI, 211
Francis, VIII, 456
GALE, Matthew, VI, 242
GALL, Edward, I, 86
GALLAHUR, Charles, XV, 166
GALLAW, David, Junior, VII, 198
GALLEGO, Joseph, XVI, 79, 95, 100
GALLOWAY, David, VII, 197
James, XII, 492
John,† XII, 206(2)
GALT, William, XV, 50
GAMBILL, Henry, VII, 22
Henry I., XVI, 57
Henry J., XV, 49

GAMBLE, Josiah, XV, 166
Robert, XII, 282; XIII, 174, 316, 588, 599; XV, 66, 419; XVI, 34, 90, 335
Samuel, XVI, 334
GAMER, Clement, VII, 21
GARCER, John, VII, 220
GARDINER, James, XIV, 394; XV, 37
John, I, 83
GARDNER, Anthony, XIV, 399
Francis, XVI, 194
Thomas, VII, 24
GARLAND, IV, 113; VI, 17
Christopher, XIV, 399
David, VI, 311, 312(3), 313(6); VIII, 442(7), 443(3), 444
David S., XV, 419, 442, 444

*Gaines †Gallaway

Edward, VI, 311, 312 (2), 313(3); VIII, 442(3), 444; XV, 155, 271, 427, XVI, 68
Edward, Junior, VI, 311(3)
Hudson M., XVI, 155
Isaac, XI, 312(2)
John, XII, 729
Peter, IV, 113
Rice, XVI, 60, 149, 318
Samuel, VIII, 443
Spotswood, XV, 149
GARNER, William G., XVI, 212
GARNET, James, VI, 172
GARNETT, Augustine, XIII, 221
Francis, XIII, 307, 308 (3), 309
Henry,* XIII, 132, 221 (3), 227(7), 307(5), 308(4), 309
James, XIII, 221,'307 (2), 308(4), 309
Muscoe, XIII, 221(2)
GARRARD, James, XII, 90, 282, 725, 726; XIII, 86, 176(2)
William, XII, 210
GARRETT, Alexander, XVI, 318
Henry, XV, 121, 464(5)
James, VII, 214
GARRATT, William, VI, 242
GARTH, Thomas, XIV, 330; XVI, 149, 318
GASCOIGNE, Anne (Fisher), VIII, 440
GASKINS, Henry L., XV, 185 (3)
Thomas, XII, 216; XV, 121
GASS, David, VII, 203
GATE, Peter, I, 86
GATES, Elijah, XV, 221
Horatio, XV, 241
Thomas, I, 3, 57(3), 58(2), 62(3), 63(2), 65, 66, 80, 81, 90, 172, 197, 263, 460†(2)
GATEWOOD, China, XIV, 268

John, XV, 378
GATLIVE, James, VII, 199
GAUDER, Frederick, XVI, 163 (3)
GAUDILOCK, Adam, VII, 203
GAULTNEY, Robert, VII, 212
William, VII, 212
GAW, Robert, XV, 99
GAY, James, VII, 198
John, VII, 197, 200
William, XII, 201
GEARING, John, I, 83
GEE, Henry, II, 554(2), 555 (2)
Robert, Junior, VII, 212
William, XIII, 132, 164 (3); XIV, 157
GEMMEL, James, VIII, 126
GENTRY, Nicholas, XII, 598 (4)
GEORGE, XV, 249, 251, 367
GEORGE I., III, 177(3); IV, 51, 58, 59, 76, 77, 96, 118, 143, 152, 153, 154(2), 155, 161, 276, 394, 429; V, 15, 27, 35, 64, 173, 357; VI, 195, 254, 257, 259, 273, 379, 383, 386, 393, 503, 504, 541; VII, 132, 144, 150, 154, 246, 302, 304, 614, 617, 619; VIII, 43, 158, 260
GEORGE II., IV, 182, 241, 296, 309, 380, 469; V, 9, 90, 100, 121, 124, 220, 310, 401, 406, 408, 528(2), 536, 559; VI, 9, 195, 217(2), 325 (2) 417(2), 425(2), 435(2), 453(2), 521 (2), 559(2); VII, 9 (2), 61(2), 69(2), 163(2), 171(2), 251 (2), 256(2), 331(2), 347(2), 367, 369, 381 (2), 382, 383, 385, 392, 403, 407, 430, 440, 441, 478, 481, 492, 500, 510, 540.

663, 602, 604, 646, 650, 652; VIII, 9(2), 11(2), 69, 113, 114, 142, 184, 186, 187, 189, 190, 191, 195, 215, 259, 261, 262, 263, 266, 295, 299, 334, 333, 336, 339(2), 343, 393, 407, 411, 430, 442, 478, 514, 515, 527, 529, 630(2), 534, 549, 555, 579, 667; IX, 92, 166, 368, 469, 679
GEORGE III., I, iv, 50; III, 506; VII, 463(2), 491, 495(2), 517(2), 639, 663; VIII, 37(2), 69, 189(2), 295(2), 305 (2), 493; 607(2), 647 (2); IX, 112, 281, 473
GEORGE, John, I, 340, 370, 432; II, 330
The Armenian, I, 425 .
William, XV, 164, 166, 212, 270
GERRARD, David, XII,607(3), Thomas., I, 86
GERRY, Elbridge, I, 36, 46
GETTY,* Dennis,† VII, 199 (2); XV, 388(3)
GEWIN,‡ Christopher, VI, 508(3), 509

GRINK, Will Ellmus, VII,217
GHOLSTON, Joseph, XVI, 411
GIBBS, William, I, 86; VII, 613
GIBSON, IV, 268, 336, 382, 383, 386, 438, 480; V, 14, 15, 144; VI, 18, 176; VII, 428; VIII, 328, 508; IX, 154, 161, 488, 511, 513, 514; X, 273, 356, 475; XI, 211, 236, 238(2), 345, 346(3); XII, 258,455; XIII, 480(2), 503; XIV, 154; XVI, 182
George, IX, 337
Hugh, XV, 240

Isaac, VII, 24
Jonathan, V, 142; VI, 173; VIII, 78, 98, 101 (2)
Josiah, VII, 206
Moses, XVI, 51
Robert, VII, 181,190(2), 191
Thomas, XV, 31
William, XVI, 379
GIFFINS, James, VII, 191
GILBERT, VI, 17
Acquiller, VII, 206
Benjamin, VII, 206
Daniel, VII, 205, 206
Felix, VII, 199
John, I, 84
John W., XIV, 266
Raleigh, I, 57, 59, 62(2), 63, 64, 66(2)
Robert, XII, 689(2), 690(7)
Samuel, VII, 206(2)
Sarah, XII, 690(2)
Thomas, XII, 206
GILES, James, XVI, 349(2)
Peggy, XVI, 349(2)
GILL, Erasmus, XIII, 98; XV, 111(3)
John, XV, 89
Richard, XV, 121
Sarah, XIII, 98
Stephen, I, 373
GILLASPEY, James, VII, 191
GILLIAM, Charles, VII, 229
Christian, XVI, 325(3)
James Skelton, XIV, 320; XV, 111, 265; XVI, 62
Robert, XI, 57
William, X, 365(2); XII, 405
GILLISON, James, VII, 23(2)
John, XV, 223
GILS, Charles, XVI, 38
James, XV, 30
GILMAN, Nicholas, I, 22
GILMER, George, XIII, 315, 316; XV, 190(5), 359, 377
GILMORE, George, XVI, 49, 211

*Getley †Denis ‡Gewen

James, VII, 195
John, VII, 191, 192; XII. 223
Thomas, VII, 191, 196
GILMOUR, Charles, VIII, 543
GILPIN, George, XII, 75; XIII, 94, 171; XVI, 48
GINNINGS, Jonathan, VII. 209
GIPSON, George, VII, 191
Josias, VII, 209
GISENS, John, VII, 183
GIST, David, X, 135
Mary, XI, 54(4)
Nathaniel, VII, 493
Samuel, VII, 129(2), 130(2); XI, 54(4)
Thomas, VII, 493
GITHINGS, John, VII, 201
GIVE, I, 196
GIVENS, James, VII, 194
John, XV, 227, 359
GLADIN, John, VII, 22
GLADY, V, 211
GLANVILL, Richard, I, 84
GLASS, Samuel, VII, 226
GLASSCOCK,* V, 143, 145; VI, 174, 176; VIII, 79, 98, 323; IX, 154, 161, 488, 511; X, 474, 475; XI, 211, 235; XII, 294; XIII, 480, 503; XV, 156(2); XVI, 182(2)
William, IV, 267; VII, 50(2), 52(3), 54
GLASSELL, William, XIV, 245
GLAZE, Conrod, XIII, 151 (2); XIV, 153
George, XIII, 151(2)
GLEADOWE, Samuel, VI,281
GLEN,† James, VII, 204
James A., XV, 380
John, XIII, 77; XIV, 406; XV, 64(2)
GLOCESTER, III, 543
GLOOR, John, VII, 23
GLOUCESTER, III, 423
GLOVER, Edmund, XIV, 240, 328

*Glascock †Glenn

William, XV, 265
GODDALE, John, III, 471
GODDART, Richard, I, 85
GODDIN, Avery, XVI, 427
Isaac, VII, 209(3)
GODFREY, Matthew, VII, 418; VIII, 154(2)
William, XV, 284
GODOLPHIN, William, I, 82, 90
GODWIN, Brewer, IX, 240
Christopher, X, 207(5)
Jeremiah, VI, 375(2); VII, 402; XIV,155(2)
Jonathan, VIII, 553
Talbot, XVI, 159(4), 267(2)
Thomas, I, 85, 386; II, 318, 330, 365
GOFF, John, VIII, 131; XI, 365; XV, 67
GOFFE, William, II, 159(4)
GOGGAN, George, VII, 23
GOGGINS, George, VII, 213
GOLDING, Simon, XIII, 608
GOOCH, Claiborne, VI,17(2); XIV, 154
Henry, II, 556
John, XV, 140
William, I, 387, 408: IV, 5(2), 240, 307, 379; V, vii, 93, 122, 407, 564; VI, 7(2), 214
GOODALL, V, 191(2)
Parke, XI, 54(3)
Richard, XI, 54, 55(4)
GOODE, Bennet, VI, 15
Bennit, V, 190
Francis, X, 477; XI, 67
John B., XVI, 268
McKerrens, VII, 223
Philip, VII, 223
Richard, XV, 418
Robert, VIII, 412, 422; X, 318: XIII, 314; XV, 31, 353
Samuel, XI, 250, 333; XIII, 193, 296; XVI, 268
GOODING, John, XVI, 337

GOODMAN, George, VII, 184
Horsley, XVI, 149
Jacob, VII, 182, 184
Joseph, VII, 201
GOODRICH, Benjamin. II,370: V, 304, 305(2)
Edward, VII, 211, 212
James, XIII, 221
John, XV, 205
Thomas, II, 165,370,378
GOODRIDGE, John B., XVI,194
GOODSON, Thomas, XVI, 426
GOODWIN, Daniel, VII, 195
Rebecca, V, 370
Robert, XIII, 549
Thomas, XVI, 100
GOODWYN, John,* XV, 122, 176, 338
Peterson, XIII, 174; XIV, 320; XV, 66,213
Robert, XIII, 289
Thomas, I, 506
GOOGE, John, I, 86
GOOSBERRY, Robert, VII, 216
GORDEN, Gilbert, VII, 215
GORDON, Alexander, VIII, 610; XVI, 37(2)
James, XII, 215(2),216: XV, 184
John, VII, 188(2); XI, 369; XII, 215
R., II, 583
Samuel, VII, 608
Thomas, II, 370,378(2), 557; XI, 57
William, VIII, 57
GORE, VIII, 132
Daniel, VII, 64
Isaac, XV, 31
Thomas, VIII, 132
GORGES, Ferdinando, I, 67,77
GORHAM, Nathaniel, I, 22
GOSNOLD, Anthony, I, 87
GOUCE, William, I, 373
GOUCH, IV, 266
Mathew, I, 239
Nathaniel, I, 236
Philip, XVI, 268(2)
GOULDING, William T., XV, 134
GOULDMAN, Francis, XIII, 221(3)

GOULSTON, Lyonell, I, 179, 203
GOUTEE, Joseph, VII, 131
GOWER, Richard, VII, 211
GOWLETT, IV, 462
Robert, IV, 462
GRACIE, Archibald, XIII, 599
GRAFFERT, Thomas, VII, 22
GRAGG, Robert, VII, 181
William, VII, 180(2), 185
GRAHAM, Edward, XVI, 403
George, III, 372; XV, 282; XVI, 236, 395
George, Junior, XVI, 236
Jacob, VII, 191(2)
James, XV, 221
John, VII, 22, 192; XVI, 90, 246
Richard, VII, 425(2), 426; XII, 372
William, VII, 192, 194, 200(2); XI, 164
GRAIES, Thomas, I, 150
GRAINGER, John, VII, 221
GRAMMAR, John, XV, 111, 218, 351; XVI, 316
GRAMMER, John, XIII, 174, 599
GRANBERRY, John, XII, 211 (2), 212; XV, 437
Josiah, VIII, 543
GRANT, Francis, VII, 23
John, XII,608; XIII,170
William, XV, 241
William F., XV, 121
GRANTHAM, III, 568(2)
GRANTLAND, James, VII, 129
GRATTAN, Robert, XIV, 308
GRATTON, Robert, XIII, 174, 589
GRAVE, Thomas, I, 84
GRAVES, I, 149; III, 471, 472 (2)
Jeremiah, XIII, 216(2)
Richard, XVI, 427
GRAVETT, John, XI, 345, 363
GRAY, IV, 524, 533(2); V, 14, 76, 136, 143, 145, 365, 366(4), 367; VI,

*Goodwin

169, 174, 176, 236, 237(4), 238(2), 239, 240(2), 352(2); VII, 532; VIII, 79, 98, 101 (2), 321, 323, 554, 556, 617(2); IX, 488, 511, 513(2), 614; X, 273, 356, 475; XI, 211, 235, 237, 238(2); XIII, 480, 504
Charles, XIV, 316(2)
David, VII, 196
Edwin, VIII, 589; IX, 314, 328; XI, 158(3), 159; XII, 386, 635; XIII, 289, 297
Elizabeth (—) (Chamberlayne), V, 118(3), 119(4), 120(5)
Ethelred, VIII, 618
Francis, II,13; XIV,336
Gabriel, XV, 176; XVI, 182
Gilbert, V, 76, 369
Henry, IV, 529
James, VII, 181
John, I, 84; XII, 607; XIII, 95; XV, 223
Joseph, VI, 285, 451; VII, 44
Mary, IV, 529
Robert, IV, 462; V, 370; VII, 230
Stephen, I, 407, 408
Thomas ,VI, 240(2)
Vincent, XIV, 394; XV, 37
William, V, 118(2),119; XIV, 336; XV, 176
William F., XII, 729
GRAYES, Thomas, I, 170, 179, 187
GRAYSON, Ambrose, VII, 327, 449
Benjamin, VII, 531; VIII, 508,509; XVI,51
Spence, XII, 684; XV, 241(2)
William, X,102(4); XII, 604, 684
GREEN, IV,112(2); XIV,156
Andrew, XIV, 277(3)

Anne, VIII, 635(2)
Berryman, XV, 48(2), 67, 172, 380
Gabriel, XV, 121, 282
George, X, 121
Griel, XVI, 346
James, VII, 214; XIV, 421; XV, 30, 121
James, Junior, XV, 282
Jeremiah, VII, 199
John, I, 424; VII, 25; XIII, 204, 297
Joshua, VIII, 635(2)
Lettice, VIII, 635(4)
Lewis, VIII, 193
Robert, XIV, 420
Roger, I, 380, 381
Samuel B., XIV, 336
Thomas, VII, 218(2). 628
William, VII, 22, 24, 232, 306; VIII, 10, 124; XIII, 219
Willis, XI, 283
GREENE, Nathaniel, X, 572 (2), 574, 581
William, XIII, 217
GREENFIELD, John, VIII, 415
GREENHILL, David, VIII, 292
Francis, V, 219(5)
Frances (Taylor) V, 216(2), 217(5), 218 (3)
Joseph, V, 216(2), 217 (3), 218(3), 219(6)
GREENHOW, James, XVI, 335
Robert, XIV, 308; XVI, 50, 197
GREENLEE, James, VII, 189 (2) ; VIII, 129
John, VIII, 129; XI, 341
GREENUP, Christopher, XI, 283; XII, 661, 631; XIII, 312
GREENVILLE, Bernard, I, 78
GREENWAY, Joseph, VII, 217
GREENWOOD, William, XIV, 426
GREER, Andrew, VII, 203
Arthur, VII, 187
Joseph, X, 325
Moses, XVI, 45

William, XVI, 45
GREGG, John, VIII, 163(3), 164(5), 165(3)
Matthew, VII, 164
Robert, XV, 121
William, VII, 194
GREGORY, John, V, 200(2); VII, 224; VIII, 129
Roger, VIII, 286; XV, 353
Walter, XVI, 47
GREIR, Arthur, VII, 195
GRENTHAM, John, Junior, XV, 121
Joseph, XV, 121
GRESON, John, VII, 23
GREVIL, Fulks, I, 78
GREY, Thomas, II, 511
GREYHAM, Isaac, XIV, 158
GRICE, Aristotle, IV, 372, 373
Edward, IV, 372, 373
John Thorp, IV, 372, 373
Thomas, IV, 372, 373
GRIER, Moses, XIII, 585, 586
GRIFFIN, Anthony, XIV, 277
Corbin, XI, 473
James, IV, 267
Leroy, II, 564
Margaret, VII, 447
Richard, Junior, VIII, 131
Samuel, XII, 635, 717; XV, 62(2)
Samuell, II, 406: III, 118, 125
William, XIII, 625(2), 626
Zachariah, XIV, 277
GRIFFING, Asabel, XIV, 428 312(2)
GRIFFITH, XV, 168
David, XIII, 311(2),
Edward, I, 529; II, 147, 197, 198(2), 205
Hannah, XIII, 311, 312
Hezekiah, XVI, 246
James, XIII, 297; XV, 270
William, VII, 219

GRIGGS, Thomas, XV, 110
Thomas, Junior, XVI, 185
GRIGSBY, Joseph, XVI, 155, 348, 398, 423, 429
Samuel, VII, 24
GRIGSON, James, VII, 215
GRIM, John, VII, 23
GRIBBES, James, VII, 198
John, VI, 508,509; XIII, 152
Robert, VII, 198
GRINDON, Sarah, II, 371
Thomas, I, 203; II, 371
GROMARRIN, Francis, VIII, 644(2)
Gillee, VIII, 643,644(4), 645, 646
Mary, VIII, 643,644(5), 645(3)
Susannah, VIII, 644
Wiltshire, VIII, 643, 644(6)
GROOM, Samuel, I, 513; III, 568
GROOTEN, Lambert, I, 499
GROTEN, Margery, XIII, 616, 617
GROVES, John, V, 370; XIII, 174, 175
GRUD, Jacob, VII, 185
GRUBBS, Higgerson, XII, 603
GRUBS, Thomas, VII, 203
GRUNDY, George, VII, 207
GRYCE, Nicholas, I, 84
GRYMES, Alice (Townley), VIII, 630(2)
Benjamin, VII, 485, 650, 651
Edward, I, 551
John, VII, 205; VIII, 630(2); XIV, 156
John Randolph, VIII, 630(3), 631(3)
Nicholas, VII, 21
Philip, VI, 418; VII, 21, 276, 288, 630, 647; XV, 442
Philip Ludwell, VII, 489, 630(3), 631; XIV, 399

GUERRANT, John, Junior, XIII, 296
GUEST, XV, 234
GUFFEY, Henry, VII, 203
GUILFORD,* IV,382, 384, 386; V, 144; VI, 172, 175, 177; VIII, 77, 80, 97, 101, 320(2); IX, 160, 489, 510, 513; X, 211, 272, 355; XIII, 482
GUILLUM, James, VII, 224
GUIN, David, VII, 196
GUM, John, VII, 181, 183; VIII, 127
GUMMERY, David, VII, 25
GUNDRY, John, II, 157
GUNN, VIII, 423
  George, VII, 199
  Thomas, VII, 202
GUNNEL, Henry, Junior, XVI, 177
GUNNELL, Thomas, XV, 178
  William, XIII, 171
GUNSON, Jacob, VII, 225
GUNTER, Charles, VII, 212
GUSMAN of Alfrach, I, 146
GUTHRY, John, XIII, 609(3)
GUTRIDGE, John, XII, 361; XIII, 183
GUTTERY, III, 219, 220(3)

GUY, George, XIV, 416
  Henry, VII, 193
  James, Junior, VII, 193
  John, VII, 189
  Robert, VII, 193
GUYAN, Isaac, XIII, 284

GWATHNEY, Joseph, XIV,266
  Owen, XIV, 266
  Temple, XIV, 268
GWATKINS, Charles, XIII, 81
  James, XII, 207
GWIN, David, VIII, 132
  Hugh,† I, 323, 371, 374, 375(2)
  Pearce, VII, 220
  Robert, VII, 189
GWINN, David, VII, 227
  John, XI, 185
GWINNETT, Button, I, 36
GWYN, VI, 493
  Francis, II, 508
GWYNE,‡ Evan, XV, 246, 291
GWYNN, Edmund, VIII, 483, 485, 486(2); X, 121
  John, VIII, 483, 484; XII, 299
  Lucy, VIII, 483, 484(2)

GYFES, Thomas, I, 66

H

HACKE, George, I, 499
HACKETT, Peter, XVI, 222
HACKETT, Thomas, I, 379
HACKLER, John, XVI, 31
HACKLEY, VI, 18; VIII, 370
  James, V, 66
HACKLUIT, Richard, I, 57, 58, 62(2), 63(2), 65, 66, 83
HACKWORTH, George, VII, 206
HARDEN, John, XII, 661
HADEN, Joseph, XV, 31
HADWAY, V, 142; VI, 173
HAGGOMAN, John, VII, 228
HAGLER, Benjamin, VII, 184
  Jacob, VII, 184

John, VII, 184
  Postine, VII, 184
HAGUE, Francis, VII, 236
HAILE, Meshach, VII, 205
HAILES, John, VII, 212
HAIN, Jeremy, I, 431
HAINES, Henry, I, 513, 514
  Joseph, XIII, 229
  Robert, XII, 672, 673
HAINGER, Peter, VII, 407
HAINS, John, VII, 225
HAIR, James, XII, 607
HAIRSTON, Andrew, VII, 208
  George, XIII, 193, 297; XIV, 316; XV, 210
  Robert, VII, 204, 208(2)
  Samuel, VII, 208(3)

HALCOMB, Philemon, VII,229
HALEY, III, 569
  George, XII, 513
HALIFAX, II, 528
HALL, Alexander, XVI, 405
  Ambrose, XVI, 269, 270
  Andrew, VII, 195
  Anne (Holling), VIII, 291(2), 292(2), 293
  Aquilla, VII, 225
  Bowling, VII, 201(2)
  Elisha, XV, 58; XVI, 76(2)
  Hezekiah, VII, 225
  Isaac, XI, 57; XV, 265; XVI, 214
  John, VII, 206, 224, 225, 227; VIII, 291(2), 292(3), 293
  Leonard, VII, 211
  Lyman, I, 36
  Moses, VII, 180
  Robert, VII, 201, 227; VIII, 127, 292
  Thomas, II, 370, 375(2), 377, 546(3); VII, 224
  William, VII, 215; XV, 67
HALLAWAY, Bennett, VII,225
HALLER, Jacob, XVI,149,179
HALLEY, Peter, XII, 672, 673
  Samuel, XIV, 428; XV, 176
HALLIS, James, VII, 202
HALLOGUAN, Patrick, VII, 209
HALLOWAY, John, IV, 49, 95; VIII, 445(3)
HALYBURTON, William, XVI, 427
HAM, Jerom, I, 501
HAMBLET, Richard, VII, 226
HAMBLETON, Moses, VII, 199
  Robert, VII, 191
  William, VII, 191
HAMBLIN, Peter, VII, 224
HAMBY, David, VIII, 131
  Jonathan, VIII, 131
HAMENER, George, VII, 182
HAMER, George, VII, 183
  Ralph, I, 84, 86, 111, 128
HAMERSLEY, Hugh, I, 85

HAMES, Edmond, VII, 226
HAMILTON, XI, 557; XIII, 165
  Alexander, I, 22; VII, 189, 197
  Andrew, VII, 194, XVI, 63
  Anthony, II, 370
  Archibald, XV, 175, 210
  Audley, VII, 195
  Frederick, XV, 426; XVI, 110
  Gawin, XIV, 277(2)
  George, XVI, 420
  James, VII, 187, 218, 236; VIII, 124; XIII, 92
  John, VII, 193, 198; VIII, 543; X, 207(2); XIII, 216; XV, 224
  Josiah, VIII, 127
  Matthew, XV, 30
  Thomas, VII, 196
  William, VII, 197; XV, 63
HAMLET, William, XIII, 173
HAMLIN, John, IV, 467
  Peter, VII, 224(2)
  Stephen, I, 386
  Thomas, VII, 224
HAMM, Robert, VII, 201
HAMMOCK, John, VII, 201
HAMMOD, John, I, 374
HAMMON, Joel, XVI, 316
HAMMON, X, 315
  Thomas, XV, 99, 245, 383
HAMMONS, John, VII, 225, 226
HAMNER, V, 191; VI, 14
HAMOND, Francis, I, 548(2)
  Manwaring, I, 530, 545; II, 10, 12, 35(2), 157
  Thomas, I, 84
HAMPSON, William, I, 85
HAMPTON, John, VII, 215, 216, VIII, 131
  Preston, VIII, 130
  Richard, VII, 24
  Thomas, I, 317
  William H., XVI, 379
HAMTON, John, VII, 201

62

HAMYLIN, II, 198
HANBURGHER, Stephen, VII, 186
HANBY, Jonathan, XIII, 161
HANCOCK, George, VII, 472; XII, 202, 675; XIII, 83, 590
  John, I, 36, 46; VIII, 635(3), 636(6); IX, 284; XI, 270; XV, 447; XVI, 329
  Margarett (Muschett), VIII, 635(2), 636(3)
  Samuel, XVI, 38
  Simon, V, 106
  William, I, 84
HAND, Thomas, XII, 672
HANDCOCK, Daniel, VII, 224
HANDLEY, James, XVI,31(2)
HANDY, George, I, 359
  John, VII, 207
  William, VII, 208
HANES, Bethany, VIII, 130
HANEY, Jacob, VII, 51
  John, I, 431
  Stephen, VII, 54
HANNAM, Thomas, I, 57, 59, 62(2), 63, 64, 66(2)
HANKINS, John, VII, 224, 227
  Richard, VII, 217
HANKINSON, George, I, 87
HANLEY, James, XV, 223
  John, XIII, 313
HANNAH, I, vii
HANNAR, IV, 267
HANSBARGER, Adam, XV,377, 378
HANSBROUGH, James, XVI, 182
HANSFORD, John, I, 84
  Sallis, VII, 22(2)
  Thomas, II, 370, 375(2), 377; III, 567(2)
HANSKAW, William, XII, 607
HANSLEY, Benjamin, VII,191
HANSON, John, I, 46; IV, 462; X, 580
  Samuel, XII, 393
HANWAY, Samuel, XII, 212, 661
HAPPY, IV, 531

HARDET, Thomas, VII, 203
HARBISON, Matthew ,VII,216
HARBOUT, Peter, XII, 404; XIV, 153
HARCUM, James, XV,236(2), 342
HARDAWAY, Stith, XVI, 410
HARDEN, George, XIII, 46; XIV, 153
HARDIDGE, Joseph, II, 370 (2), 379(2)
  William, III, 60
HARDIMAN, John, VII, 206
HARDIN, Edward, VII, 21, 217
  John, VII, 198, 216
  Mark, VII, 214, 215
  Martin, VII, 136(2), 426(2)
HARDING, Joseph, XV, 228
HARDMAN, John, VII, 205
HARDRES, I, xxi
HARDRICKE, II, 473
HARDY, XIII, 567
  George, I, 236, 283, 289, 370*
  John, XIII, 46; XIV,156
  Richard, IX, 240
  Samuel, XI, 571(2), 574(2), 575
HARDYWAY, Daniel, XV, 259
HARE, William, X, XV, 182
HARGRAVE, Jesse, XIV, 243, 268
  Samuel, XIV, 268(3)
HARGROVE, James, VII, 211
HARKRIDER, John, XIII, 586
HARLOE, Peter, I, 84
HARLOWE, John, I, 506, 548 (2), 550; II, 36(2)
HARMAN, XV, 18; XVI, 244
  Henry, Junior, XV, 217
HARMANSON, George, IV, 268
  Gertrude, IV, 377; VIII, 665
  John, XII, 364
  Matthew, V, 391
  Sophia, VIII, 665, 666 (2)
HARMAS, Charles, I, 170, 179, 187

HARMENSON, Thomas, II, 302(2), 475(2)
HARMER, Ambrose, I, 289, 322, 338
  George, X, 300(2), 301(6), 371(4); XI, 35 (2), 36(3), 257(3); XV, 190(2)
  John, V, 402, 403(2); X, 300(3), 301, 371; XI, 35(2), 36(6)
HARMON, XV, 218
  Adam, VII, 200
  John, XII, 601(2)
HARMOND, George, VIII, 126
HARNESS, George, XIV, 378; XV, 274
  George, Junior, XV, 67; XVI, 51
HARNETT, Cornelius, I, 46
HARPER, XIV, 153
  Adam, VII, 179,180,183
  Charles, XVI, 225
  Jacob, VII, 182, 183; VIII, 126
  Jeduthon, VII, 222
  John, I, 83; XIII, 48, 49 (3)
  Joseph, XIV, 157; XV, 123(2)
  Philip, VII, 182, 183; VIII, 126
  Robert, VII, 401
  Samuel G., XV, 123(2)
HARPUR, Robert, X, 561
HARQUIP, II, 34, 39
HARRING, Leonard, VII, 188
HARRINGTON, V, 559
HARRIS, III, 567
  Benjamin,* VI, 291;
XIV, 426
  Charles, VII, 206
  Hugh, VII, 219
  Isham, VII, 211
  James, VII, 201
  Joel, XV, 227; XVI, 149
  John, I, 138, 147; VII, 202, 220; X, 112; XIII, 608; XIV, 425; XVI, 60, 68
  John, Junior, VII, 202, 220; XIV, 319

Joshua, XIV, 334
  Lazarus,XV, 463
  Nathan, VII, 212
  Overton, XV, 240
  Robert, XVI, 36(4)
  Thomas, I, 86, 129, 327, 340; II, 156; XIV, 278(3), 337
  William, I, 373, 379, 414, 422, 426, 429; VII, 201; VIII, 606; XIV, 243; XV, 155
HARRISON, Anne (Carter), VII, 455(5), 456
  Benjamin, I, 36, 229, 23G; III, 181, 202, 461, 540(2); IV, 356, 530; V, 300, 368(3), 369(2); VI, 291†,298, 303, 304(2), 305(8), 306(8), 307, 308, 415, 416; VII, 288, 455(3), 456; VIII, 66(4), 67 (2), 68, 257(3), 149, 578; IX, 176; X, 5, 659, 678, 581, 582; XI, 5, 147, 405, 548, 551, 552, 571; XII, 639, 716; XIII, 149; XIV, 320; XV, 240, 265(2); XVI, 214, 268(5)
  Benjamin, Junior, III, 182, 425, 428, 430(2), 431, 477(3), 538(5), 539(3), 540(4)
  Burr, VII, 406; VIII, 624; XII, 604, 684
  Carter R., XV, 255; XVI, 214, 268(2), 269
  Carter Henry, VII, 455(2), 456(3), 457 (3), 626(4), 627(4)
  Cary, XIII, 149
  Charles, VII, 201
  Collier, XV, 408
  Cuthbert, XI, 631, 676
  Daniel, VIII, 127
  Edmund, XIII, 570; XIV, 390
  Edward, I, 83
  Elizabeth, III, 538(4).

64

539(2), 540(7)
George, XII, 631, 676
Gideon, VII, 188
Harman, I, 84
Henry, IV, 78; VII, 456; VIII, 66
James, XVI, 268
John, VII, 188(2)
John Peyton, XII, 605
Mathew, VII, 406, 475; XVI, 174
Nathan, VII, 181
Nathaniel, III, 539; IV, 78; VI, 280(6); VII, 186, 188(2), 569; VIII, 66(5), 67(6), 68(6), 174(2), 175(5), 176(6), X, 559; XI, 57
Ralph, I, 83
Reuben, XV, 132
Richard, XV, 343
Robert, XIV, 241; XV, 132
Ruben, VII, 194
Susannah, VIII, 67, 68 (2)
Theophilus, XIII, 625; XV, 240
Thomas, VII, 570; X, 295; XV,99; XVI,194
William, XI, 250; XIV, 241, 267; XV, 111
William B., XV, 223
Willy, XV, 240
HARROBACK, Jacob, VII, 23
HARROD, James, XII, 223, 580(2), 581, 631
HARSTON, George, XV,95,160
— Samuel, XV, 95, 160
HART, Edward, XV, 166
John, I, 36
Martha, VIII, 628(2)
Mary, VIII, 628(2)
Silas, IX, 420
— Thomas, XII, 76
HARTLAND, Anthony, II, 378
HARTSHORNE, William, XI, 511; XII, 393, 479; XIV, 308; XV, 89, 249, 383
HARTWELL, Henry, II, 560,

567, 568, 569
HARVEY, John, I, 4(7), 147, 153, 166, 168, 178, 185, 191, 202, 214, 223(2); XI, 393; XII, 639
Matthew, XIII, 83, 171
Robert, XII, 202; XIII, 83, 171; XVI, 43
Thomas, XIV, 331(4)
William, VII, 225; XIII, 100; XIV, 331(3)
HARVIE, John, I, 46; XI, 390; XII, 280; XIII, 174, 229, 599; XIV, 155, 308; XV, 419; XVI, 34, 90, 335
Lewis, XVI, 335(2)
Robert ,XV, 44
HARWELL, Thomas, I, 82
HARWOOD, I, 111
Edward, I, 83
George, II, 156(2)
Leonard, I, 86
Thomas, I, 139, 148, 154, 203, 236, 250, 289, 356, 357, 359, 372; IV, 179
William, V,371; VI,437, 524; VII, 13, 76, 588
HASBARGER, Christian, XV, 31
HASELRIG, Francis, I, 85
HASKINS, Christopher, XIII, 151(2); XIV, 156
HASTING, George, VII, 201
HASTINGS, Joseph, XII, 661
HATCH, Margaret, I, 209
HATCHER, Benjamin, VII, 206, 209; XV, 374; XVI, 100
John, XV, 30
William, I, 283,359,369, 387(4), 506; II, 551 (4)
HATCHILL, Abraham, XVI, 410
Stephen, VII, 225
HATTON, Samuel, XV, 284
HAUGH, Joseph, XVI, 245
HAULCOM, Thomas, VII, 212
HAUSEY, John, I, 146

HAVEN, Edward, VII, 216
Nicholas, VII, 182
HAVENER, Jacob, VII, 185
Nicholas, VII, 164, 185; VIII, 126
HAWES, Aylett, XV, 121
HAWK, Isaac, XII, 625
HAWKIN, VII, 478(3), 479 (3)
HAWKINS, Richard, I, 78
HAWKINS, Charles, I, 85
John, I, 83; VIII, 127; XII, 725, 726*; XIII, 171
Pinkithman, VII, 225, 226, 227
Thomas, I, 203; II, 330, 406
HAWKS, Richard, VII, 202
Uriah, VII, 202
HAWL, John, VII, 195
HAWLEY, I, 82
HAWSON, Richard, XV, 172
HAY, Andrew, VII, 196
Charles, XIII, 330
George, XVI, 34, 335(2)
James, VIII, 129
John, VIII, 618; XIII, 320(3); XVI, 51
William, I, 506; VIII, 618; XI, 496; XII, 420; XIII, 229, 318, 320(3)
HAYDON, Jeremy, I, 84
HAYES, II, 318
James, VI, 243
John, VII, 22
Richard, I, 247(2), 279
Thomas, VI, 243
William, VII, 21
HAYLEY, John, III, 564
HAYMOND, Colder, XV, 31
John, XIII, 292; XIV, 322
William, XII, 209, 295; XVI, 224
HAYNE, I, xi
HAYNES, George, VII, 205
Henry, VIII, 128; XIV, 315
James, VIII, 129
John, VII, 210

Thomas, V, 14
William, VII, 201, 205, 206; XV, 55, 223
HAYNIE, Anthony, XV, 121
HAYNS, William, XIV, 375
HAYRICK, Thomas, I, 149
HAYS, Andrew, VII, 192,196; XVI, 423
James, XVI, 149(2),178
John, VII, 196; XI, 164; XVI, 432
Nancy, XVI, 432
Nicholas, VII, 204, 208
HAYWARD, George, I, 82
John, I, 387
HAYWOOD, James, I, 86
HEADLEY, William, XII, 672
HEALE, George, VII,50; VIII, 63(2), 64(4), 65(4)
John, VIII, 63, 64(2), 65(3)
HEARTWELL, Henry, III, 571
HEATH, Andrew, IX, 264
Henry, XV, 374
John, VII, 228; XV, 121 (2)
Jonathan, IX, 425
HECKS, Henry, VII, 191
HEDGES, John, XII, 584
HEDGMAN, Peter, VI,292(5), 303(2); VI,262; VIII, 216(2)
HEDRICK, Adam, VII, 186
George, VII, 185
HEELE, Warwick, I, 82
HEINZMAN, Henry, XVI, 162
HEISKILL, Adam, XIV, 323, 378; XV, 65
HELM, Achilles, XIV, 416(4)
Leonard, XIV, 416(2)
Linaugh, VIII, 625
Thomas, XII, 217
HEMPHILL, Samuel, VII, 188
HENDERSON, XV, 248, 264 (2), 436, 436(2)
Alexander, XIV, 308, 394; XV, 37; XVI, 158, 174, 236, 334
Alexanderson,VIII,550; XII, 60, 604

*Hawkings

Bennett, XIII, 42(3),87, 88, 481(2); XIV,* 331(2)
Daniel, VII, 180
David, VII, 221
Elizabeth (Irwin), XVI, 83
Jacob, VII, 207
James, VII, 179, 190, 226; XII, 72; XIII, 95, 293; XV, 161, 259; XVI, 410
John, VII, 195; XII,512, 514; XIII, 218, 219 (2); XIV, 157; XV, 49, 133
John G., XV, 223, 224
Matthew, XVI, 212
Michael, VII, 190
Richard, IX, 564, 571 (2), 572(3); X, 55, 159; XIII, 258, 504; XV, 139
Robert, XIII, 284; XIV, 158
Samuel, VII, 190
William, VII, 194; XI, 61, 100; XIII, 105; XIV, 422
HENDLEY, Nathaniel, VII, 220
HENDRICK, Humphrey, VII, 201
John, VII, 201
HENDRICKS, James, XII, 393
HENING, George, XIV, 336
I. G., XV, 276
John, XVI, 395
William Walter, I, xxii, xxiv; II, ii; III, 7; V, vi; VI, iv; VII, 5; VIII, 3; IX, v; X, ii (2), iii; XI, ii,iv; XII, 7; XIII, iii; XIV, 2 (2); XVI, 60, 212, 292, 335, 374(3)
HENLEY, Hezekiah, XII, 374
HENRY VIII, II, 89(2)
VIII, III, 178
Daniel, III, 472; XVI, 197(2)
Edward, XIV, 241

James, XII, 760
John, X, 5553; XVI, 79, 44,9
Patrick, VIII, 367, 494, 578; IX, 7, 119; X, 5, 9; XI, 5, 250, 272; XII, 8, 639
Robert, VII, 196
William, XIII, 170
HENSEY, Patrick, VII, 208
HENSLEY, Benjamin, VII,203
Samuel, VII, 214
HENSON, Bartlet, VII,205
Nimrod, VII, 202
Philip, VII, 203
Thomas, XIV, 202
HEPBURN, Thomas, XV, 459
William, XIV, 263, 404
HERBERT, I, 82
Christopher, XIII, 223 (6), 224
James, XIII, 223(4),224
Maximillian, XV, 447(2)
Pascow, XIV, 282
Philip, I, 81
Thomas, XIII, 318(3), 319; XIV, 158, 282, 332
William, XIII, 94, 312, 592, 609
HERDMAN, Samuel, XVI, 159
HEREFORD, XIV, 153
John, X, 104; VI, 19
HERING, Alexander, VII, 189
HERMAN, John, VII, 201
HERMON, Caleb, VII, 192
HERNDON, Edward, XVI, 420
John, X, 370
John M., XVI, 420
William, XVI, 90(2)
HERON, James, XII, 479; XIII, 599; XV, 66
Peter, XI, 254(3)
HERREN, Leonard, VII, 188
HERRING, Elias, X, 124
HERRON, Leonard, VII, 181
HERVEY, John, VIII, 149
HETH, Andrew, XII, 397
William, XI, 310, XV, 129, 130(2)
HEWES, Joseph, I, 36
HEWETT, John, I, 376(3)

HEWITT, William, IX, 311
HEXTON*
HEYRICK,† Henry, I, 283, 289
Thomas, I, 150
HEYWARD, Thomas, Junior, I, 36, 46
HICK, VIII, 543; XV, 122, 176
HICKIE, John, VII, 219(2)
HICKLINS, Thomas, VII, 192, 406(3)
HICKMAN, XI, 345, 346(2); XII, 83, 116, 580
Adam, XVI, 171(3), 238(4)
John, XII, 672, 774(2)
R., I, 8, 129, 223, 224
William, IV, 529; XVI, 409
HICKS,‡ IV, 372, 373, 374
Baptist, I, 82, 90
Nathaniel, XIV, 322
Richard, Junior, VII,224
William, XV, 413
HIDE, John, I, 86
HIGBEE, Joseph, XIII, 175
HIGGASON, XIV, 185
HIGGINBOTHAM, Aaron, VIII, 128
David, XV, 271; XVI, 149
Thomas, XVI, 100
HIGGINS, John, XV, 245
HIGGINSON, V, 13(2), 494
HIGGISON,§ Humphrey, I, 239, 288, 372, 378, 408
HIGGONS, Peter, I, 86
HIGHT, John, VII, 223
HILEY, George, XII, 297
HILL, I, vii; III, 69, 415; VI, 242; XV, 233
Adkin, XII, 631
Amos, XIV, 278
Ann, XIV, 278(3)
Daniel, XVI, 38(2)
Edward, I, 236, 283, 289, 321, 339, 348, 369, 386, 387(5), 392, 403, 406, 422, 423, 426, 499, 505(2), 506, (2), 526; II, 199(2),

330, 364(5), 365, 546, 547; III, 93(3), 181, 202
Francis, XVI, 268
Henry, XIII, 143
Isaac, VII, 131
Jacob, XVI, 33
James, VI, 242; XII,407
John, I, 236; II, 198
Leonard, XVI, 176(2), 406(3)
Nicholas, II, 31,197,198, 249; VII, 24
Richard, I, 528; II, 205
Robert, I, 83; XIV, 266; XVI, 223
Swinfield, XIII, 585(2); XV, 50
Thomas, VII, 224; XVI, 45
Tristian, I, 86
William, VII, 201; XIII, 607, 608; XIV, 268, 408; XV, 110
HILLIARD, Joseph, Junior, XIII, 287; XIV, 266
HILTON, X, 369
HINDS, Andrew, XI, 470; XII, 631
HINES, Andrew, X, 293; XIII, 313
HINKSON, III, 677
HINSHAW, Thomas, I, 85
HINSON, Tobias, I, 86
HINTON, Benjamin, XIII,545
Christopher, VII 201
Griffith, I, 83
John, XIII, 545(2)
Robert, VII, 203
William, VII, 204
HIPKINS, John, XIV, 308
Judith, XVI, 432
William, XVI, 432
HIRE, Leonard, VII, 182
HITCHCOCK, Caleb, XV, 221
Jane, VII, 225
HITE, Abraham, VII, 25; XIII, 148
Alexander, XI, 57; XVI, 47
Catharine (Obanion). IX, 557

*See Keeton †Heyricke ‡Hick §Higginson

George, XIII, 204; XV, 99, 110
Isaac, VII, 475; VIII, 415, 624; XI, 155(3); XIII, 48, 313; XIV, 153
Jacob, VII, 214; VIII, 624; IX, 577
John, VII, 23(3), 232, 236; VIII, 415, 624
Joel, XIV, 420
Thomas, IX, 247, 576
HIX, X, 364
John, VII, 203, 212; XIV, 257
Thomas, VIII, 131
HIXON, Benjamin, XVI, 273
ILLESON, Benjamin, XIV, 242

HOARD, James, XII, 400
Thomas, XIV, 156
HOARDS, Thomas, XIII, 48
HOBART, V, 659
Henry, I, 90
HOBB, III, 59; V, 142, 144; VI, 172, 176, 492(2); VII, 480,481,482,583; VIII, 78, 98; IX, 400 (3), 488, 510; X, 272, 365, 475, 497; XI, 188, 210, 235; XII, 301, 515; XIII, 479, 502.
HORDAY, John, IX, 310
HOBSON, Samuel, XV, 173
HOCKADAY, James, VIII, 209
William, I, 378, 379, 380
HODGE, Samuel, VII, 193
Thomas, VII, 431, 569
HODGES, Edward, I, 86
Joseph, XIII, 205(2)
HODGSON, John, I, 85
William, XIII,175; XIV, 387
HODIN, John, I, 239, 283
HODSDEN, Joseph, XVI, 229 (4)
William, VI, 275, 288 (2), 289(2), 310(3); VII,156; X,124; XIV, 154, 155
HOE, XI, 18

Rice,* I, 202, 262, 278, 289, 322; IV, 93
Robert T., XIV, 308
HOEDRITCH, Jeoffrey, XVI,83
HOFFMAN, Philip, XI, 57
HOFMAN, Nicholas, VIII, 126
HOG,† Peter, VIII, 10, 124, 127
William, VII, 191
HOGAN,‡ James, XI, 345; XII, 83, 580(2), 581
HOGSHEAD, Michael, VII, 185, 187
HOLCOMBE, John, XII, 591
Philip, Junior, XV, 121
HOLCROFT, Thomas, I, 78, 82 (2)
HOLCROFTE, Jeffrey, I, 82
HOLDEN, Alexander, XIV, 242
George, VII, 64
Robert, II, 370, 380
HOLDER, William, I, 375(3)
HOLDMAN, Jacob, XI, 57
HOLL, Assy, XIII, 284; XIV, 168
HOLLADAY, Anthony, V, 369
John, X, 228
HOLLAND, Albridgton, XI, 129(3)
Gabriel, I, 129
John, XI, 253(4)
Peter, XV, 187(2)
HOLLENBACK, George, XVI, 46
HOLLES, I, 82
John, I, 82
HOLLIDAY, John, IV, 179; VI, 17
HOLLINBOUGH, George, XIII, 284; XIV, 158
HOLLIS, James, VII, 221
HOLLOWAY, David, XVI, 355
John, IV, 115(2), 117, 135(3), 137, 138(4), 142, 150(2), 181, 240, 267, 308, 379, 433; XI, 428
HOLLZELAW, Catharine, VII, 230
HOLM, VI, 399
HOLMAN, George, I, 83

HOLMES, George, VII, 221
Hugh, XV, 67, 99, 465; XVI, 52, 100, 271, 423
Jacob, XIII, 218
John, VII, 194
Joseph, XI, 511
Samuel, XV, 52
HOLT, I, 422; VI, 492; VII, 583
Christopher, I, 84
James, VII, 435, 437; VIII, 269, 539, 570; IX, 103; XV, 447
John, I, 84; V, 368(5); VI,240; VII,515; XV, 31
John E., XV, 447; XVI, 40, 58, 100
Thomas, XIV, 423
William, XV, 31
HOLTON, Samuel, I, 46
Richard, I, 86
HOME, George, IV, 197
HOMES, Mary, IV, 378(2)
Robert, VII, 184
William Wilson, IV, 378
HONE, Theophilus, I, 373; II, 157, 159(4), 249, 250, 94, 592; XV, 89
Sarah, XIV, 408
Thomas P., XVI, 379
HOOVT, Richard, VII, 201
HOOK, XIII, 188(2); XIV, 153, 241
James, VIII, 369
William, VII, 186
HOOKER, George, I, 87
HOOKE, XV, 76
Jeremiah, II, 555, 253
HOOD, VIII, 79; XI, 448; XII, 581; XIII, 480, 503
John, VI, 13, 352(4)
William, IV, 528
HOOE, XIV, 152
Bernard, XIII, 137; XV, 179
James H., XVI, 337(2)
John, XIII, 283; XIV, 153, 429
Robert Townsend, XIII, 188
HOOKS, James, VII, 188

John, V, 74(2)
Robert, V, 74
William, VII, 181, 187
HOOME, VIII, 158
HOOMES, John, XI, 467(5), 468(3); XII, 618(2), 619(6), 698; XIII, 108, 174, 287, 576(4), 577, 622(3); XIV, 668, 417(2)
HOOPER, James, VII, 129
William, II, 36
HOOVER, Jacob, XII, 625
HOP, Adam, XV, 270
HOPE, George, XIV, 308, 323
John, I, 548(3); XVI, 422(3)
HOPKINS, XI, 310
Archibald, XII, 188(2)
Charles, XIII, 175
John, I, 87; VII, 181, 188; XII, 95, 96, 690; XIII, 699; XIV, 322; XV, 66; XVI, 56
Joshua, XI, 129
Samuel, XIII, 193, 296
Stephen, I, 36
HOPKINSON, Francis, I, 36
HOPPER, William, VII, 214
HOPSON, XIV, 156
Joseph, XIV, 258(2), 259
HOPTON, Ralph, IV, 515(2), 516(2)
HOPWOOD, Moses, VII, 222
HORD, James, XII, 511; XIV, 157
William, XIII, 284
HORDEN, John, VII, 215
HORE, Christopher, I, 84
Edward, X, 325
William D. Meriwether, XV, 271
HORNBACK, Benjamin, XIV, 411
HORNBERRY, Jacob, VII, 183
HORNBY, V, 143; VI, 174; VIII, 79, 98
HORNER, Gustavus Browne, XII, 685; XIII, 92; XVI, 226, 379
John, XVI, 408(2)

*Hooe †Hogg ‡Hogans
69   70

John, Junior, XVI, 408 (2)
William, XV, 282; XVI, 225, 226, 408
HORNSBY, Joseph, XII, 496
Thomas, VII, 569
HORSELEY, XIV, 262(3); XVI, 70
HOSSEY, Stephen, I, 379
HORSLEY,* John, XIII, 273 (3), 481(2), 505, 565, 587
HORSMENDEN,† Warham, I, 429, 432, 501, 504, 505, 506, 512(2), 514, 515; II, 322(6), 323
HORTON, Alexander, VI, 304 (2), 305(2), 306
Daniel, IV,528(2); XVI, 310
John, VI, 305
Joseph, IV, 528
Sarah, VI, 304, 305(3), 306
William, VI, 290(3)
HOSIER, Adam, XVI, 280(2)
HOSKINS, Anthony, I, 370
Bartholomew, I, 359,386
HOSMER, Titus, I, 46
HOUCRINS, Edward, XVI, 241(5)
HOUGH, Francis, I, 240
John, VII, 21; VIII, 550; XII, 600
Mahlon, XV, 459
William, XV, 271
HOUSE, John, VII, 210
HOUSLING, VIII, 497
HOUSTON, XVI, 54
George, XIII, 297
James, XIV, 266
HOVER, Postern, VIII, 127
HOWARD,‡ I, v; II, 458; III, 8(19); XII, 89; XV, 168
Abraham, VII, 203
Allan, VII, 126, 423(2)
Allen, VII, 202
Benjamin, VII, 475; VIII, 369; IX, 335
Edward, VII, 198

John, I, 85, 247; XV, 182
John, Junior, XII, 665
Moses, VIII, 218
Theophilus, I, 81, 90
William, II,15; VII,222, 226; IX,334(4); XIV, 155, 156
How, Daniel, I, 384
HOWE, John, I, 154, 170, 179, 187, 203
William, XV, 121
HOWELL, James, XV, 425
Stephen, VII, 201
HOWERTON, Thomas, XV,380
HOWLE, Richard, I, 86
Thomas, VII, 223
HOWLET, IV, 266
HUBARD, Frances (Morton), VII, 637(6); VIII, 169(3), 170
James,§ IV, 535; VII, 636, 637(7), 638(2); VIII,168, 169(4), 170 (4), 347, 501, 649(2); IX, 131
William, XIII, 315
HUBBARD, Benjamin, V, 396
James, Junior, VII, 361, 499, 568
Matthew, V, 371
Nicholas, XV, 61(4)
Robert,|| I, 378, 383, 425
Thomas, XV, 160
HUBERT, Robert, I, 427
HUDDLESTON, Daniel, X, 325
John, XVI, 334
HUDGETT, James, VI, 242
HUDGINS, I, vii
HUDNALL, Richard, XV, 236 (2), 342
HUDSON, I, 649
Christopher, VII, 220 (2), 221, 592; XIII, 626; XVI, 60, 68
Ephraim, VII, 226
James, VII, 223
John, VII, 198, 216
Richard, VII, 223
Thomas, VII, 196

William, VII, 201, 223; XIII, 553; XV, 120
HUES, John, VII, 211
HUESTON, William, XIV, 431 (3)
HUFF, Joseph, XIII, 218
Lewis, XIII, 315
HUFFEN, Randolph, XV, 59 (2)
HUFFMAN, Nicholas, VII, 181, 182
Philip, VII, 475
HUFMAN, Honicle, VII, 187
Nicholas, VII, 183
Philip, VII, 184
HUGART, James, VII, 197
James, Junior, VII, 198
Thomas, VII, 198
HUGH, XIII, 558
James, VII, 217
John, VII, 236
HUGHART, Thomas, XIV, 266
HUGHES,* VII, 402; VIII, 300; XVI, 204
Aaron, VII, 204
Andrew, XIII, 171, 582
Archelaus, IX, 568; XII, 227; XIII, 582; XV, 316
Ashford, V, 250(2); VI, 15, 16
Charles, VII, 204
James, VII, 216; VIII, 127; XI, 21(4), 22
Jerry, XV, 210
John, XV, 67
Matthias, VII, 204
William, VII, 216, 493
HUGHLETT, Thomas W., XV, 121(2)
HUGIIS, XV, 379
John, VII, 191, 210
William, VII, 217
HUGINSTON, James, VII, 195
HULETT, Sarah, VII, 82(2)
HULL, Henry, XVI, 56
Peter, I, 28J; XIV, 322; XV, 56, 161
HULLS, Arnold, I, 84
HULM, Bell, VII, 202
Thomas, VII, 202
HULTON, Mores, IX, 425

HUMBLE, Richard, I, 83
HUME, James, Junior, XV, 223
HUMES,† Andrew, XIII, 582
HUMPHREY, Ralph, XIV, 153
HUMPHREYS, Alexander, XIII, 588
Ralph, XI, 442
HUMPHRIES, XII, 595
Joseph, VII, 51
HUNDLEY, Caleb, VI, 243
Richard, VI, 242
Robert, VI, 243
HUNGAR, IV, 336, 382, 384, 386; V, 143, 145, 146, 364; VI, 19, 173, 177 (2), 443(2), 445, 496, 510, 511; VII, 79, 80, 98, 100, 222, 223, 263, 279; IX, 154, 160, 488, 489, 511, 513; X, 273, 356, 475, XIV, 152
HUNGERFORD, Edward, I, 78
HUNT, V,107; VII,225; XIV, 156
David, XIII, 275; XV,97
George, II, 322(6), 323
James, VI, 495; VII, 588
Samuel, IX, 310
Tamar (Fisher), VIII, 440
Thomas, I, 85; VII, 205; X, 325
William, II, 370, 374, 376(3), 377(2); VII, 223
HUNTER, VIII, 426(2); XIV, 154
Alexander, XIII, 297; XV, 210
Archibald, VII, 569
David, XIV, 308, 378; XV, 99, 385; XVI, 321 (2), 423
Ichabod, XV,117(3),120
James, III, 315,326(2), 329(2), 447(2), 451 (2); IX, 303, 304(5), 305(6), 306(3); XI, 322; XII, 238, 242; VII,

*Mursley †Horsmenden ‡Edlingham §Hubbard ||Huberd
71   19   72

204(2), 208, 435, 437;
VIII, 269; XIV. 270;
XVI, 334
John, C., XVI, 177, 395
Moses, XIV, 270, 308
Nathaniel. Chapman,
XII, 373
Robert, VII, 195
William, VII, 265, 569;
XIII, 94
William, Junior. XIII.
94, 174
HUNTINGTON, I, 101
Samuel, I, 36, 46; X, 549
HUNTLEY, John, I, 84
HUNTON, James, XVI, 168,
225
Robert, XV, 120
Thomas, XV, 121; XVI,
226, 379
William, XV, 121
HUNTS, Thomas, II, 12(2)
HURD, Joshua, XV, 267
HURST, Thomas, XIV,419(3)
HURT, James, VII, 202
James, Junior, VII, 202
Joel, VII, 202
Mary, XIII, 82
Mourning, XVI, 329
William, VII, 202
HUSBANDS, Richard, I, 613
HUSE, Joseph, VII, 223
HUSHMAN, Holerick, VII,187
HUSON, William, VII, 221
HUSS, II, 257
HUSSEY, Isaac, VII, 218
HUSTAN, Robert, VII, 193
HUSTON, Archibald, VII,187.
194(2)
George, XVI, 49, 56, 211

I

ILES, John, II, 370

INGERSOL, Jared, I, 23
INGLES, Ann* (Bray), IV,
371; VI, 413(2)
John, XVI, 217
Judith (Bray), VI, 413,

James, VII, 194, 196,
216, 217
Samuel, VII, 195
William, XV, 164
HUTCHERSON, William, VII,
202
HUTCHESON, John, VII, 191;
XIII, 95(2); XV, 181
(3), 188(2), 221
Thomas, XIII, 215
HUTCHINGS, John, VI, 227;
VII, 435, 437; VIII,
269, 530; IX, 149; XI,
57, 58, 157(4); XIII,
226(4); XIV, 280(3)
John, Junior, VII, 437
Joseph, VIII, 539, 570;
XIII, 612(4)
Moses, XV, 334
HUTCHINS, Thomas, XI, 555,
556
HUTCHINSON, Jeremiah, VII,
21
Robert, I, 239, 283, 289,
339
William, I, 169, 187
HUTCHISON, Benjamin, VII,
21
William, VII, 191
HUTCHYSON, William, I, 179
HUTSON, Richard, I, 46

HYLAND, Ferguson, XIII321
HYLTON, Daniel Laurence,
XII, 375; XV, 419
Lawrence, XII, 280
HYNDMAN, Alexander, XV,
240
HYNES, Andrew, XII, 282,
676, 719

415(4), 416(2)
Mongo, III, 425; IV,371;
VI, 413
William, VII, 588; XIV,
156
INGRAM, Joseph, II, 384, 395,
461; III, 567, 568(2)

*Anne
73

INNES, Harry, XII, 400, 602;
XIII, 164
Hugh, XIV, 316; XVI,
77(3)
James, XIII, 8
INNIS, Robert, XVI, 45

IRBY, Edmund, XVI, 410
William, XV, 161; XVI,
410
IRESEN, James, VII, 216
IRONSIDE, Richard, I, 83
IRVIN, XIII, 563
Abraham, XII, 602
James, VIII, 658
IRVINE, David, VII, 210
Samuel, XVI, 100
William, VII, 209(2);
VIII, 128; XII, 603;
XIII, 87; XVI, 31
IRVING, XIV, 166
Charles, XI, 450(3);

XIII, 175, 316(2)
IRWIN, Elizabeth, XVI, 83
James, XIII, 174; XVI,
83
John, Junior, XVI, 83
Joseph, XIII, 305
Robert, XVI, 83(3), 84
(3)

ISAAC, Nicholas, I, 86
ISHAM, XI, 431
ISLES, John, II, 461, 661
ISMON, Henry, III, 564
ISRAEL, Michael, VII, 204

ITSON, Boys, XV, 419

IVERSON, Abraham, I, 379
IVY, Francis, VIII, 126
Thomas, III, 95

IZARD, VI, 449

J

JACK, VIII, 642; XIII, 83
James, VII, 216, 217
John, XV, 67, 274, 291;
XVI, 162
Thomas, VII, 553
JACKSON, I, 551; XIII, 165
(2); XV, 990
Christopher, IV, 448
Edward, XIII,152; XIV,
158; XV, 243; XVI,
274, 407(2)
George, XI, 318, 367;
XII, 403, 639; XIV,
157, 242, 322; XV,
243, 346; XVI, 197
Henry, I, 83; VII, 212
Jesse, VII, 217
John, I, 178; VII, 205;
XV, 178, 346; XVI,
177
John (Mrs.), I, 145
John, Junior, XII, 639;
XIII, 152
Mark, VII, 211
Peter, VII, 211

Robert, VI, 282
Samuel, VII, 200, 212,
631, 632, 633; XVI,
246, 279
William, I, 23, 24; VII,
201, 218
JACOB, John, I, 384
John I., XV, 274, 291*
JACOBS, William, VII, 215
JACOBSON, Peter, I, 86
Philip, I, 86
JACOBY, Francis, VII, 214
JAMEISON, Andrew, XIII,174
JAMES I., I, iv(2), 57, 76, 80,
98; II, 525; IV, 157,
554(3), 555; V, 531;
IX, 118, 130; XIV,
200
JAMES II., III, 28(2), 29, 40,
550, 563(3), 560, 563;
VI, 198
JAMES, Catlett, XIII, 322(2)
David, VII, 216
Humphrey, I, 83
Isaac, XVI, 179

*Jacoba
74

Joseph, VII, 213
Mildred, XIII, 322
Richard, VIII, 606
Thomas, I, 67, 77, 513
William, XIV, 276(2),
277
JAMESON, IX, 320; XI, 157
Alexander, VII, 203;
XV, 138
Andrew, VII, 197
David, VII, 570; IX,
126; XI, 473; XIII,
143; XV, 176
Edmund, XVI, 136
Elizabeth, XV, 138(3)
George, VII, 197
John, VII, 181; XIV,
245; XV, 63, 209
Thomas, VII, 203
JANNEY, Mahlon, XV, 271
JARMAN, William, XVI, 149
JARRELL, Thomas, VI, 285
JARRET, John, V, 369
JARRETT, Daverix, XIV, 315
Elizabeth, XIV, 315
William N., XV, 235
JARROTT, Hezekiah, VII, 224
JARVIS, Thomas, III, 59
JASON, II, 374

JEE, Andrew, XII, 83; XIV,
157
JEETER, Charles P., XVI, 420
(2)
Mary, XVI, 420(2)
JEFFERIES, II, 560
William, III, 545(2)
JEFFESS, Edward, XV, 66
John, XIV, 308, 320
JEFFERSON, Field, VI, 495
George, XVI, 100
Peter, V, 378(2); IX,
662, 664; XIV, 326
Peterfield, XII, 659
Randolph, XIV, 155
Thomas, I, iv(2), vii,
viii, x(3), xi, xxii,
xxiii, xxiv, 3, 36, 121
(3), 137, 147, 153,
223(2), 224, 230, 238,
282, 288, 322, 339,
352, 358, 363, 369,

370(2), 429, 506, 516,
526, 551; II, vii, 9,
17(2), 18, 33, 42, 149,
163, 249, 509; III, 8,
9, 229, 482; IV, 5,
VIII, 149, 326, 385,
477; IX, 175(2), 176,
X, 5, 9, 318, 568(3),
569, 570, 575; XI,
434, 562, 571(2), 574
(2), 575; XII, 324,
419; XV, 69
JEFFREYS,* Herbert, II, vii
(4), viii(3), 404, 420,
424, 430, 548, 549,
555, 557, 564, 565
JENIFER, Daniel of St. Thom-
as, I, 22; II, 545; X,
553; XII, 50
JENINGS, Edmund, III, 423,
460
Peter, I, 530
William, VII, 25
JENKINS, XVI, 234
Henry, IV, 529(3)
Joseph, VII, 181, 187;
XIII, 661
Samuel, VII, 218(2)
JENNING, VIII, 546(2)
JENNINGS, I, 3; XIV, 315
Charles, XIII, 106; XIV,
323
Edmund, III, 8(2), 431;
IV, 5
John, I, 516(2); VIII,
131
Jonathan, VII, 205
Peter, II, 150, 197, 198
(2), 205, 225, 226
Thomas, I, 86; XVI, 225
William, XII, 672
William, Junior, XV,339
JENNY, John, XV, 459
JENYNGS, II, 250
JERDON, Thomas, VII, 447
JERDONE, Francis, VII, 129
(4), 130(2)
Thomas, VII, 458
JERMYN, Henry, IV, 515(2)
XV, 374
Elizabeth, II, 374
JERVISE, Thomas, II, 472

Jeffereys, Jeffries, Jeffryes
75

JETER, Ambrose, XV, 30
JETT, James, Junior, XV, 30
John, XV, 30
Stephen, VIII, 139(3),
140(5), 141
Thomas, VII, 431; IX,
332
JOANNY, John, III, 228
JOB, Moses, VII, 215
JOBAN, George, I, 65
JOHN, I, 432
Henry, I, 86
William, XII, 639; XIV,
272
JOHNS, John, XII, 661; XIV,
300; XV, 120
JOHNSON, XIII, 571, 572,
573(2), 579(2), XIV,
154; XVI, 17
Andrew, XV, 425; XVI,
403
Anne, VIII, 461
Benjamin, XIII, 91
Daniel, VII, 216
Dorothy, VIII, 467
Edward, XIII, 155(3),
156, 479(2),503; XVI,
409
Elizabeth, VIII, 461,
462(2), 463
Elizabeth (Bray), VI,
413, 414(8), 415(2);
VII, 247(6), 248, 452
(4), 453(5); VIII,
461(10), 462, 463(2)
Garret,* II, 400(3); III,
479(2)
Jacob, II, 447(3); III,
95, 479(2)
Jael, (Mrs.), IV, 179
James, XVI, 310(2)
James Bray, VIII, 461
James, Junior, XII, 407
John, I, 84, 545; II, 370,
375(2), 377; VII,
183; XV, 182; XVI,
31(2)
Joseph, I, 236,262; XIV,
322
Martha, VII, 160; VIII,
461

Martin, XV, 30
Nicholas, V, 115(6),
116(5), 117
Patrick, VII, 210
Peter, VII, 408; XV, 121
Philip, VII, 413, 414(7),
415(3); VII, 64, 83
(3), 84, 175(3), 247
(6), 248(4), 259, 260
(2), 316, 360(2), 361,
452(3), 453(7), 454
(2), 498(3), 668;
VII, 146, 460(4),
461(8), 462(6), 463
(6); IX, 69; XII,
716(2)
Rebecca, VIII, 461
Richard, I, 86; II, 434;
V, 114(3), 115(3),
116(5), 117(2); VII,
159, 160(2), 161(2);
VIII, 391, 455(8),
456(5), 457(3); XVI,
338(5)
Robert, I,' 82, 84; XV,
263; XIII, 170; XV,
234
Stephen, VII, 216
Thomas, I, 84, 85, 323,
370, 379, 386; V, 114
(4), 115(2), 116(2);
VI,395; VII, 160(5),
161; VIII, 457, 461
William, I, 86; II, 155
(2); V, 114(2); VII,
23, 160; VIII, 133(2),
461; XIII, 218, 546
(2); XVI, 330
William Samuel, I, 22
Zachariah, XI, 341
JOHNSTON, VI, 17
Aaron, IX, 576(3); XI,
60(2), 61
Benjamin, XII, 384(3),
385(2); XIV, 245
Benjamin W., XV, 365
Christopher, XII, 615
Daniel, VII, 215
David, VII, 213; XVI,
403
Edward, XV, 447

*Garratt
76

Elizabeth (Moorman),
XII, 614
Frances, IX, 576(2)
Francis, XI, 60(2), 61
George, VIII, 165
Hugh, VII, 216
James, VII, 208
John, VII, 180(2)
Malcom, XIV, 422
Peter, VII, 570; XI,273;
XIV, 390; XV, 166,
270, 274, 435, 436;
XVI, 158
Robert, VII, 493; XII,
391; XIII, 183(2)
JOLLY, Henry, XV, 379
JONES, XIV, 157
Abner, XV, 30
Albridgton, VII, 624;
VIII, 660
Allen, VIII, 34(2), 35
(2), 61, 62(3)
Anthony, I, 239
Batte, VIII, 276
Benjamin, XV, 176;
XVI, 136, 346
Britton, XIV, 281
Calesby, XI, 369(2);
XII, 64(2); XV, 121
Daniel, VIII, 292
Drury, XIV, 390
Edmund, X, 209
Elizabeth, XI, 65(3)
Frederick, III, 431; IV,
371; VI, 294; VII,
402; XIV, 156, 314,
322(2)
Gabriel, VII, 120, 200,
282, 236; VIII, 446;
IX, 374, XIII, 588
George, XIV, 321; XV,
167
Griffin, IX, 573
James, VII, 210, 216;
IX, 244; XIV, 321;
XV, 167, 259; XVI,
410
John, I, 87; VI, 485,
507; VII, 210(2), 216,
486; VIII, 160(6),
264, 580; XII, 721;
XIV, 167, 312; XV,

G3; XVI, 136, 334, 346
Jonathan, VII, 191, 209;
VIII, 131
Joseph, VII, 21; VIII,
220, 521(2), 494, 660;
IX, 95, 574(2), 575;
XI,204, 382, 405; XII,
591, 792; XIII, 599;
XIV, 320; XV, 111,
207, 213, 216, 259,
297(3), 351, 364;
XVI, 62, 376
Joshua, VIII, 131
Josias, XII, 661; XIII,
587; XIV, 311
Levi, VII, 215
Lewellin, VIII, 276(7),
277(5)
Meriwether, XV, 353;
XVI, 34
Minitre, XV, 30
Nathaniel, V, 370
Peter, II, 328; VII, 206,
209, 602, 603
Peter B., XVI, 410
Philip, IV, 479
Rice, VIII, 159(2),
160(10), 161(3)
Richard, VII, 225; VIII,
276(2), 277(2), 292,
369; XV, 161; XVI,
410
Robert, II, 370(2), 550;
IV, 267; V, 142; VI,
172; VII, 208, 210
Robert, Junior, VI, 285,
298
Rowland, XVI, 309
Samuel, VII, 402; XIV,
156
Skelton, I, 76; XVI, 34
Thomas, IV, 372(2),
374; VII, 202, 208,
222, 224(3), 602;
VIII, 130; IX, 244;
XVI, 335
Thomas B., XV, 334
Thomas, Junior, XII,
605; XV, 323
Tignal, XIV, 241
Walter, XI, 369; XV,
121

Walter, Junior, XVI,
235
Widow, III, 470
William, I, 370, 507; II,
429,531; VIII,160(2),
625
Wood, VII, 202
Zachary, I, 83
JOPLIN, Thomas, VI, 375
JORDAN, IV, 528; V, 143, 145,
233(2); VI, 169(2),
173, 175, 226; VII,
533; XIV, 155
Alexander, XVI, 58
George, I, 283, 506, 512;
II, 31, 330
James, XVI, 246
John, IV, 458
Michael, XIV, 422(3)
Samuel, VI, 16; VII,
232; VIII, 149
Thomas, V, 370
William, V, 285; VI, 211
JORDAYNE.* George, I, 322,
339, 342
JORDEN, Thomas, I, 169, 179
William, XV, 444
JORDON, Benjamin, IV, 529
Charles, IV, 529
John, VII, 181

Joshua, IV, 529
Thomas, I, 145; IV, 529
William, IV, 529
JORNIGAN, Thomas, IV, 528
Thomas, Junior, IV, 528
JOSIUA, John, I, 85
JOSEPH, VIII, 66(2), 67(2)
JOUET,* John, XII, 282, 400,
602
JOUIT, John, XIII, 159, 160
JOUITT, Robert, XIV, 308
JOURDAN, V, 136
Samuel, V, 250
JOURDAYNE,I Thomas, I, 130,
154, 187
JOUSLIN, Elizabeth, VII, 146
James, VII, 145, 146(2)
Richard, VII, 145
JOYCE, Thomas, VII, 226
JOYNER, VIII, 440
Lewis, XIII, 547(2),
548
JOYNES, Levin, XII, 364

K

KAVENAUGH,§ Charles, VII,
447
KAY, Joshua, XIV, 330
KEAN, David, XIV, 375, 426;
XV, 55
John, XIII, 315
KEARNES, John, XI, 405;
XIII, 159, 175, 599
Michael, XII, 213
KEARSLEY, John, XIII, 174
KEASY, Thomas, VII, 223
KEZ, Aaron, XVI, 56
James, XI, 57
KEEF, Reuben, VII, 208
KEELING, Leonard, VII, 223
KERN, William, XV, 380

KEENE, Newton, XVI, 395
KEENY, XV, 168
Abraham, VII, 191
KEETON,|| John, II, 447(3);
III, 479(2)
KEISELL, George, XIII, 297
(2), 298
KEITH, Isaac S., XII, 393
James, XVI, 48, 379
Reuben, VII, 226
KELDERMAN, Herman, II,
308(2); III, 479(2)
KELKE, Charles, I, 82
KELLAR, Abraham, XI, 57
George, XI, 57
KELLER, Conrad, XIV, 221
John, XIV, 257

*Jorden   †Jouett, Jouit   ‡Jourdan, Jordon, Jurdain
§Kavenaugh ||Kenton

KELLEY, George, XI, 332
KELLIGREW, Robert, I, 76
KELLO, Richard, VII, 624;
IX, 314, 328
Samuel, XIII, 173, 297
KELLY, David, VII, 212
George, XI, 58; XII,
479; XIII,599,619(3)
Isaac, XVI, 329(3)
John, XVI, 60, 149, 318
Michael, VII, 195
KELSOR, Robert, XIV, 120
KEMP,* IV, 266, 267, 335(2),
383, 385, 387; V, 136,
142(2), 144(2); VI,
169, 173(2), 176(2),
352, 492; VII, 583;
VIII, 78(2), 80, 98
(2),100, 101, 323(2);
IX, 577(2); XI, 270,
448; XIII, 480, 503
James, III, 95; XVI,
225, 379
Matthew, II, 36, 454,
646(2)
Richard, I, 4, 5, 238,
282, 288, 322, 339; II,
319; VI, 510
William, I, 133, 196;
XVI, 225
KEMPER, Henry, VII, 24
KENADAY, James, VII, 195
William, VII, 195
KENDAL, II, 198, 205
William, III, 28
KENDALL, John, V, 84(5), 85
Joshua, V, 84(2), 85(3)
Mary, VI, 443(4), 445;
VIII, 278(7)
William, I, 431; II, 15,
197, 250, 549(2); VI,
443, 445(2); VIII,
132, 278(2), 279
KENDELL, William, XII, 631
KENDRICK, Benjamin, XV,
267
KENERIDCBURG, Richard, I,
86
KENNEDY, XIV, 153
Clement, VIII, 193;
XIII, 283

David, VII, 493
John, X, 135; XII, 631
Thomas, X,I, 603
William, XI, 223, 456,
602
KENNER, George, VII, 24
Rodham, III, 167(2); V,
15; VI, 175
KENNON, VI, 13; VIII, 97,
321, 323; IX, 488,510,
513(5); X, 272, 365,
475; XI, 210, 235, 238
(3)
Richard, V, 142, 144;
VI, 172, 175, 298, 307;
XIII, 193; XV, 114
Robert, VI, 277; VII,
212
William, VI, 277, 294;
VII, 569; VIII, 77;
XI, 147(4), 148
KENNY, Edward, VII, 189
KENT, XV, 217
Isaac, VIII, 164
KENTON, Simon, XIII, 182
(2)
KER, David, VII, 569; VIII,
456
Edward, Junior, XII,
682(3)
George, XII, 682(3)
KERCHEVILLE, William, XVI,
197(2)
KERN, Michael, XVI, 235
Michael, Junior, XVI,
456
KERNS, Adam, XV, 224
Michael, XIV, 389
KERR, David C., XVI, 47
Edward, VII, 130(6);
XII, 364
George, VI, 241; VII,
50(4), 52(2), 54; XI,
148(3), 149(2)
John, XVI, 31
William, VII, 191
KERRE, Samuel, VII, 187
KERRIL, Richard, I, 83
KERSEY, VI, 18; XIV, 153
KESLER, Sandcœur, VII, 209
KESINGER, Mathias, XIII, 95
(2)

KETLEY, Thomas, I, 86
KETTLE, Abraham, XIV, 411
Jacob, XV, 274
KETTLEBY, John, I, 87
KETTRICK, Anthony, VII, 54
KEY, XIV, 153
Gersham, VI, 18
Henry, VII, 202
Joshua, XVI, 149, 318
Thomas, I, 148
William, VII, 24
KEYE, XV, 246, 291(2)
KEYS, James, XV, 360
Samuel, XV, 240(3),
262

KIDD, Andrew, XV, 228
James, VII, 226
John, XIV, 399
KIGER, George, XIII, 315
KILLICREW, Robert, I, 82, 90
KILPATRICK, John, VII, 197
KINCHLOE, Daniel, XV, 379
KINCKELVE, Robert, XV, 298
KINDLEY, Benjamin, VII, 186
KINDLER, Jacob, VII, 187
KING, VII, 141; XIV, 164;
XVI, 334(2)
Alexander, XV, 67
Andrew, VI, 239
Charles, VI, 242
Edmund, XIII, 278
Faith, V, 367; VI, 240
George, VII, 187, 195;
XV, 169
Henry, VIII, 653; IX,
68, 70
Jacob, XVI, 405
John, VII, 187, 195;
VIII, 653; XI, 332;
XVI, 231
Joseph, XVI, 194
Miles, IX, 466; XI, 405;
XII, 97, 635; XIII,
106; XV, 447
Rachael, VII, 130
Ralph, I, 84
Robert, IV, 93; VI, 16
(2)
Rufus, I, 22
Sackville, XIV, 308
Thomas, XIII, 300, 567

Walter, VI, 241; IX,
234; X,300(6); XI,36
William, I, 84; XV, 426;
XVI, 32, 110, 140, 167
(2), 181, 346
KINGE,* Henry, I, 145(2)
KINGSMELL, Richard, I, 129,
138, 145
KINGSTON, Thomas, I, 139
KINKADE, James, VII, 203
John, VII, 189
KINKEAD, Thomas, XVI, 161
Thomas, Benjamin, VII, 179,
180, 181, 183†
KINNEY, Jacob, XVI, 94, 100,
379
KINSEL, Cunrod, VII, 185
KINSEY, Benjamin, VII, 198
William, VII, 186
KIPLINGER, XV, 377
KIRBY, Benjamin, XIII, 289
John, XIV, 418
Obadiah, XV, 378
Richard, XV, 378
Samuel, XIII, 91
KIRKENDALE, Benjamin, VII,
25(2)
John, VII, 25(2)
Nathaniel, VII, 25(3)
KIRKMAN, Sarah, II, 559
KIRKPATRICK, Samuel, XIII,
617
KIRKUM, Robert, VII, 128
KIRTLEY, Francis, VII, 185
KIRTON, Josias, I, 84
KISER, Andrew, XVI, 233
KITE, Abraham, VIII, 252
Gabriel, VII, 185
George, VII, 185, 186
Jacob, VII, 185
Valentine, VII, 185
William, VII, 183

KNIGHT, III, 25
Charles, VII, 225, 226
Peter, I, 362, 431, 530;
II, 327; VII, 226
KNOWLES, Sands, II, 552(4),
553(2)
Thomas, I, 85
KNOX, Geo., XVI, 31
Robert, XV, 168

*Kynge   †Kinly

KOONTZ, John, XV, 99, 132;
  XVI, 400
KOPPIN, Robert, I, 84
KOPPING, George, I, 78
KOYDES, Edward, II, 201

KYCEK, Daniel, XVI, 274

KYGGAN, Carberry, I, 405(4),
  406(2)
KYLE, David. XIII, 587
  Jeremiah, XVI, 57
  Valentine, VII, 182
KYTH, IX, 184(2); XI, 258
  (2)

LARGENT, James, XII, 702;
  XIV, 153
LARK, Robert, VII, 224
LARUE, Isaac, XVI, 246
LATHAM, Peter, I, 84
  Philip, XV, 178
  Robert, XV, 176
LATHRAM, Robert, XIV, 418
  (2)
LATIMER, James, XIII, 299;
  XIV, 169; XV, 309
LATON, John, VII, 22
LAUCKE, Peter, XIV, 323
LAUDCRAFT, Nathaniel, XVI,
  179
LAUREL, Henry, VII, 182
LAURENCE, Richard, II, 184
LAURENS, Henry, I, 46
LAWLER, Michael, VII, 213
LAWN, V, 75(2), 76; IX, 184
  (2); XI, 258(2)
  John, VII, 179, 180
LAWRENCE, III, 568, 569; IV,
  266,* 334, 382, 385,
  387, 480; V, 14, 136
  (2), 142, 145; VI,
  169(2), 173, 177, 472
  (2)
  Henry, I, 510(3), 511
  James, VII, 186
  Richard, II, 370, 376,
  377, 461
  Robert, I, 546
  Thomas, VII, 183, 184
LAWRY, Gawin, VIII, 658
LAWSON, VII, 613
  Anthony, V, 106; VIII,
  653; XI, 270
  Christopher, VII, 50
  Gavin, X, 196
  Gawin, XIV, 154
  John, II, 371, 372; VII,
  204, 205, 493; IX,
  233; XIV, 157, 394;
  XV, 37; XVI, 174
  Robert, XI, 272
  Thomas, I, 87; VII, 427
  William, I, 83
LAYMAN, Daniel, XIII, 585
LAYNE, William, VII, 205
LAYTON, IV, 267, 336, 383,
  386; V, 137, 142, 144;

VI, 169, 172, 175;
  VIII, 78, 98, 323, 421,
  423; IX, 154, 488, 510,
  513; X, 272, 355, 475;
  XI, 210, 235; XIII,
  479, 502
  William, XIII, 218

LEAHY, James, XV, 228
LEAR,† John, II, 249, 330;
  VI, 174
  Tobias, XV, 465
LEDBETTER, William, VII, 212
  William, Junior, VII, 212
LEDGEWOOD, William, VII,
  193
LEE, IV, 462; V, 559; VIII,
  279; XI, 84, 345, 346
  (2)
  Ambrose, VII, 202
  Anna, III, 59; VI, 443
  (3), 444, 454(4); VIII,
  278
  Arthur, XI, 571(2), 574
  (2), 575; XIII, 131;
  XVI, 58, 140
  Betty, VIII, 469
  Charles, IX, 576; XI,
  60; XII, 393; XIII,
  94, 592; XV, 183
  Clement, VII, 220
  Daniel, XVI, 29
  Francis, II, 569; V, 370
  Francis Lightfoot, I, 36,
  46; VII, 236, 459, 460
  Godfrey, IV, 529
  Hancock, III, 59; VI,
  443(4), 445; VIII,
  278(7), XI, 345;
  XIII, 222(3), 307
  Henry, I, 84, 288, 370;
  VII, 229, 232, 427,
  568; VIII, 158, 165,
  489, 627, 664; IX, 62;
  XII, 361, 372, 608,
  633, 725, 726; XIII, 4,
  183; XIV, 387, 407;
  XV, 66
  Henry, Junior, XI, 204
  James, VII, 199
  John, II, 309; IV, 462;
  XV, 97

L

LACASSAGNE, Michael, XIII,
  91
LACEY, Elliott, VII, 206
  Israel,* XV, 214, 223,
  242, 383
  Joseph, XV, 242
  Theophilus, VIII, 130
LACKLE, Adam, VII, 204
LACOSTE, Stephen, XIII, 100,
  699
LACY, Drury, XVI, 183
  Theophilus, VII, 307
LADD, XV, 442
  Benjamin, VII, 21
  Noble, VI, 21
LAFAYETTE, X, 569(4), 576;
  XI,553(3); XII,30(3)
LAFERTY, Ralph, VII, 193,
  197
LAFTWICH, William, X, 109
LAIDLEY, James G., XVI, 209
  Thomas, XIV, 272
LAKE, Walter, VII, 218
LAMAN, John, VII, 216
LAMB, James, XI, 129
  William, XII, 361; XIII,
  183
LAMBERT, David, XII, 690
  Jacob, XV, 65; XVI, 47
  John, XV, 190
  Thomas, I, 284, 359, 370,
  373; II, 158
LAMPKIN, Richard, XVI, 329
LANCASTER, Nathaniel, XV,
  120
LANE, Anna Maria, XVI,
  432(2)
  John, XVI, 432
  John Burk, VII, 203

Joseph, XIII, 580; XV,
  134(2)
  Mary, XIII, 580(2), 581
  Presley Carr, XIII,
  580(3), 581
  Thomas, V, 287(3); VI,
  317
  William, A., XVI, 388
  (2)
  William, Junior, XIII,
  580; XVI, 395
  William, Third, XIII,
  580
  Willoughby W., XVI,
  195
LANGDON, John, I, 22
LANGHORNE, VIII, 301, 302
  John, II, 470
  William, IX, 68, 70
LANIER, David, XIII, 297
  James, XIII, 88,176(2);
  XVI, 60
  Robert, VII, 212
LANGDON, Joseph, VII, 406
LANGLEY, Ralph, I, 422
  Robert, VI, 240
LANGSTON, John, II, 461
LANCTON, Thomas, I, 83
LANGWORTHY, Edward, I, 46
LANKFORD, Benjamin, XV,97
LANNUM, William, XIV, 272
LANQUESTER, James, II, 371
LANSDALE, Benjamin, VII,53
  Peter, I, 649
LAPESLEY, William, VII, 195
LAPSLEY, Joseph, VII,189(2)
  Samuel, XII, 223
LAPWORTH, Michael, I, 111
LARAMORE, III, 668
LARD, David, VII, 184

Kendall, VIII, 278(3),
  279(6), 469
  Ludwell, XII, 604; XIII,
  94, 592; XV, 69, 214
  Mary (Kendall), VI,
  443(4), 445; VIII,
  278(7)
  Philip Ludwell, VII,236,
  309(2), 431; VII, 78,
  320(2), 622
  Richard, I, 339, 515; II,
  201, 563, 569(2); III,
  657, 570; VII,427(2),
  570; VIII, 124, 278,
  391, 640(2); IX, 62;
  XI, 369; XV, 379
  Richard Bland, XII,605;
  XIII, 171; XIV, 378;
  XVI, 177, 395
  Richard Evers, XIII,
  219, 220(2); XV, 437,
  447; XVI, 100, 130,
  346
  Richard Henry, I, 36,
  46; VII, 427, 431, 459,
  460, 570; VIII, 391,
  640(2); XI, 204; XII,
  685; XVI, 40, 58
  Sarah, IV, 529
  Thomas, V, 143, 194(2);
  VI, 7, 173; XII, 373;
  XIII, 137
  Thomas Ludwell, VII,
  450, 460; VIII, 494,
  627, 670; IX, 49, 95,
  175, 305; XIV, 387;
  XV, 214
  William, III, 125; VIII,
  278(2); XI,405; XVI,
  215(3)
LEECH, I, 111
LEED, X, 356; XI, 188, 211,
  235; XII, 301; XIII,
  504; XIV, 172; XV,
  312; XVI, 182
LEEK, Vincent, XV, 270
LEEPER, Gaun,* VII, 187, 195
LEET, Daniel, XVI, 408(2)
LEFFINGWELL, Samuel, XVI,
  164
LEFTWICH, Jabez, XVI, 155,
  338

Jesse, XVI, 52
  Thomas, VII, 225; XV,
  233, 234
  Uriah, XVI, 38
  William, VII, 225; XI,
  61, 171; XIII, 81†;
  XIV, 422; XV, 137
  William, Junior, XIV,
  418(2); XV, 160
LEFTWICK, Augustine, VII,
  206
LEGAT, Alexander, VII, 197,
  200
  James, VII, 216
LEGRAND,‡ XIV, 157
  Alexander, XIV,425(2),
  426
  Baker, XIV, 425
  James, VIII, 369
  Josiah, XIV, 425
  Peter, VII, 232, 592
LEIGH, Emanuel I., XVI, 129
  Ferdinando, VIII, 286
LEITCH, James T., XVI, 100
LEMAYEUR, John, XIV, 426
LEMEN, Robert, VIII, 415
LENDAR, Lawrence, VII, 216
LEONARD, John, VII, 183
  Robert, XV, 137(3)
LEPRADE, John, XVI, 62(2)
LE ROY, James, VI, 239
LERUE, Isaac, XVI, 56
LESLIE, Thomas, XV, 459
LFSTER, Bryan, VIII, 132
LET, Richard, I, 85
LETHAM, John, III, 167
LETRAY, James, XV, 23
LETT, James, VII, 224(2)
  John, VII, 225
LEVER, Thomas, I, 84
LEVET, John, I, 87
LEVIL, George, VII, 224
LEVINZ, I, xxi
LEVINGSTON, William, IV,
  237(3)
LEWELLIN, Maurice, I, 85
LEWIS, Aaron, XII, 603
  Andrew, VII, 493; VIII,
  127, 546, 552; XIV,
  275(2), 327; XVI,
  217, 331(5)

Benjamin, XIII, 228,
  229(2); XIV, 257;
  XV, 359; XVI, 49,
  211
  Charles, VII, 24, 218,
  377(2), 378(11), 379
  (5); VIII, 60, 149,
  478(3), 479(6), 546,
  644; X, 474; XIII,
  616; XIV, 433; XV,
  223, 362, 377; XVI,
  211
  Charles, Junior, XV,362
  Charles, Lilburn, XIII,
  87
  Daniel, XVI, 177
  David, V, 74; VII, 203,
  204
  David, Junior, V, 74
  Edward, I, 85
  Fielding, VIII, 10, 167,
  216(2), 220, 221(2),
  281(2), 494, 601; IX,
  72, 574; X, 196; XIV,
  154, 334(2)
  Francis, I, 36, 46
  George, VII, 179, 180
  Henry, VI, 411
  Howell, XIII, 87; XIV,
  433; XVI, 182
  Ivenon, XIV, 399
  James, VII, 129, 130; X,
  370; XIV, 330; XV,
  223; XVI, 60, 149,
  212, 318
  John, V, 198(4),199(2),
  399; VII, 202, 219,
  377(2), 378(4); VIII,
  59, 60, 61, 208, 478
  (2), 497(7), 480(4);
  IX, 573, 574; XII, 86;
  XIV, 266; XV, 49, 67;
  XVI, 53, 161
  Joseph, XV, 214
  Lucy, VII, 130
  Lucy (Thornton), IX,
  573
  Margaret, XIII, 166
  Mildred, IX, 573, 574
  (2), 575(3)
  Nicholas, VIII,149; XII,

83; XIII, 175; XIV,
  155
  Priscilla (Churchill),
  VII, 168
  Robert, VII, 378; VIII,
  59, 60(10), 61(2);
  XII, 682; XV, 120;
  XVI, 420
  Samuel, XI, 139
  Susannah (Gomarrin),
  VIII, 644
  Thomas, VII, 120, 232;
  VIII, 10, 124, 127,
  646; X, 521; XII, 202;
  XIII, 284(2); XIV,
  158, 312, 322, 378;
  XV, 67; XVI, 78, 314
  (2), 315
  Thomas W., XV, 427
  Warner, VII, 409,410(8),
  411(2)
  William, VI, 449; VII,
  193, 195, 377, 475;
  XII, 383, 400, 479;
  XIII, 171, 175, 589;
  XV, 362; XVI, 49,
  211, 231
  Zachary, VI, 411(2)
  Zebulon, VII, 211
LEY, XIV, 154
  Thomas, VI, 17(2);
  VIII, 423(2)
LEYBROOKE, Henry, XIV, 408
LEYBURN, John, XV, 442;
  XVI, 403, 429*

LIGHT, John, XVI, 401
  Peter, XV, 125
LICHTFOOT, Anne, VIII, 459
  (2)
  Armistead, VIII, 457,
  458(7), 459(4)
  Elizabeth, V, 112(3)
  Francis, V, 111, 112(4),
  113(3)
  Francis, Junior, V, 112
  Philip, III, 565(2); IV,
  535; V, 111, 113(2),
  114(2), 371; VIII,
  457, 458(3), 459, 460
  (2); XV, 175

Phillp, Junior, V, 112
(6), 113(10)
William, V, 370; VII,
213, 211, 570; VIII,
405, 458; XVI, 50,
197, 246(2)
Liggon, Joseph, XV, 49
Ligon, John, XIII, 293
Richard, XVI, 417(3)
Thomas, XV, 30
William, IV, 307; XV,30
Linch, James, VII, 212
Lind, George, XVI, 47
Lindsey, Richard, I, 82
Lindsay, John, VIII, 415
Lindsey, Isaac, VII, 215, 216
James, VII, 216
John, VII, 220
Matthew, VII, 196
Thomas, VII, 216
Lince, John, II, 9(2)
Link, Barton, VIII, 131
John, VIII, 131(2)
Linn, James, XV, 380
Linnor, IV, 462
Linsey, Edward, VII, 215
Francis, VII, 223
Matthew, VII, 196
Thomas, VII, 215(2)
Linton, John, XII, 684
William, XII, 373, 684;
XVI. 174
Liny, Robert, II, 456
Lippencott, Samuel, XIV.
822
Lithgow, Alexander, XII,
372
Little, Adam, VII, 184, 185
Andrew, VII, 179, 180,
185, 187
Charles, XII, 75; XV,
177; XVI, 177
James, XIII, 88, 176(2)
John, XV, 260
Stokeley, XIV, 408
William, XII, 371
Littlefield, Edward, I, 84
Littlejohn, John, XV, 214
Joshua, XII, 690
Littlepage, IV, 113, 381,
383, 385; V, 145; VI,
169, 177, 492; VII,

532; VIII, 210, 323,
508(2); IX, 154, 161,
488, 511, 513(2); X,
273, 356, 475; XI, 211,
235, 238(2); XII,
581; XIII, 480, 503;
XVI, 385(2)
Edmund, V, 108
James, VIII, 466(2),
467(2)
John Carter, IX, 68,
146(3); XIV, 266
Richard, V, 117, 119,
120(2), 143, 190; VI,
17(2), 173, 211; VIII,
79, 98, 100; XIII, 623,
624(5)
Thomas, XII, 407
Littleton, Charles, VII,215,
216
Nathaniel, I, 356, 371,
384
Solomon, VII, 216
Southy, II, 545
Lively, Mark, VII, 203
Livingston, Philip, I, 36
Robert R., XI, 549
William, I, 22

Llewellin,* Daniel, I, 239,
283, 322, 373
Lloyd, Cornelius, I, 283, 340,
370, 373, 379
Edward, I, 289, 323
Philip, II, 520

Locard, William, VII, 215
Lockart, Charles, VIII, 129
James, VII, 181, 191
Locke, Joseph, XV, 186(3)
Lockett, James, VII, 201
Lockhart, Joseph, VIII, 472
Patrick, XI, 341, 450;
XII, 202, 675; XIII,
83
Lockheart, Randal, VII,476
Lockringk, James, VII, 193
Lodge, Luke, I, 86
Loffbury, John W., XIII,
292
Logan, Benjamin, XI, 283;

XII, 223, 232(2), 282,
396(2)
David, Junior, VII, 223
George. VIII, 570
James, VII, 195
John, VII, 227; XII,
396; XIII, 184
Login, John, VIII, 131
Logue, Samuel, XV, 345
Locwood, William, XI, 431
(2)
Lomax, Elizabeth, V, 86, 87,
88
Lunsford, V, 289(2);
VI, 227, 394
Thomas, XI, 204
London, John, VII, 206
Long, Arthur, II, 371, 379
Armistead, XIV, 336
Daniel, VII, 185; XIV,
336
David, VII, 493
Gabriel, XVI, 182
Henry, III, 473; VII,
186, 191
John, VII, 181, 191
Reuben,* VII, 213, 214,
326, 447
William, VII, 190, 197
Longest, Elizabeth, VI, 243
(2)
Looney, David, VII, 194
Joseph, VII, 204
Peter, VII, 191
Robert, VII, 190, 194
Loony, XII, 117
Lord, Abner, XIV, 428(2),
429; XV, 176(3)
John, II, 16, 160(2), 151
Thomas, XIV, 428; XV,
176
Lorimore, Thomas, VII, 194
Loson, David, VII, 205
John, VII, 205
Loudoun, VII, 62
Love, Charles I., XVI, 395
Ephraim, VII, 187
John, XIV, 394; XV, 37,
120(2)
Joseph, VII, 194
Marion, XII, 408(3)
Philip, VII, 493

Samuel, XII, 75; XIII,
171, 580; XIV, 378;
XV, 242
William, XII, 408(4);
XVI, 37
Lovell, James, I, 46
Robert, IV, 438; VI, 18
William, XV, 58
Loveinc,† Thomas, I, 283,
430
Lovelace, William, I, 83
Lovett, III, 471
Lovin, Adam, VII, 220
Loving, John, VII, 202
William, XII, 665; XIV,
322; XV, 182(3)
Lovince, Thomas, I, 322
Low, John, VII, 25, 197
Vincent, I, 86
Lowry, VIII, 78, 98; IX, 154,
161, 488, 511; XI, 211,
235; XII, 581; XIII,
480, 503; XIV, 154;
XVI, 182
John, VII, 193, 195, 196;
XVI, 334, 335
Mary,‡ IV, 379(3)
Patrick, VII, 195, 196
William, IV, 379*; VI,
18(2); VIII, 370(2);
XIII, 174
Lowther, Uriah, XVI,51 (3)
William, XV, 223, 224;
XVI, 355
Loyall,§ George, XVI, 40
Paul, VII, 435,437; VIII,
269, 539; XI, 58, 185,
405, 530; XII, 299;
XIV, 169; XV, 309;
XVI, 40
Loyd, Cornelius, I, 239, 385
Edward, I, 82

Lucar, Thomas, I, 431
Lucas, Burton, VII, 493
Edward, VII, 216
John, VII, 223
Mary, V, 370
Peter, XV, 120
Thomas, II, 197, 198(2),
205, 260

*Lluellen, Luellin
85

*Rueben   †Loveinge
86

*Loury   §Loyal

Luckett,* Levin,† XV, 214;
XVI, 51
Lucks, William, VII, 205
Luddington, William, I, 323
Ludlow, George. I, 239, 282,
288, 322, 339, 372,
408; III, 360
Mary, II, 153
Thomas, II, 153(2)
Ludlowe, George, I, 235
Ludwell, Philip, II, 330,
544, 545, 546, 547,
548, 549, 551(2), 554,
559(2), 560, 563; III,
136, 428, 431, 552,
557, 568(2); IV, 113;
V, 368(2), 371; VI,
230, 240
Philip, Junior, III, 425,
426
Thomas, II, 39, 56, 137,
201(2), 203(2), 211,
225, 226, 245(2), 313,
316(3), 320, 325, 359,
418, 422(2), 423, 430,
431, 432, 455, 457,
518, 519(2), 521, 529,
537, 538, 557
Lukens, John, XI, 555
Lukin, Edwin, I, 85
Lumpkin, George, XIV, 321
Thomas, XV, 137
Lumpkins, Thomas, XIII, 81
Lundy, Joshua C., XVI, 60,
346
Lunsford, John, XVI, 334
Lushington, Thomas, II,371
Lusk, Robert, VII, 195, 198
Luttrell, John, VII, 24
Lutz, Mary, XIII, 303(4)
Philip, XII, 303(3)

Lyddall, George, II, 328,
347
Lyle, VIII, 423
Daniel, VII, 196
James, VIII, 422; X,

477; XIII, 314, 589;
XV, 418
James, Junior, XIII,
174; XV, 418
John, Junior, VII, 195
Joseph, XV, 240
Matthew, XVI, 183
Samuel, VII, 196; XI,
164
William, XIV, 308
Lynch, M., 574; XII, 258,
398, 456, 572, 582,
629(2); XIII, 480(2),
504; XVI, 77
Charles, V, 250(2),
378(2); VI, 15; XI,
134, 135, 250; XII,
398, 512; XIV, 279
Edward, VII, 125
Head, XII, 206
John, X, 459(2); XI,
38(2); XII, 66(4),
398, 399(2); XIII,
273, 296, 298, 481,
578; XIV, 155, 266,
389(3); XVI, 220
Thomas, Junior, I, 36
Lyne, X, 55
*Edmund, XII,282; XIII,
183
Edward, XII, 361
George, IX, 69
Henry, XIV, 316
John, VIII, 456
William, VIII, 456, 633;
X, 103, 210; XIV, 268
William, Junior, XIV,
268
Lynx, John, VIII, 130
Lynn, Michael, VII, 24
Lyon, James, VIII, 130;
XIII, 582
Joseph, VIII, 216
Lyons, Peter, VIII, 272(2),
349(2), 350(4), 351;
XII, 770
Thomas, XV, 270

M

Mabry, Hinchia, X, 115(2)

McAfee, Samuel, XII, 631
McAlhaney, John, VII, 191
McAlister, XI, 571
Charles, XV, 262
James, IX, 569
McAlly, John, XII, 209
McAmish, James, XIII, 615
(3)
McAnally, Charles, VII,196
John, VII, 204
Macashan, Richard, VI, 242
McBridge, Daniel, VII, 191
McCabe, Henry, X, 488(2)
Henry, Junior, X, 488
(5)
McCall, George, VII, 50(4)
McCalley, John, XII, 661
Mary, XVI, 51
McCallum, Daniel, XIII,
104; XV, 381; XVI,
41(2)
McCarney, Robert, VII, 179
McCarrol, John, XVI,37(3)
Lodowick, XVI, 169(3)
McCartin, Daniel, XV, 177
McCarty, Daniel, IV, 58, 75,
76; V, 194(2); VI,
396, 397; XIV, 407
Dennis, IV, 331; V, 233
Edward, XIV, 389; XV,
249, 267, 291, 465
McCab, James, VII, 193
John, VII, 183, 188
Robert, VII, 185
McChesney, Robert, XV,240
Samuel, XV, 266, 267
McClanahan, VII, 189
Alexander, VII, 195
Eledge, VII, 475
Elijah, VII, 190
Robert, VII, 23
Thomas, VII, 229(3)
McCleery, William, XIV,
272, 389; XV, 62
McClelan, Abraham, VII,
208
McCleland, Thomas S., XV,
442; XVI, 100

McClellan, Joseph, VIII,
129
McClenahan, Elijah, XVI,
231
McClenny, James, XV, 347
(3)
McClerry, William, XII,639
McClintock, Alice, XIII,
616, 617
McClong, James, VII, 195
John, VII, 195
McCloskey, Patrick, VII,
196
John, XV, 262
Samuel, XV, 63
William, XV, 181(3),
186(2)
McClunge, Joseph, VII, 198
Thomas, VII, 198
McClure, Alexander, VII,
192
Arthur, VII, 195
James, VII, 181,184,187
John, VII, 181
Moses, VII, 193
Robert, XV, 54
McClurg, James, XIII, 599
James R., XVI, 335
McClurn, Halbert, VII, 191
McCockle, James, XI, 164
McColley, John, XIV, 279
(3)
McCollom, Hendrey, VII,
198
Henry, VII, 195
McComb, Thomas, VII, 185
McCome, Thomas, VII, 195
McComey, Robert, VII, 188
(2)
McConnal, John, VII, 223
McConnell, William, XVI,
31
McConnico,* Christopher,
XII, 479, 792; XV, 66,
111, 218
McCormack, Joshua, VII,
189, 199
Thomas, VII, 225
McCormick, Adam, VII, 183

*Lucket   ‡Leven
87

*McConico
88

23

Francis, VII, 215
Joshua, VII, 189
McCORNE, Thomas. VII, 187
McCOWN, John, VII. 192
McCOWNALD, William, XI.
100
McCOY, Enos, XV, 264
John, VII, 181, 198
Oliver, XIV, 322; XVI.
56
Robert, VII, 23(3), 179
William, VII, 218; XIV.
322; XVI, 56, 395(2)
McCRAE, John, XII, 373, 663
(3)
Robert, XIII, 174
McCRAW, William, XV, 48
(2), 57, 173
McCRIMAR, Francis, VII, 216
McCROSKEY, David, VII, 196
(2)
John, XVI, 38
McCUE, John, XIII, 588
McCULLEY. John. VII, 198
McCULLOCH, Roderick, XIII.
816(2)
McCULLOCK, George, XII.
599, 661
Robert, XVI, 149
William, XIII, 218
McCULLOM, Henry, VII, 196
McCULLY, John, XII, 295
McCUTCHIN, William, VII,
200
McCUTCHINSON, Samuel,
VII, 197
McCUTCHISON, James, VII.
197
William, VII, 190, 197
McDADE, Patrick, VII, 205
McDANIEL, XIII, 276, 278
(3), 279
Edward, VII, 207
Henry, XVI, 38
Joseph, VII, 207(2)
Tarrance, VII, 224
William, VII, 22, 220;
XIII, 278; XV, 120
McDAVID, Patrick, VII, 206
McDONALD, Edward, VII,
192, 194

William, VIII, 129; XV,
425
McDONNALL, Bryan, VII.
189(2), 199*
McDOUALL, John, VII, 569
McDOWEL, John, XVI, 94.
100
McDOWELL, VIII, 423
James, VII, 195; XII.
521; XV, 44, 262, 442.
444; XVI, 403
John, XII, 725, 726
Joseph, VII, 216
Samuel, VII, 196; XI.
164, 283; ·XII, 602;
XIII, 184
William, XII, 602
MACDOWELL, Samuel, VIII.
646
McDUEL, Charles, IV,529(2)
McELHERIN, Daniel, XVI,54.
158
McELVAN, Alexander, VII.
198
McFALL,† Daniel, VII, 210
James, VII, 210
McFARLAND, Alexander,
XIV, 280(4)
McFARLANE, James, XVI,
366
McFARLIN, John, VII, 200
William, VII, 181
McFERRAN, Martin, XIII,
171; XVI, 72, 348
McFERRIN, James, VII, 199
John, VII, 199
Samuel, VII, 199
Thomas, VII, 199
McGAREY, Edward, VII, 187
Hugh, VII, 188
Robert, VII, 188(2)
McGAVOCK, David, XIII, 583
James, XIII, 77, 590
McGEARY, Robert, VII, 181
McGEE, William, VII, 194
McGILL, Archibald, XVI,100
John, VII, 216
William, VII, 180
William, Junior, VII,180
McGLAMERY, John, XIII, 609
McGOVERAN, Mark, XVI. 55

McGRAW, Charles, XV, 189
(3)
McGRIGGER, John, VII, 219
McGUIRE, Francis, XVI, 412
(2)
Thomas, VII, 25
William, XIII, 90, 204;
XV, 121
McHENRY, James, VII, 198
McHENRY, James, I, 22
MACHIN, John, VI, 242(2)
Thomas, VI, 242
MACHIR, John, XII, 608
McILHENY, James, XII, 600
McILLHANEY, James, XV,
214
McINTIRE, Alexander, XV,49
Andrew, XVI, 275(3)
McINTYRE, Nicholas, VII,216
McINTOSII, X, 572
George, XVI, 100
Robert, XIV, 378·
McINTYER, John, XIV, 424
McKAY, Andrew, XIV, 421
(4)
John, VII, 180, 181
Robert, VII, 180; XIV.
420, 421(4)
MACKCLURE, Hugh, VII, 191
McKEAN, Thomas, I, 36, 46
McKEAND, John, XIII, 228,
229(2)
McKEE, Alexander, XI, 283;
XII, 395, 396
William, XI, 164, 341;
XIV, 266, 276(2)
McKEEVER, Paul, XII, 625
McKENNAN, William, XV,
169
McKENRY,* Henry, VII, 215
Patrick, VII, 215
Tully, IX, 576; XI, 60
McKENZIE, Robert, VII, 493;
X, 288(2); XI, 283
William, XII, 492
MACKENZIE, Duncan, XIII,
198
Mordock, VII, 23
MACKEY, James, VII, 205
John, Junior, VII, 205
Robert, XII, 227(3);
XV, 250; XVI, 62, 100

McKIE, Alexander, X,288(2)
MACKIE, Alexander, VII,128,
194
Andrew, VI, 288
James, VII, 206
McKINLEY, James, XIII, 183
McKINNEY, William, VII,195
MACKLEMARE, Thomas, VII.
198
McKOWN, Gilbert, XII, 607
MACKY, John, VII, 205
Robert, XV, 99
MACLAINE, Archibald, XII,
492
MACLANAHAN, Alexander,
VIII, 549
MACLAUGHLAN, Duncan, XII,
682
McLAUGHAM, Alexander,
VII, 493
McLEAN, John, XI, 111(3)
MACLIN, Frederick, VII, 211
Thomas, VII, 210; XVI,
268
William, XV, 122
McMACHAN, Benjamin, XVI,
54, 158
William, XII, 514
McMAHAN, XV, 49
McMECHAN, William, XIII,
297
McMIGHT, Daniel, VII, 180
McMILLIAN, John, XII, 604;
XIII, 137
McMILLION, John, XV, 241
(3)
McMILLON, John, VII, 24
McMULEN, Alexander, VII,
204
McMULLAN, Alexander, VII.
196
McMULLIN, William, VII,199
McMURRAY,† Samuel, VII,
198, 200
William, VII, 199
McMURTRY, James, VII, 205
McMURTY, Joseph, VII, 208
McNAMAR,‡ Thomas, VII,
179, 180, 197
McNEAL, John, VII, 191, 226

MACNEAL, Hector, VI, 528
McNEALE, Archelus, VII, 206
McNEALEY, Hugh, XV, 249
McNEELEY, Michael, XIII,87
McNEELY, Hugh, XIV, 272
McNEIL, Daniel, IX, 425
John, VII, 493
McNEILL, Alexander, XIII.
288, 289(2)
John, VII, 669
McNELLY, John, VIII, 133
McNELY, Denis, VII, 198
McNESS, John, VII, 223
McNIGHT, Daniel, VII, 179
George, VII, 493
MACOCK, Samuel, I, 111
MACON, John, XIV, 268(2)
William, VII, 455; VIII,
391, 494; XII, 383;
XV, 353
William H., XVI, 427
McI'HERSON, VIII, 423
Isaac, XIV, 429(5)
McQUEEN, Charles, VII, 213
McRAE, XIII, 480, 504
Alexander, XIV, 308,
320, 350; XV, 66;
XVI, 34, 335(2)
John, XVI, 316, 376
MACRAE, Allan, VII, 424,426,
427; VIII, 158
McROBERT, Alexander, XIII,
228, 229(2)
McROBERTS, Archibald, XI,
273
McIIONALDS, James, VII, 204
McRUNNALS, James, VII,208
McSHAN, Edward, XIII, 565
McWHORTER, Robert, VII,
204
McWILLIAMS. Samuel, XV,
132; XVI, 400
MADDISON, James, VIII, 167,
281, 282
John, VII, 232
MADDOX, VI, 351
David, VII, 224
MADDY, William, XIII, 95
MADILL,* Alexander, XIV,
336(3); XV, 176(2);
XVI, 60, 136
MADISON, XV, 81, 346

Gabriel, XII, 282, 400,
456
James, X, 521, 524, 528,
530, 531(2), 532, 533
(2), 534(2), 535; XI,
272, 554(2), 555; XII,
219(3); XIV, ·322;
XVI, 50, 197, 351
John, VII, 120
Thomas, IX, 319, 320;
XII, 202; XIII, 171;
XIV,275(3),308; XV,
44, 65, 66
MAESHOUCK, Paulus, I, 362
MAGARY, Hugh, XII, 631
MAGAVOCK, James, VII, 195
MAGERY, Robert, VII, 185
MAGET, Nicholas, VIII, 660
MAGILL, Archibald, XIV,
308; XV, 121,250,387
Charles, XV, 274, 387;
XVI, 246
James, VII, 217(2)
John, VII, 217
MAGINIS, Francis, VII, 216
MAGITT, Samuel, V, 369
MAHAFFY, Hugh, XV, 360
MAHIXON, VII, 481, 482
MAINEY,† David, XV, 267
MAIS, Joseph, VII, 190
MAITLAND, David, XV, 187
Robert, XV, 187
MAJOR, Edward, I, 323, 370,
378, 379, 384
MAKENRY, William, VII, 181
MALAND, Adam, VII, 23
MALCOM, John, VII, 161(2)
MALCOMB, George, VII, 184
John, VII, 184(2)
MALLAR, Michael, VII, 181
MALLAY, Philip, I, 549(2)
MALLER, Thomas, VII, 126
MALLET, John, I, 78
MALLORY, VIII, 474
Francis, VIII, 264
John, I, 82
Philip,‡ I, 424; II, 34
(2), 39(2)
MALLOW,§ George, VII, 185
Michael, VII, 179, 182,
184, 185, 187
MALTRAVERS, Henry, I, 552

MAN, Abel, VII, 201
Charles, VII, 185, 201
George, VII, 186
Jacob, VII, 186
MAND, Josiah, I, 86
MANEAR, David, XIV,256(8)
MANIER, David, XVI, 222
MANIN, Peter, VII, 219
MANK, Daniel, VII, 215
Henry, VII, 215
Reudy, VII, 215
Richard, VII, 215
MANLEY, William, IV, 36;
VII, 205, 206, 209
MANN, XV, 217; XVI, 72,
272
Elizabeth, XV, 136(2)
John, VIII, 127
Samuel, VII, 201
Thomas, XV, 136
MANNER, Andrew, VII, 129
MANNERING, Stephen, II,370,
379
MANNIN, John, VII, 224
Thomas, VII, 211
MANSEL, Robert, I, 81, 90
MANSFIELD, Robert, I, 78
MANSIL, David, I, 370
MANWOOD, Peter, I, 81, 90
MAPES, Francis, I, 84
MAPLES, Richard, VII, 210
(2)
Thomas, II, 555(2) ·
MAPLESDEN, Richard, I, 84
MAR, William, VII, 192
MARCH, John, I, 85
MARCHEL, George, VII, 192
MARCKLE, Charles, Junior,
XVI, 324
MARK, John, XIII, 174
MARKHAM, Bernard, XI, 57,
393; XIII, 314; XIV,
265
George, XIV, 390
John, VII, 230; XIII,
275
Vincent, XIV, 319
MARKLAND, Nathan B., XV,
435, 436
MARKS, John, XII, 662
Nathan, XIV, 418
Silky, XIV, 418

MARMILLOD, VIII, 628, 629
·Henrietta (Walthoe),
VIII, 627, 628(5), 629
MARS, John, XI, 250
MARSIN, Wiltshire, VII, 186
MARSHALL, II, 518; VII, 569
Benjamin, XV, 274
Charles, XVI, 226
George, VIII, 438(2),
439(6)
James, XIII, 297; XV,
169; XVI, 412
James M., XV, 203(2)
John, I, vii; XII, 280;
XIII, 8, 174, 599;
XIV, 360; XV, 23(3),
59, 359; XVI, 34, 335
John, Junior, XII, 282
Richard, XIII, 210(4)
Robert, XVI, 334
Roger, I, 327(3)
Thomas, VI, 376; VII,
24; VIII, 10, 124, 489;
XI, 283; XII, 369,
391, 605; XV, 274
William, XV, 114; XVI,
249
MARSHART,* Michael, I,142,
171(2), 196
MARSHEL, James, XV,119(2)
MARSTELLER, Philip, XIII, 94
MARSTON, Thomas, II, 566
MARTAIN, John, VII, 209
MARTEN,† Nicholas, I, 129,
179, 203
MARTIN, IV, 267; V, 143; VI,
174; VII, 213; XVI,
26
Abner, XIII, 148
Abraham, VII, 224
Abram, VII, 211
Absalom, XIV, 424
Andrew, VII, 226
Anthony, VIII, 646
Brice, XV, 210,234,435,
436(2)
Charles, VII, 217
David, VII, 203
Edmund, XIII, 283
Edward, VII, 215
George, IV, 462
Henry, XI, 442; XII,

645; XIII, 315, 316;
XV, 31, 182(3)
Henry, Junior, XIV, 156
Hugh, VII, 197, 199
James, VII, 204, .224;
XV, 339(5), 340(3);
VII, 77(2), 220
Jesse, VII, 21, 217; XII,
511, 512; XIII, 284;
XIV, 157(2)
John, I, 83, 86; II, 645;
III, 568; VII, 204,
231; IX, 526
John, M., XI, ii(2); VII,
4(2)
Joseph, VII, 21, 24, 218;
XIII, 284; XIV, 241,
316; XV, 95, 160, 234,
435, 436
Luther, XIII, 49; XIV,
153
Richard, I, 86
Robert, VII, 205, 206,
224
Samuel, IX, 233, 234
Solomon, I, 515(2)
Thomas, IV, 529; XIII,
287; XIV, 268
Thomas Bryan, VII,
236; IX, 247; X, 124;
XIV, 153
William, VII, 203, 211;
XII, 227; XVI, 31(2),
52(3)
MARY, QUEEN, III, 423
MARYE, William S., XVI, 379
MASE, Richard, VII, 198
MASON, I, 82; XIV, 163;
XVI, 169(2)
Anne, V, 252(2)
Edward, XVI, 60
George, II, 150(2), 151,
330, 332, 433; III,
21(2); IV, 363; VI,
19; IX, 49, 175; X,
55, 537; XII, 50, 639;
XV, 379
James, I, 386; XVI, 231
John, X, V, 177(2)
John R., XVI, 140, 346
Lemuel,* I, 430,506,512.
629; II, 197, 205, 330

Littlebury, IX, 146(2)
Lyonell, I, 386
Samuel, VII, 215
Stephens   Thompson,
XIV, 432; XV, 465
Thomas, VII, 236; XIV,
430(6); XV, 119(2).
241
Thompson,† VIII, 550;
XII, 403; XIV, 153;
XV, 177; XVI, 337
MASSEY, John, VII, 186
William, VII, 218; VIII,
149
MASTERSON, Edward, VII, 21
MASTIN, Charles, XVI, 29
MATHEWS, Thomas, XIV,
419(3)
MATHEW, William, VII, 215
MATTHEWS, Archer, XI, 139
Arthur, VII, 226
Eliaha, XV, 178
George, VII, 193, 195;
VIII, 549
Griffin, VII, 24
Jacob, VII, 225
John,‡ I, 46; II, 827;
VII, 192, 194, 195(2);
XVI, 53
John Twitty, VII, 226
Joshua, VII, 195
Lawrence, VII, 226
Richard, VII, 24, 195
Sampson, VII, 192, 193,
195; VIII, 549; XIII,
588; XIV, 266
Samuel,§ I, 5(4), 140,
145, 147, 150(2), 163,
169, 171(2), 175(2),
177(2), 178, 187, 196
(2), 202, 221(2), 235,
238, 370, 371, 373,
379, 385, 386, 408(2).
425, 426, 428, 431,
432, 492, 498, 499,
500, 501, 502(2), 504,
515, 516, 527, 528(4),
529(5), 537, 543, 544
(2), 646; II, 14(3),
319, 472; III, 472(2)
Thomas, XII, 639

*Lemuell Masonn   †Thomason   ‡Mathews
§Mathews, Mathewes, Matthewes
93

William,* I, 146; VII,
195; VIII, 126
MATTHIS, William, VII, 198
MATTOCKS, John, VII, 209
MATTOON, John, III, 479(2)
MATTOONE, John, II, 302
MATTOX, John, VII, 206
MAUPIN, Chapman, XVI, 149
Daniel, VII, 203
John, VII, 203
William, VII, 203
MAURICE, Stephen, VII, 24
MAURY, Abraham, VII, 218,
219(2), 232
Fontaine, XIII, 599;
XIV, 245, 308; XV.58
MAUZY, Richard, XVI, 329
MAWDET, Otho, I, 83
MAXSON, Zebulon, XIV, 322
MAXWELL, Daniel, XIII, 211
James, XIII, 211
John, VII, 192(2), 194,
199
Robert, XII, 639; XIII,
48; XIV, 411
MAY, VII, 126
David, XII, 202
John, X, 286; XI, 283;
XII, 580, 633(2);
XIII, 183
MAYCOCK, III, 470; V, 136,
143, 145; VI, 169, 176
MAYCOX, XIV, 155; XV, 50
MAYES, John, VII, 196
Joseph, VI, 13(2), 495;
VIII, 126(2); XVI,
323(3)
MAYHOW, I, 142
MAYLE, Thomas,I, 85
MAYNARD, XIV, 156
MAYO, XIV, 156; XV, 377
John, XII, 220(2), 221
(3); XVI, 79(2), 82,
258
Joseph, VIII, 643, 644,
645; XII, 611(4), 612
(3), 613; XIV, 155
(2); XV, 49
Philip, VII, 568; VIII,
412, 644(2), 645(3);
IX, 233, 234
William, XVI, 178(2)

MEACOM, Ann, X, 350,351(2)
John, X, 350(4),351(2)
MEAD, Abel, VII, 209
John, VII, 209
William, VII, 207
MEADE, Andrew, XI, 333
David, VIII, 470(2),
471(7), 472(8), 473
(2); XV, 259
Everard, XI, 272; XII,
591; XIV, 390; XV.
259
Richard Kidder, XV,
216, 242
Sarah (Waters), VIII,
470(2), 471(2), 472
(2), 473
Susunnah, VIII, 471(2)
William, VII, 207, 208,
475; XI, 171
MEADES, Thomas, I, 389
MEADOWS, I, 82
Benjamin, VII, 201
Josiah, X, 325
MEAKS, Joshua, VII, 218
MEALEY, Patrick, VII, 52
MEAMACK, James, VII, 215
MEARES, Thomas, I, 289, 323
MEAS, William, VII, 199
MEASE, Robert, XIII, 174
MECOM, Elizabeth, XIV, 418
James, XIV, 418
John, XIV, 417, 418(3)
Matthew, XIV, 418
Samuel, XIV, 418
Thomas, XIV, 418
MEDLEY, John, VII, 191
MEEK, Samuel, XV, 360
MEERES, Thomas, I, 340
MEES, Henry, II, 154(2), 250
MEGARY, Edward, VII, 181
(2)
MEGGENSON, IX, 567
MEGGINSON, Joseph Cabell,
XIV, 156
Michael, IV, 75
William, VII, 55
MEGGS, Robert, XIII, 304(2)
MELCUM, John, VII, 180(2)
Joseph, VII, 180(2)
MELDRUM, William, VIII,415
MELLIN, William, I, 379

*Matthewe
94

MELLINGE, William, I, 431
MELONEY, Thomas, XVI. 422
(2)
MELTON, John, VI, 19
MENDENHALL, John, VII,217
MENEFIE, I, 138, 142
MENEFY, George, I, 235
MENNIS, Callohill, XV, 95
MENSER, Jonas, XII, 721
MENZIE, Alexander, VII, 493
MERCER, I, vi; II, 197, 239;
III, 223
George, XII, 365(6),
366(7), 367(9), 368
(5), 369(4)
Hugh, XII,210(2); XVI,
47
James, VII, 569; VIII,
426(3); IX, 49, 95;
XII, 365(4), 366(10),
367(6), 368(5), XIII,
8; XIV, 382
John, VIII, 220(2); XI,
210
John Francis, X, 470;
XI, 571
William, XII, 210(3)
MERCHANT, Henry, I, 46
Jourdan, XV, 228
Philip, VII, 218
William, VI, 242(2)
MEREDITH, VI,492; VII,583;
XII, 301; XIV. 172;
XV. 312
John, V, 74
Joseph, V, 74(2)
Sampson, V, 74
Samuel, VIII, 128; XI,
229; XIII, 296, 315,
316; XIV, 322; XV,
353, 419
Sarah, V, 74
MERGEE, Edward, VII, 216
(2)
MERIWETHER, IV, 335, 383,
387; V, 14, 137, 142,
144, 234(2); VI, 169
(2), 172, 176; VII,
532, 533; VIII, 78, 98,
100(3), 236, 321, 407,
416(2); IX, 154, 159,
160, 468, 510, 513(3);

X, 474, 475; XI, 210,
235, 237(2), 238(3).
310; XI, 581; XIII,
479, 503
Charles, XV, 173, 380
David, IV, 267; V, 257;
VI, 301(2); VII, 129;
XII, 395
Elizabeth, V, 257
George, X, 288, 293
Mildred, VIII, 54(2),
55(5), 56, 57(2)
Nicholas, V, 115, 257;
VI, 301; VII, 222;
VIII, 54(2), 55(2).
56, 57, 60
Richard, VI, 15
Susanna, VI,405(4),406
Thomas, VI, 301(6),
302(2), 405(5), 407;
VIII, 60, 456; XV, 121
William, IV, 142, 376;
V, 257(5), 258(6),
301(2); VIII, 283;
XV, 30, 259
William Douglas, XIII,
175; XV, 427
MERRICK, John, I, 83
MERRIOT, William, V, 368
MERRITT, Henry, XV, 52
MERRYMAN, Jesse, XVI, 241
(2)
Thomas, XVI, 241(3)
METAPPIN, II, 155
METEER, James, VII, 181
MEWTIS, Thomas, I, 83
MEYCOT, Cavallero, I, 82

MICHAEL, Elizabeth. XVI.
402(3)
John, III, 479(2)
MICHAELL, John, II, 447(3)
MICHAUX, Jacob, IV, 532;
XIV, 155, 150; XVI,
246
Joseph, XII, 591
MICHEAUX, Jacob, VI, 20
Paul, V, 190; VI, 15
MICHELL, William, I,431,501
MICHIE, William, XIV, 330;
XVI, 149(2)

MICHILBOURNE,* Edward, I.
78, 81
MICKIE, David, XVI, 212
MICOU, VI, 492; VII,583(2);
VIII, 100, 323; IX,
513; XI, 188; XII,
301; XIV, 172; XV,
312
MIDDLETON, Arthur, I, 36
Helland, VII, 21
Robert, I, 84
Thomas, I, 62; III, 210
William, XVI, 177
MIELES, John, VII, 192
MIFFLIN, Daniel, XI, 131
Thomas, I, 23
MIFORD, George, XII, 633
MIGGINSON, XV, 32
MILBOY, John, II, 157(3)
MILBURN, David, XV, 63
MILDEBARLER, Nicholas, VII,
186
MILES, IV, 266; V, 142, 144;
VI, 172, 176
Joab, XVI, 318(2)
Joseph, XVI, 318(2)
MILIGAN, James, VII, 198
MILITIN, XVI, 244
MILLAN, Thomas, XVI, 204,
221, 222
MILLER, Adam, VII, 186, 187
David, VII, 199
Elizabeth, IX, 577
Francis, VII, 663
Harman, VIII, 369;
XIV, 157
Isaac, XII, 90, 159;
XIV, 330; XVI, 60
Jacob, VII, 186, 406(2),
407
James, XIV, 308
John, VII, 185, 190,215;
XIII, 87, 184; XIV,
308; XV, 379
John Frederick, VII,
219
Mary (Obanion), IX,
577
Peter, VII, 186
Robert, VII, 569; XIV.
322
Samuel, XVI, 56

Simon, X, 196; XIV, 154
Thomas, XI, 29; XVI,
273(2), 330
Tobias, XIII, 536
William, VII, 215, 475;
XII, 672, 673
MILLS, I, 83
James, VII, 569; XII,
204(2)
John, VIII, 552; XII,
203(2), 204(7)
MILLSAPS, Thomas, VII, 194
MILLWOOD, James, VII, 206
MILMAN, Thomas, VII, 131
MILMAY, Robert, I, 86
MILNER,† VII, 233, 321, 322,
543, 544; IX, 154, 159,
161, 488, 511, 513,
614; X, 273, 356, 475;
XI, 211, 235, 238;
XIII, 480, 503
George, II, 372, 384
John, V, 242, 243; VI,
508
Robert D., XV, 120
Thomas, III, 330,506(2);
III, 25(2), 26, 27, 97,
107, 125; VI, 247(2);
472; VIII, 79, 98, 100,
101, 552, 553
MILSTEAD, John, XIII, 94, 95
(3)
MILTON, John, XV, 121, 242;
XVI, 100
MIM, Gilbert, XV, 224
MIMS, Martin, XVI, 388
Randolph, XVI, 355
MINEAR, Adam, XIII, 565
John, XIV, 44
John, VII, 201
MINER, David, XIV, 321
MINGE, James, II, 310, 340
John, VI, 13
MINICE, Robert, VII, 180,
183, 185
MINIFIE, George, I, 282, 297
(2)
MINNIS, Robert, VII, 180,
181(2), 187, 168
MINOR, Dabney, XVI, 149
Doodes, II, 308(2); III,
479(2)

*Michelborn   †Millner
96

25

Garret, XI. 508
George, XV, 177
John, XIII. 73; XIV.
268; XV. 242; XVI.
47, 236
Nicholas, VII, 217, 222,
234, 235(2). 236
Thomas, XII. 729
Vivion. XIII, 73
MINSER, Jonas. XIV, 157
MINTER,* William, VII, 179,
180(2), 184(2)
MIRES, Nathan, IV, 529
MISCAMPBELL, Andrew, VII.
196
MISKELL, Austin, XV. 120
Teige, II. 161(4)
MISKIMMINS, David, XV, 49
MITCHELL, Bartholomew, I.
78
Bernard, I, 86
Isaac, I, 86
James. XV, 270
Thomas, XV. 55
MITCHELL, Abraham, VII,
208; VIII, 660
Cornelius, VII, 22
David, VII, 199
Edward, XIII, 151(2);
XIV, 156
Francis, VII, 212
Ignatius, XII, 608(3)
James, VII,126(2); XII,
699
John, VII, 196, 225, 227;
XII, 595; XIII, 321;
XVI, 29, 30(5)
Joseph, IX, 669
Lockett, XIII, 608, 609
(2)
Robert, VII, 179, 180;
XIII, 316; XIV, 308;
XVI, 189
Samuel, XII, 202
Thomas, XIV, 306(4);
XV, 185, 210
William, VII, 225; XI,
100; XV, 185(3), 186,
210; XVI, 79
MITCHUM, John, VII, 209
MIXER, Isaac, XV, 268

MOFFET,† George, VII, 195;
VIII, 127, 546; XI,164
MOLSON, William, VII, 227
MOLSWORTH, Guy, II, 10, 11
(2)
MONCK, I, xlv, 528, 529
MONCURE, John, VII, 427;
XVI, 22(2)
MONEY, Bryan, VII, 216, 217
MONFORD, Edward, XIV, 390
MONGER, James, I, 84
MONMOUTH, II, 528
MONROE, Andrew, II, 16;
XIII, 222(3), 307
James, I, viii; XI, 571
(2), 574(2), 575; XV,
397, 469; XVI, 22
John, XV, 30(2)
William, VII, 226
MONSON, Thomas, I, 82
MONTAGUE, Edward, VII,
276, 277(4) 374(3),
375, 376(5), 377; XII,
366(4)
Henry I, 67, 77, 82, 90
James, I, 81, 90
Peter, I, 373, 379, 431
MONTFORD, Filmer W., XVI,
177(2)
Thomas, I, 84
MONTGOMERY, I, 102
Alexander, XIII, 174,
175, 316
James, VII, 199
James, Junior, VII, 199
John, VII, 191, 195, 199;
XI, 164, 335, 336;
XIV, 266, 306
Joseph, VII, 199
Robert, VII, 199, 230
Samuel, VII, 199
Thomas, XII, 604
William, VII, 210; XII,
396, 456
MOODY, Henry, II, 11
Joseph, XV, 205
Matthew, VII, 316(2)
MOONE, John, I, 370, 386
MOOR, David, VII, 190. 194
George,‡ I, 67, 77, 82
James, VII, 191

MOORE, VI, 492; VII, 583;
XI, 188; XII, 301;
XIII, 173; XIV, 172;
XV, 312; XVI, 27(2),
314, 315, 318(2)
Alexander, XVI, 43
Andrew, I, 84; XI, 164,
341; XV, 44, 442
Anna Catharine, VIII.
477(2)
Augustine, VII, 285(2),
286, 287(2). 446, 476
(2), 478(2)
Bernard, VI, 411(3);
VII, 64, 298, 327(2).
328(3). 330, 449(3),
450(2), 451, 483, 484
(4), 485(2), 489;
VIII, 30(2), 31(3),
32(3), 33(4), 434(2),
476(5), 477(5); XII,
407
Cato, XII, 371
Conrad, IX, 425(3)
David, VII, 195
Edward, IV, 529(2);
XIII, 87; XIV, 330;
XV, 271
Elizabeth, VIII, 476(2)
Francis, VII, 224, 227;
VIII, 129
George, VII, 202
Harbin, VII, 300
James, VII, 199, 207,
209; XII, 672, 673;
XV, 270
James Francis, XII,396,
397; XIII, 148
John, I, 83(2); V, 75
(4); VI, 296(3); VII,
183, 192, 196, 202,
205, 212; XVI, 43(2)
Levi, XI, 129(3)
Mary Anne, XVI, 43(5)
Richard, III, 552(2);
VII, 220
Robert, XV, 66
Samuel, VII, 22,23; XV,
262
Thomas, VII, 223, 669;
VIII, 285(3), 286(4),
287; XII, 605; XIV,

389; XV, 343
Tobias, VII, 212
William, I, 84; IV, 529;
V, 75(2); VII, 189,
198; XI, 204; XV, 444
MOORING, Christopher, V,
369
John, V, 368
MOORMAN, Achilles, XV, 359
Agnes, XII, 614
Charles, XII, 613(3),
615, 616(2)
Elizabeth, XII, 614
James, XII, 614
James C., XVI, 129
Mary, XII, 614, 615
Micajah, VII, 126; XII,
398
Robert, XII, 613,614(5)
Thomas, XII, 614(3)
MORAN, John, XV, 184(2)
MORE, Samuel, VII, 218
MOREHEAD, Charles, VII, 625
Jane, VII, 51
MORETON, Ralph, I, 84
MORGAN, XII, 297,515; XIII,
42, 80, 86(2), 518,
553,588; XIV,410(3);
XV, 67(2), 229
Benjamin, VII, 23(2)
Charles, I, 82; VII, 230
Daniel, XI, 310; XV,121
Edward, VIII, 131
Evan, VII, 205, 207
Francis, I, 339, 370, 379
Gideon, XIII, 174; XVI,
49, 211
Haines, XIII, 275; XVI,
401
John, VII, 205, 207, 214
Morgan, XVI, 224
Samuel, XVI, 410
Stephen, XV, 31; XVI,
224
Thomas, VII, 205, 207,
218
William, VII, 205, 206,
209; XII, 512(2);
XIV, 157(2)
William, Junior, VII,207
Zackquill,* XI, 255(2);
XII, 212, 213, 214;

XV, 31; XVI, 54
MORGIN, John, VII, 209
MORLAND, Young, V, 370
MORLATT,* Thomas, I, 129
MORLEY, William, I, 527
MORAES, XV, 63
MORRIL, Samuel, VII, 423
MORRIS, IX, 330
Carroll, XV, 466
Dabney, XVI, 410
Daniel, VII, 207
Elizabeth, XV, 458(4),
459(3)
George, II, 39, 159
Gouverneur, I, 23. 46
Jacob, VII, 21
James, VII, 208, 215,
216; XIV, 308
John, XII, 605; XIV,
312, 322
Joshua, XVI, 78
Leonard, XIV, 312, 322
Lewis, I, 36
Richard, IX, 145(2),
146(2); XV, 210
Robert, I, 36, 46; XI,
68(2)
Thomas, I, 84
William, IV, 266; VII,
21; XII, 282,672,673;
XIII, 215; XIV, 321,
322(2), 408; XV, 63;
XVI, 50(2)
MORRISON,* Charles, II, 330,
546
Francis, I, 403, 424, 426,
428, 526; II, iii, vii
(2), 9, 13, 34, 37, 56,
134(3), 137, 148, 149,
156, 160(2), 428, 513,
519, 521, 529, 537,
538, 546, 549, 555;
III, 570
Isaac, XII, 631, 676, 719
James, VII, 204; XII,
631, 676, 719
Michael, VII, 204
Robert, I, 320(4)
MORROW, John, XIII, 174;
XV, 139; XVI, 232
William, XV, 63
MORSE, David, VII, 208

MORSLAY, Robert, I, 516
MORTIMER, Charles, XIII,100
MORTON, V, 144; VI, 176;
VII, 583; VIII, 323,
508, 626(2); IX, 154,
161, 488, 511, 513;
XIV, 156
Frances, VII, 637(6);
VIII, 169(3), 170
Frances (Colton), VII,
637(2)
George, V, 142; VI, 173;
VIII, 78, 98, 101
James, XIII, 556; XIV,
390, 425; XVI, 183
John, I, 36; VII, 592;
XI, 273; XIII,153(2),
550
Joseph, V, 250; VI. 18,
212; VII, 220,637(2);
VIII, 169(2)
Joseph, Junior, VI. 291
Samuel, VII, 224; XIII,
48; XIV, 157
Thomas, VII, 228
William, IV, 515(3),
516(2), 517, 518(3);
XI, 250, 273; XIII,
193, 565
William L., XIV. 136,
346
MOSGY, John, XI, 283
Littleberry, XIII, 293
Poindexter, VII, 213
Richard, VI, 15(2)
Robert, XII, 223, 400
MOSERY, V, 190
Richard, V, 190
MOSELLEY, Arthur, XIV, 328,
422
Charles, XIII, 587
David, XV, 120
Edward, V, 106; XI,
250; XV, 184(3)
Edward Hack, VI, 221†;
VIII, 156(3), 454
Edward Hack, Junior,
VIII, 470
John, XIII, 587(3);
XIV, 240, 269, 328
Samuel, VII, 212

Thomas, V, 104; VI, 15
(2); XIV, 240, 269,
311, 328
William, III, 95; XIV,
319, 337(3); XVI,
335
William, Junior, V, 106
MOSELY, George. VI, 240(2)
Hillery, XVI, 409
John, XII, 661
Sampson, VII, 212
Thomas, VII, 221(2)
William, II, 309; XVI,
34
MOSES, George, VII, 183
Peter, VII, 182, 183
MOSS, David, VII, 212
John, VII, 222; XV, 63
John, Junior, VII, 222
William, XV, 419; XVI,
379
MOTTRAM, John, I, 370
MOTTROM, Spencer, III, 60
MOULSOE, John, I, 84
MOUNSEL, Peter, I, 85
MOUNT, Ezekiel, XVI, 51
MOUNTAINE, James, I, 86
MOUNTJOY, John, XIII, 585
Thomas, XIII, 585; XV,
298(5)
MOUNTS, Providence, XII,
599(3)
MOUSE, George, VII, 182, 184
MOXLEY, Richard, VII, 22
MOYERS, Jacob, VII, 186
MOYSEE,* Theodore, I, 138,
148

MUHLENBERG, Frederick
Augustus, I, 29
Peter,† XI, 309; XIII,
621
MULDER, Joshua, II, 302(3);
III, 479(3)
MULFORD, IV, 528
MULLINS, Matthew, VII, 203
MUMFORD, Edward, XV, 30
Robert, IV, 266, 334
MUNDAY, Christopher, VII,
206
Isaac, VII, 224
MUNDELL, John, XVI, 100

MUNFORD, IV, 479(4)
Edward, XIII, 153(2)
George W. XIV, 436
(2); XV, 471(2);
XVI, 441(2)
James, V, 212
Robert, VIII, 141, 292;
X, 124
Thomas Bolling, VIII,
192
William, XV, 114; XVI,
110, 135, 136, 185(2),
292, 336(2)
MUNKS, Lawrence, I, 86
MUNROE, John, VII, 43
MURCHIE, John, XI,57; XIII,
314
MUROIN, I, xl
MURFEE, Miles. VII, 22
William, VII, 220
MURFEY, Richard, VIII, 130
MURFY, John, VII, 224
MURPHEY, Anna, VIII, 275
Lawrence, VII, 198
MURPHY, XIV, 166
Archibald, XV, 210
John, VII, 208; XIII,
90
John, IX, 334
Luke, VII, 208(2)
Richard, VII, 215
MURRAY, Elizabeth, IV, 529
(4)
James, IV, 529(4), VI,
507
John, VII, 24; VIII, 5
(4), 320; XIII, 174,
585
Richard, VII, 202
Samuel, XII, 600
William, XI, 57; XIV,
390
MURRELL, Samuel, XV, 427
MUSEY, Anthony, XIII, 149
John, VII, 425(3), 426
Thomas, VII, 206
MURTY, Joseph. VII, 209
MUSCHAMP, Christopher, II,
556(2)
MUSCHETT, James,† XIV,
308, 394; XV, 37;
XVI, 174

Margaret, VIII, 635, 636(3)
MUSE, Daniel, XV, 183(3), 188(4)
  George, VII, 213
  Hudson, XI, 369
  Laurence XV, 363
MUSGROVE, William, VII, 21
MUSTOE, Anthony, XIII, 174; XIV, 266

NALL, William, XII, 82(3); XIV, 277
NALLE, Martin, VII, 23
  William, VII, 22
  William, Junior, VII,214
NANCE, VI, 412, 415(2), 416
  Robert, VII, 212
  Thomas, VII, 212(2)
NAPIER, Thomas, IX, 325; X, 112
NASH, James, VII, 23
  John, VI, 291; VII, 229, 232; XI, 272
  John, Junior, XIV, 390
  Paul, XVI, 100, 316
  Thomas, VII, 592
  Thomas, Junior, XIII, 223
NASSAWADDOCK.* IV, 268, 384, 386
NAYLOR,† IV, 267, 335, 383, 385; VI, 492; VII, 583; XI, 188; XII, 301; XIV, 172; XV, 312

NEAL, XV, 224
  Charles, XVI, 270(2), 271
  Elizabeth (——), XVI, 270(2), 271
  James, XV, 223, 224
  Joseph, VII, 24
NEALE, Thomas, III, 112(3), 113, 114(2)
NEALY, William, VII, 217
NEAVILL, John, IX, 13

MUTER, XI, 310
  George, XII, 602

MYERS, Jacob, XVI, 29
  John, XII, 209
  Moses, XIII, 599; XV, 437
  Samuel, XVI, 79, 95
MYRE, XII, 86

N

NEBUS, Joshua, VII, 53
NECTOWANCE, I, 323(4), 324 (5), 325(5), 453(2)
NEEDHAM, Joseph, XIV, 323
NEEL, William, XIV, 314
NEELY, Hugh, XV, 360(3)
  James, VII, 207
  William, XII, 202
NEIL, Abraham, XIV, 378
  William, XV, 164
NEILL, Abraham, XIV, 323
NEILLE, Abraham, XIV, 308
NEILSON, Charles, VI, 239
  John, VII, 208
NELSON, V, 321, 402(2),403; X, 573, 574; XIII, 621; XIV, 154
  Alexander, XIII, 589
  Arthur, IX, 585; XIV, 153
  Hugh, XI, 473; XVI,309
  James, XIV, 424
  John, XV, 114, 115(3), 116(2), 180(5); XVI, 54
  Nathaniel, XII, 97
  Thomas, V, 71; VI, 227, 291, 418, 511(2), 512 (3); VII, 138, 276, 288, 568, 647; VIII, 365, 378, 406, 539, 578; X, 439; XI, 465; XII, 479
  Thomas, Junior, I, 36; VIII, 378, 432; X, 6, 478(2); XI, 473

William, 11, 533; III, 229(2); V, 321, 371; VI, 197, 291, 418; VII, 138, 276, 288, 568, 646; VIII, 5(2), 55, 56, 365, 378, 406, 539, 578; XII, 698, 729; XVI, 50, 197
  William, Junior, VIII, 580; XIII, 131
NETTLES, Abraham, XIII, 207(2), 208(4)
NEUCE,* Thomas, I, 111
  William, I, 111, 115
NEUSOM, John, XVI, 274
NEVETT, II, 511
NEVIL, Henry, I, 78, 81, 90
  James, VII, 202
NEVILL, James, VII, 202; IX, 568
  John, VII, 24
  Robert, VII, 24
NEVISON, John, XIII, 159, 175; XVI, 58, 197
NEW, Anthony, XII, 698; XIII, 73, 576; XV,363
  Edward, VI, 304
  John, VI, 303, 304, 305, 306(7), 307(3)
  Margaret (Bland) (Tan-ner), VI, 304,305,306
  Richard, I, 381
NEWBERRY, Samuel, VIII,129
NEWBRIDGE, Joseph, I, 86
NEWBY, Henry, VII, 50(3)
NEWCASTLE, V, 589
NEWCE, George, I, 85
  Henry, I, 85
NEWCOMBE, Henry, II, 138
NEWELL, James, XIII, 583; XVI, 174
NEWHOUSE, John, I, 85
NEWLAND, Charles, VII, 21
  John, XVI, 38
NEWMAN, II, 11
  Daniel, VII, 220
  James, XVI, 329
NEWPORT, II, 528
  Christopher, I, 83
NEWSUM, William, V, 367 (2); VII, 313; XV, 447; XVI, 197

NEWTON, George, XVI, 58
  John, VII, 231
  Nathaniel, XVI, 58
  Thomas, VII, 434(2), 435, 437; VIII, 269, 454; XIII, 211, 326 (2); XIV, 280(4); XV, 228, 437, 447; XVI, 39(2), 130
  Thomas, Junior, VIII, 539, 570; IX, 149; XI, 58, 450; XIII, 226(4), 541,599,623(3); XIV, 308; XVI, 58
NIBLETT, John, XV, 52
NICE, William, XIV, 281(2)
NICHOLAS, XIII, 42, 175; XVI, 70
  George, XII, 639
  John, VII, 232; VIII, 369(2); IX, 61; XI, 29; XIV, 155; XV,427
  Peter,† XIII, 297
  Philip Norborne, XVI, 79, 90, 95, 100
  Robert Carter, VII, 13, 19, 39, 40, 49, 58, 69, 76, 82(2), 83(3), 84, 167(3), 175(4), 259 (3), 260, 276, 336, 350(4), 353, 360(3), 361, 466, 468, 498(4), 569, 647; VIII, 149; 191, 211(4), 212, 315, 337, 342, 348, 360, 365, 378, 463, 502, 532, 578, 648, 662; IX, 56, 67(2), 70, 71, 138, 145, 148(2), 199, 201, 222, 223; X, 318; XII, 716; XIII, 211
  Wilson Cary, XIII, 42 (2), 48, 87, 316(2), 481(2), 504; XIV, 156, 330, 425; XV, 66, 427
NICHOLLS, John, XV, 124
NICHOLS, Austin, XV,176(2)
  Christopher, I, 83
  Edwin, XVI, 49, 66

John, II, 431, 432; X, 124
  Thomas, I, 83; VII, 181; XV, 168
NICHOLSON, Andrew, XV, 374
  Francis, III, 8(4), 97, 107, 199, 203, 215, 217, 223, 226, 228, 428
  George, XIII, 229
  James, VI, 239
  John, XIII, 216, 217
  Robert, V, 367
  Robert, Junior, XI, 473
  Thomas, XIII,627; XIV, 338; XV, 138, 296
NICKOLLS, James Bruce, XIII, 175; XV, 89
NICOLSON, George, XIII, 325 (2), 326(2); XVI, 256, 257(2), 258(2)
  Thomas, XIII, 206(2); XIV, 282, 283; XV, 187, 242, 389, 411
NIX, William, VII, 209
NIXSON, John, XIV, 321

NOBLE, VIII, 98, 100,101(3), 283; IX, 154, 159,161, 488, 511, 513(4), 514 (2)
  Anthony, IX, 569
  George, VIII, 79, 98; XII, 76; XIV, 334(2)
NOELL, Cornelius, Junior, XV, 419
NOFFSINGER, XIII, 77; XIV, 406
NOFTSINGER, John, XVI, 45
NOLAND, XIV, 153
  Thomas, IX, 585
  William, XIV, 214
NOLDES, Elizabeth, VI, 243
NORFLEET, VIII, 544
  Edward, V, 200(2)
  Henry, XI, 129(3)
NORMAN, IV, 531; VIII, 25, 26(3); X, 365; XIV, 154
  Clement, VII, 24

Thomas, XVI, 182
  William, XV, 210
NORMENT, Samuel, IV, 93
NORNICOT, Thomas, I, 87
NORRELL, Francis, VII, 225
  James, VII, 224
NORRIS, John, V, 559
  Richard, XV, 175; XVI, 379
  Thadius, XVI, 225, 226
NORTH, George, XV, 110; XVI, 185
  William, XIV, 331(3)
NORTHAMPTON, II, 528
NORTHSINGER, John, XIII, 585
NORTON, John, V, 306, 307 (2), 308(3); VI, 227, 437, 524; VII, 13, 76, 138, 294(2)
  John Hatley, IX, 145, 146
  Thomas, VII, 220
  William, I, 116
NORWELL, Spencer D., XV, 223
  William, IX, 70, 71, 201; XII, 717; XIV, 308
NORWELL, Hugh, III, 425
  Reuben, XIV, 389
NORWOOD, Charles, I, 388, 392, 393, 406, 424(2); II, 57
  Henry, II, 137, 517, 519, 520(2)
  Samuel, VII, 191
  William, I, 405(2), 406
NOSLER, Puston, VII, 187
NOTT, Edward, III, 8(2), 431, 481; IV, 562, 563
NOURSE, Gabriel, XV, 110
  James, IX, 247, 576
NOWELL, William, I, 247
NOWLING,* Bryan, VIII, 131
  Bryant Ward, XII, 653; XV, 97, 233, 234
NOY, VII, 489
NUCKLE, IV, 528
NULL, Nicholas, VII, 186
NUNNALLY, John, XV, 30

NUSUM, John, XV, 243
NUTALL, James, Junior, X, 121

O

OAKES, Isaac, XV, 48(2), 67, 173, 380
OBANION, Bryan, IX,576(4), 577(3); XI, 60(2), 61 (4)
  Catharine, IX, 577
  John, IX, 577
  Mary, IX, 577
  William, IX, 577
O'CALLIS, William, XV, 121
ODAM, John, IV, 529(2)
O'DANIEL, William, VII, 218
ODEN, Lewis, VII, 25
ODEON, Charles, XIII, 223
ODLE, Jeremiah, VII, 215
  Jonathan, VII, 215
OEWIN, William, II, 35
OFFLEY, Robert, I, 84
OGDEN, Samuel, XIII, 218
OGLE, John, I, 92
OCLESBY, Jacob, XIV, 257
  Robert, VII, 206
  Thomas, VII, 206(2)
OKAIR, Edward, VII, 208
OLD, James, XVI, 68
OLDHAM, William, XI, 470
OLERON, IX, 203; X, 98
OLIVER, Achilles, XVI, 411 (3)
  Benjamin, XV, 70
  Benjamin, Junior, XV, 353
  James, XIV, 243
  John, XIV, 266
  Patsey, VII, 411(2)
  Thomas, XIII, 315

121
NUZAM, John, XVI, 336(4)

O

ONEAL, Edward, VII, 24
ONEIL, John, XV, 31
OPPECHANKENO, I, 319
ORANGE, William, VII, 437
ORCHARD, James, VII,210(2)
ORME, I, 82
OSS, Alexander D., XIII, 183
  John, VII, 224, 431; XIII, 580
ORRACK, John, VII, 210
ORWELL, Lewis, I, 82
OSBORNE, VI, 224, 226, 362, 473; VII, 532, 533, 582; VIII, 78, 100(3), 101(4), 236, 321, 322; IX, 154, 159, 160, 488, 510, 513(2); X, 273, 356, 475, 497; XI, 187, 210, 235, 237(2); 238; XII, 258, 455, 515; XIII, 479, 503, 518, 575(2); XIV, 171, 258(2), 260, 261(2), 262; XV, 312
  Edward, VIII, 412
  James, XIV, 336(2); XV, 30
  John, VI, 174, 176; XIV, 308; XV, 218, 351; XVI, 214
  Thomas,* I, 138, 147, 154, 168, 171, 178, 186, 202; VII, 21
OSBY, Robert, IV, 30
OTEE, John, XIV, 308
OTEY, Isaac, XVI, 379
  John II., XV, 12
  Walter, XVI, 324
OTIS, Samuel A., I, 29, 51
OTT, Jacob, XVI, 29

OVERALL, Nathaniel, VII, 24
OVERALL, John, XV, 120
OVERSTREET, Thomas, VII,
208, 209
OVERTON, James, VII, 222;
XII, 400, 628
John, XV, 121
Richard, XIII, 73
Samuel, XV, 185(2),240

OWEN, John, XII, 360(3),
361; XIV, 156, 256
John Cockey, XIII, 42

PABLEY, John, VII, 214
PACA, William, I, 36; X, 533
PACE, II, v
Henry, XV, 323
PACKET, John, XV, 121
PACQUETT, Jeremy, II, 302
(2); III, 479(2)
PAD, XIII, 165
PAGE, IV, 383, 387, 481; V,
137, 142, 144, 234(2),
325(2); VI, 169, 172,
176, 224, 473; VII,
532, 533, 601; VIII,
78(2), 98, 100(5),
236, 321, 322, 390,
407; IX,154, 159, 160,
488, 510, 513(4); X,
273, 356, 475; X1,210,
235, 237(2), 238(3);
XII, 258, 455; XIII,
83, 479, 503; XIV, 154
Carter, V, 278, 279(6),
280(2), 300(2); VIII,
446(2); XV, 30, 99
Francis, III, 39(3), 550;
V, 279
Henry, II, 370, 375(2),
377, 546(2)
James, VIII, 131
John, II, 380, 546, 547,
563; III, 428, 482(2);
552, 657, 569; IV,267;
V, 278, 279(4), 280,

William, XV, 362
OWENS, John, IX, 685
Nicholas, II, 257
Thomas, VII, 210
William, XIV, 322; XV,
30
OWING, John C., XII, 719(2)
OWSLEY, John, VII, 222
William, VII, 21

OXENBRIDGE, William, I, 83

OZBAN, John, VII, 186

P

281, 282, 284; VI,407,
411(3), 418, 437, 524;
VII, 13, 76, 475; VIII,
445, 446(6), 447(5),
466(2), 485, 578, 580,
653; IX, 49, 95; X,
121, 209, 446(2); XI,
555; XII, 698; XV,67;
XVI, 34, 277, 335
Judith, VIII, 445(3),
446
Judith (Wormeley),
446
Lucy, V, 279(3), 280
Mann, IV, 376(3); V,
277(2), 284(3), 300,
325; VI, 411(3); VII,
480(2), 481(8), 482
(4), 483(2), 568, 601;
VIII, 162, 230, 445
(2), 446, 637; X, 470;
XI, 204, 405; XII,
210; XV, 242
Mann, Junior, V, 278,
279(5), 280(3), 281
(7); 282(4), 283(3),
284(6); VIII,669; IX,
72; XV, 67
Mary, V, 279(3), 280;
VIII, 162(2)
Matthew, III, 181, 202,
482; V, 278, 279(3),
280, 282
Matthew, Junior, XV,70

Ralph, V, 278(5), 279
(2), 280(2), 283;VII,
480; 481
Robert, V, 279(3), 280;
XIII, 624(5); XV,
70(2)
Robin, V, 300
Thomas T., XV, 241;
XVI, 48
PAGET, William, I, 102
PAGETT, Anthony, I, 138
PAGNAM, I, 82
PAINE, XIV, 241
Florentine, I, 506
Robert Treat, I, 36
Thomas, X, 534
PALMER, IX, 320
Anthony, I, 78
John, VII, 83, 176, 260
Martin, II,159(5); VIII,
265
Miles, I, 85
Richard, VII, 300
Roger, VIII, 285
Thomas, I, 138, 147,168,
186
William, I, 84; VII, 21
PALSLEY, Jacob, XVI, 390
PANCAKE, John, XII, 403;
XIII, 171; XIV, 411
PANKAKE, John, XIV, 153
PANNELL, Samuel, VII, 214;
XV, 125, 233, 234
William.* III, 472, 473;
XII, 372
PANNILL, Samuel, XV, 359
PANTON, Thomas, I, 82
PAREPOINT, Francis, XII,631
PARFITT, Roger, II, 16
PARHAM, Matthew, VII, 356
William, VII, 211, 226
PARIS, George, XVI, 245
PARISH, David, VII, 226
John, VII, 211; XIII,
287; XIV, 169; XV,
309
Joseph, VII, 212
PARKE, Daniel, II, 225, 226,
249, 313, 320, 422,
431, 432; IV, 29(2);
VI, 319, 320(3), 321
(2)

Daniel, Junior, VI, 319
(3), 320
Frances, VI, 319
John, VII, 216
Joseph, XI, 273
Lucy, VI, 319(2)
PARKER, VII, 614
Alexander, XV, 221
George, VII, 25(2),635;
VIII, 287(2), 288(5);
XII, 364
James, VII, 131
John, IV, 528; VII, 213
Joseph, XV, 457, 458
Josiah, IX, 69; XI, 152,
332
Nathaniel, VII, 213
Rice, XIII,618(3); XIV,
153
Richard, VII, 214; IX,
124; XIII, 41(2), 42
Robert, XII, 403; XV,
231
Thomas H., XV, 447;
XVI, 100, 130
William, I, 57, 59,62(2),
63, 64, 66(2), 81, 90
Winslow, XV, 368(2)
PARKERSON, Joseph, IX, 546
PARKES, Daniel, II, 325, 569
PARKHURST, Robert, I, 84
PARNS, John, VII, 326, 447
Richard, VII, 22, 214(2)
PARR, John, XIV, 277(2)
PARRAMORE, Thomas, VII,
568, 635
PARROT, VI, 18(2); VIII,
650(2)
PARROTT, Benjamin, VII, 202
PARRY, William, I, 512; VII,
484(2)
PARSLOW, Giles, I, 86
PARSONS, David, VII, 25;
XV, 463(3); XVI,
162(2)
Isaac, XII, 404; XIII,
90; XIV, 153
James, XVI, 162
John, V, 271
Major, XIV, 331(3)
Samuel, XIII, 316
William, VII, 211, 225

*Pannel
106

105

PARTRIDGE, Elizabeth, II, 35
John, II, 156(2), 157(2)
Richard, I, 85
Roger, II, 35
PASHALL, Edmond, I, 86
PASTEUR, William, VIII, 461
PATE, Anthony, VII, 205, 210
Cornelius, XVI, 179
Jacob, VII, 205, 206, 210
Jeremiah, VII, 205, 206
John, II, 15; VII, 205,
206, 210
Matthew, VII, 205, 210
Richard, I, 379
Thomas, VII, 226
PATERSON, Erwin, VII, 226
Thomas, VII, 185
William, I, 22
PATOUN, I, 394
PATRICK, Charles, VII, 191
John, VII, 190
William, XV, 270; XVI,
405
PATTEN, Matthew, VII, 180
PATTERSON, XIV, 257
David, XIII, 314; XVI,
40
James, VII,180,187,190,
195, 206(2); XIV,322
John, XIV,322; XVI,172
Jonathan, VIII, 149
Nathaniel, VII, 204, 208
Nelson, XIV, 390
Robert, VII, 181, 187,
195; XI, 100
Samuel, VII, 187, 188,
195
Thomas, VII, 180, 187
William, IX, 569
PATTISON, Charles, XI, 29;
XIII, 587
David, X, 477; XI, 393;
XIV, 265; XVI, 379
John, XVI, 72
PATTON, James, V, 188(3),
189(2); . VII, 189;
XIII, 91; XVI, 316
Matthew, VII, 180, 182,
187, 189, 190
Robert, XIII, 599; XIV,
308; XVI, 47, 100
Samuel, XIV, 266

William, XVI, 37(3)
PATY, Jesse, VII, 209
PAUL, Audley, VIII, 129; IX,
421(2)
Thomas, XIV, 282(2)
PAULIN, Henry, VII, 202
PAULING, Henry, XII, 396
PAULY, Lewis* A., XVI, 117,
157(2)
PAUP, John, XV, 52
PAVIES, Webley, III, 473
PAWLETT,† Thomas, I, 168,
186, 202
PAXTON, John, VII, 193
Joseph, XII, 674; XIII,
228
Joseph, Junior, XII, 674
Samuel, XV, 262
Thomas, VII, 196
PAYN, Philip, XIV, 266
PAYNE, XI, 516, 524(2);
XIII, 188(2); XV, 76
David, VIII, 165
Edward, VIII, 550
Francis, XV, 178
George, XIII, 296, 298
Jacob, XVI, 325, 326
James, XV, 31
John, VII, 382; VII, 218
John, Junior, VII, 475
Nicholas, XV, 348(2)
Philip, XV, 97, 359
Richard, XV, 30
Robert, I, 82; V, 305;
IX, 335; XIV, 267
William, I, 84; XIII,
225, 553; XVI, 177
William G., XVI, 310(2)
PAYTON, John, VII, 213, 214;
XV, 274

PEACHY,‡ Anne, XIII,97(2),
98(3)
Thomas Griffin, XII,
792; XIII, 174, 599;
XIV, 320
William, VII, 269
William S., XV, 265
PEAKE, Humphrey, XVI,379,
395
William, VII, 24
William, Junior, VII, 21

PEAL, Robert, III, 219
PEALE, Malachy, III, 69
Robert, III, 471; VI, 14;
XIV, 155
PEARCE, Isaac, VII, 217
PEARIS, Richard, VIII, 129
Robert, VII, 216
PEARPOINT, Larkin, VII, 161,
184
PEARRY, Daniel, XIII, 586
PEARS, Edmund, I, 86
PEARSALL, Job, VII, 26
PEARSE, I, 82
PEARSON, Robert, XVI,31(2)
Simon, IV, 331(2)
PEARSTE, Jeremy, I, 85
PEARY, John, VII, 161
PEASLEY, Henry, VII, 41(2),
42, 43
Robert,* III, 219, 471
PEATE, Peter, I, 85
PECK, XV, 64
John, XVI, 403
PEEBLES, Robert, VII, 211
PEEINE, William, I, 129
PEERY, William, XV, 270
PEGRAM, XVI, 376
Edward, XII, 778; XIV,
320; XV, 351
George, Junior, XVI,
216(3)
John, XV, 213
PEIRCE, William, I, 140, 153,
171, 178, 196, 202,
235, 282, 288
PELHAM, Peter, VII, 351,
361, 499; VIII, 347,
501, 649; IX, 68; XV,
52
Thomas, XV, 338
PELL, Richard, VII, 218
PEMBROKE, I, 117
PENCE, Jacob, VII, 185
PENDALL, Jacob, XIII, 230
PENDLETON, Edmund, VI,
394, 624; VII, 13, 64,
75, 83(3), 175(3),
289, 327, 449, 485,
568; VIII, 30, 33, 272
(2), 349(2), 350(4),
351, 390, 580; IX, 7,
49, 95, 175, 213; X,

209, 210; XI, 204,548;
XII, 698; XIII, 131,
287, 576
Edmund, Junior, XII,
698; XIII, 287, 576
Edward, XV, 30
Henry, VIII, 434, 669
Henry, Junior, XV, 120
James, VIII, 139(2),
141; XIII, 143, 287;
XIV, 268, 418; XV,
411
John, IX, 175; XV, 120;
XVI, 90, 217(2)
John Junior, IX, 68;
XIII, 174
Nathaniel, XVI, 306
Philip, IX, 247, 569;
XIV, 266, 270; XV, 99
Philip C., XVI, 423
Reuben, XV, 343
Spice (Freeland), XI,
65(3)
William, XIII, II
William F., I, ii(5); IX,
....
PENET, XIII, 323(2)
PENINGER, Henry, VII, 180,
181, 187
PENN, Abraham, XIII, 582;
XIV, 316
Gabriel, XII, 229; XIII,
315, 316
George, XIII, 582; XIV,
241, 316
Greenville, XV, 210;
XVI, 136, 346
James, XIV, 308, 422;
XVI, 335
John, I, 36, 46
William, X, 522, 523,
526(4), 527
PENNINGER, Henry, VII, 182
Henry, Junior, XVI, 56
PENNINGTON, Robert, I, 85
PENNOCK, William, XIII, 106
(4), 107(5), 108, 325
(2), 326(2),622; XV,
437; XVI, 63, 130
PEO, Hugh, II, 197
PEPPER, Robert, VII, 207

*Louis   †Paulett   ‡Peachey
107

*Peasley
108

23

Samuel, VII, 207; XIII, 283; XIV, 158
PERCIE, George, I, 81
PERCIVAL, Richard, I, 83
PERCY, George, I, 3
PERGGOY, Edward, VII, 219, 220
PERKEY, Henry, XV, 359; XVI, 49
PERKIN, Edward, I, 84
  Thomas, I, 83
PERKINS, Aden, I, 85
  Charles, VII, 23
  Christopher, I, 82
  Elizabeth, II, 169(5)
  Hardin, XII, 657,
  Isaac, VII, 217, 236
  Peter, XI, 250
  Thomas, II, 160(7)
  Thomas, Junior, II, 160 (2)
  William, XIII, 316(2)
  William, Junior, XII, 661; XIII, 149, 587; XIV, 240; XV, 99, 120
PERKINSON, Josiah, XV, 31
PERRELL, John, Junior, XV, 245
PERRIE, Henry, I, 432
PERRIN, John, VII, 224(2)
PERROT, Henry, VI, 402(2), 403(2)
  Margaret, VI, 402, 403
  Mary, VI, 403(5), 404 (2)
  Richard, VI, 402(4), 403(5), 404(3)
PERRY, Elizabeth, I, 516
  Franklin, VII, 218
  Henry, I, 373, 386, 408, 499, 505, 526
  Hildebert, XVI, 432
  Holaway, VII, 216
  Ignatius, XIV, 334(3)
  James, XVI, 412
  John, XVI, 194
  Micajah, V, 287(3), 288(2); VI, 316
  Nicholas, II, 12(3), 39
  Richard, V, 287(3), 288(2); VI, 317
  Sarah, XVI, 432

William, I, 138, 148, 150, 154(2), 178, 202
PERRYMAN, David, VII, 224
PERSEY, Abraham, I, 145(3)
PERSIE, V, 66; VI, 15
PERSON, John, VIII, 177
  William, VII, 201
PET, Arthur, I, 84
  Phineas, I, 85
PETANGER, Peter, VII, 215
PETER, IX, 421; XV, 168(2), 466
PETERBOROUGH, II, 528
PETERFISH, Gunrod, VII, 186
PETERS, Christian, XVI, 37, 38
  John, IV, 528
  Stephen, XIII, 585
PETERSEN, VII, 214
PETERSON, Christian, II, 339 (2); III, 479(2)
  Edward, VII, 199
  Jacob, VII, 182, 184
  John, III, 479(2); VII, 179
  Martin, VII, 184
  Samuel, VII, 188
  Thomas, VII, 179, 188
PETIS, Stephen, XV, 120
PETRE, John, I, 81
PETRO, Philip, VIII, 127
PETTERSON, Peter, II, 204
PETTIES, Thomas, II, 319
PETTOS, Thomas, I, 288, 322, 339
PETTUS, Dabney, XV,458(4), 459(5)
  Elizabeth (Morris), XV, 458(4), 459(3)
  Stephen, II, 158
  Thomas, I, 235, 239,372, 378, 408, 432, 499, 504, 526; VII, 443
PETTY, Francis M., XIII, 278
  Joseph, XV, 120
PETTYJOHN, John, XII, 83: XIV, 187
PETTYPOOL, Colwell, VIII, 643, 644(2), 645(2)
  Mary (Gomarrin), VIII, 643, 644(5), 645(3)

PETWAY, Joseph, V, 368; VI, 239
  Robert, V, 367(4), 368 (2)
PEWMAN, VIII, 464, 467(2)
PEWTHERER, James, XIV,428
PEYTON, VI, 173, 175, 224; VII, 310
  Francis, VIII, 550, 664; IX, 62; XII, 75, 605
  Francis, Junior, XIV, 376
  Henry, VII, 232, 427
  John, VII, 213; X, 121; XII, 227(3); XIII, 136(6), 137(5), 138, 139(6), 140(7), 141 (3), 143, 144, 315; XVI, 62, 232(3)
  John R., XIII, 585
  Mary, XIII, 137, 143
  Robert, III, 565, 566
  Valentine, IV, 479; XII, 207; XIII, 585
PHELPS, Edward, II, 371
  Elisha, XV, 216
  Hugh, XV, 171, 221,224, 232, 298; XVI, 209
  John, VII, 204
  William, VII, 210
PHETTIPLACE, Michael, I, 84
  William, I, 84
PHILBY, William, VII, 224
PHILIPS, Benjamin, VII, 213
  George, XII, 375
  John, VII, 217; XV, 265
  John, Junior, VII, 243
  Josiah, IX, 463(3), 464 (3)
  Martin, VII, 183
  Philip,* XII, 676, 719
  Richard, VII, 205
  Samuel, VII, 217
PHILLIPS, X, 209
  Frederick, X, 209
  Richard, VIII, 474
  Thomas, XIII, 170
PHILPOT, John, V, 292, 293 (2)
PRIPS, Robert, I, 86
PRRIPP, Matthew, VIII, 539

PICKETT, George, XIII, 618 (2); XVI, 34, 95, 335
  George B., XVI, 226
  Martin,† XII, 685; XIII, 92; XIV, 394; XV, 37
  William,† XII, 217, 685; XIII, 92
  William S., XV, 30
PICKFORD, Christopher, I, 85
PICKINS, Gabriel, VII, 184
PIERCE, Daniel, XIII, 218
  Elisha, VIII, 131
  John, XII, 496; XIII, 297; XVI, 197
  John Baptist, XIII, 283
  Joseph, VII, 216
  Peter, VII, 24
  Thomas, X, 124; XIV, 155; XVI, 229(3)
  William, IX, 146(2)
PIERPOINT, John, XII. 514
PIGOT, I, 83
  John, VII, 228
PIKCLE, John Frederick, VII. 220
PIMMITT,† John, II, 447(8); III, 479(2)
PINCE, John, XVI, 56
PINCHAM, Richard, XV, 31
PINCKNEY, Charles, I, 23
  Charles C., I, 23
PINE, XVI, 244
PINKNEY, John, IX, 145(2). 146(2)
PINNER, John, IV, 529, 530
PIPER, John, XVI, 179
PIT, George, I, 84
PITTS, IV, 268, 382, 384, 386; V, 141, 144, 146; VI, 172, 175, 177; VII, 64 (3), 127(2), 128, 129, 130; VIII, 77, 80, 97, 101, 324; IX, 153,160, 488, 489, 510, 513; XI, 97(2), 210, 211, 235, 238; XIII, 479, 482, 502
  George, VII, 221
  Henry, IX, 240, 310
  Robert,§ I, 247, 359,370, 379, 384, 386, 506,

*Philip †Picket ‡Primmitt §Pitts

512, 528; II, 318(2); VII, 131
  Thomas, I, 326, 327
PITTE, John, II, 199
PITTMAN, Ann, XIV, 335
  John, XIV, 335
  Mary, XIV, 335
  William, XIV, 335(3)
  William, Junior, XIV, 335
PITTS, Catherine, VII, 131
PLACE, Rowland., II, 569
PLACKITER, Peter, IV,530(4)
PLATER, George, X, 553
PLATT, I, vii
PLEASANT, VI, 224
  Beaufort, VI, 239
PLEASANTS, II, v(2)
  Isaac W., XIII, 296; XVI, 330
  James, XIV, 316
  John, VI, 223, 281, 352; VII, 306*; VIII, 78
  John, Junior, XII, 647
  Robert, XIII, 316
  Samuel, IV, 3; V, iv(2); XIII, 293; XIV, 319
  Samuel, Junior, I, xxiii; XV, 323; XVI, 292(3)
  Thomas, XII, 682; XIII, 316
PLEYDALL, Thomas, I, 86
PLUMMER, Robert, XV, 270
  Thomas, I, 87
PLUNKETPETER, John, VII, 23
PLUNKETT, John, VII, 196
POAGE, George, XIV, 266
  Thomas, XII, 601(4)
  William, XII, 72
POE, I, 82
  William, VII, 214
POGECE, Robert, VII, 203
POGUE, William, VII, 203
POINDEXTER, V, 258(5), 259
POINTER, VIII, 645(2)
  Thomas, VII, 186
POLLARD, Benjamin, XV, 363
  James, XV, 184(2), 185
  Robert, XI, 36; XIII,

621(3); XIV, 266; XVI, 35, 79, 95, 100, 223(2)
Thomas, XV, 262
William, XII, 729; XV. 70, 353
POLE, Stephen, I, 82
POLLERT, John, VII, 225
POLLETT, Thomas, VII, 224
POLLIN, Thomas, VII, 52
POLLINGTON, John, I, 129
POLLOCK, Alexander, XVI,29
  Oliver, XIII, 326(2)
POLOC, William, VII, 196
POLSON, Joseph, VII, 216
POMET, Richard, I, 83
POMFREY,† Reason, XII.721;
  XIV, 157
  Richard, II, 370, 461,551
POOL, Benjamin, VII, 21
  Elizabeth, IV, 458
  George, IV, 458
POOLE, I, 142, 143
  Henry, I, 339
  Stephen, I, 90
  William, VII, 224(2)
POORE, Andrew, VII, 211
  Michael, VII, 211
POPE, VI, 271
  Benjamin, XI, 470
  John, XII, 373
  Matthew, XI, 473
  Nathaniel Junior, XV, 223
  William, X,293; XI,470;
  XVI, 409
POPEHAM, Francis, I, 67, 77
POPHAM, George, I, 57, 59, 62(2), 63, 64, 66(2)
POPKTON, William, I, 138
PORTER, Charles, XII, 219, 375
  John, III, 158, 198(3);
  III, 95(2); VII, 196
  Patrick, VII, 195
  Samuel, VII, 24
  Thomas, XIII, 94, 592
PORTERFIELD, Robert, XIII, 588; XVI, 405
PORTEUS, Robert, IV, 112;
  VII, 628
PORTLOCK, John, XIII, 223

POSY, John, I, 84
POSEY, John, VI, 375; XIII, 152
  John Price, XII, 692(3)
POSTON, Elias, XII, 625, 702;
  XIV, 153
  William, XVI, 32
POTITE, Benjamin, XV, 164
POTT, XIII, 77
  John, I, 4(4), 111*, 128, 131(2), 132, 137, 145 (3), 147, 171, 196, 208
POTTER, III, 568
  Cuthbert, III, 543
  Roger, II, 328
POTTINGER, Samuel, XII, 631
POTTLET, Nathan, VII, 208
POTTS, John, XIV, 387; XV, 64
  John, Junior, XIII, 178
  William, II, 371, 379, 557(2), 658(2)
POUNTIS, John, I, 111, 120, 128(2)
POVEY, Thomas, VI, 303(3), 305, 306, 307(2), 308
POWEL, V, 189; XV, 37
  Nathaniel; I, 111
  William, I, 85
POWELL, VI, 19; VIII, 79;
  XIII, 556; XIV, 153;
  XV, 166; XVI, 170
  (3), 192(3)
  Alfred, XVI, 423
  Benjamin, IX, 239
  Burr, XII, 606; XV,383;
  XVI, 51, 380
  Charles, XV, 184
  David, XII, 378
  James, II, 330
  John,† I, 179, 430, 529;
  II, 15, 197, 250; VII, 203, 213
  Joshua, VIII, 130
  Levin,‡ X,135; XII,605;
  XIII, 311,313(2),580;
  XIV, 378
  Levin, Junior, XIV, 378
  Lucas, IX, 567; X, 370
  Richard, VII, 203
  Robert, XV, 233, 234
  Thomas, II, 371, 379§;

VII, 186, 203
William, XV, 30
William H., XV, 214
POWER, James, VI, 230, 418, 437, 454, 524, 528;
  VII, 13, 39, 40, 59, 64, 76
  Joseph, VII, 51
POWERS, John, XII, 295, 639
POWLET, I, 111
POYTHERES,|| Francis, I, 283, 289, 318(2), 319, 339, 353, 359
POYTHRESS, Peter, XV, 230;
  XI, 57
  William, VI, 485
  William, Junior, VII,608
PRAT, John, I, 85
PRATER, Jonathan, VII, 219
  Nehemiah, VII, 220
PRATHER, Charles, XIII, 151
  (2), 518; XIV,167(2)
  Donne Basil, XIII, 148
  Thomas, VII, 205, 207
PRATON, Ningum, VII, 220
PRATT, John, VII, 208; VIII, 445
PRENTIS, John, VII, 231;
  VIII, 406
  Joseph, IX, 131, 201,314, 328; XII, 97, 639;
  XIII, 8, 131
  Robert, IX, 68, 201
  William, V,413,414(3), 415, 416(2); VII, 75, 173, 233, 234, 257, 349, 359, 371, 382, 465, 502; XVI, 627, 309, 434
PREFEST, Michael, VII, 192
PRESCOTT,£ Edward, I, 549 (2); II, 15(2)
PRESLEY,** William, I, 340;
  II, 197, 198, 250
PRESNAL, James, VII, 210
PRESTON, Amias, I, 81, 90
  David, VII, 207
  Elizabeth, VII, 189, 190
  Francis, XII, 674; XIII, 590; XV, 426; XVI, 167(2), 181

*Potts †Powel ‡Levin §Yowell ||Poythres **Preslye

James P., XV,133; XVI, 72
John, XII, 674; XIII, 585, 590; XV,66, 133; XVI, 53, 403
Moses, VII, 206
Philip, VII, 207
Thomas L., XVI,377(2), 379, 403
Walter, XIII, 644
William, VII, 189, 475; VIII, 127, 546, 552; XI, 134, 135
PRETTY, George, I, 84
PREWITT, Henry, VII, 223
PRICE, VI, 352; XIII, 79
Anger, XV, 30
Anne, II, 157(3)
Arthur, I, 289
Daniel, VII, 186
Henry, I, 85
Jacob, XIII, 207(3), 208(4)
Jenkin, II, 11
John, VII, 21; XII, 383
Leonard, VII, 493, 569
Thomas, VII, 216, 569; XIII, 132, 205(2), 206(2); XIV, 268; XV, 155
Walter, I, 138, 148
William, VI, 352; VIII, 79; XV, 419; XVI, 335
PRICHARD, Rees, XIV, 153
Roger, I, 146
Thomas, VII, 183
William, XV, 228
PRICKET, Jacob, VII, 215,216
Josiah,* XIII, 48; XIV, 157; XV, 31, 49
PRIDE, Halcot, XI, 382(2)
James, VII, 568
John, XII,591; XIII,293
William, V, 66, 364(2); VI, 15, 16(2), 294; VII, 127; XIV, 155
PRIMM, James, XV, 456(2), 457; XVI, 176(2),406 (2), 421
PRINCE, Edward, I, 289

Thomas, XIII, 73
PRIOR, Allyn, XIV, 322; XV, 362
Richard, VII, 204
PRISNALL, Daniel, VII, 201
PRITCHARD, II, 330
Rees, XIII, 152
Richard, VII, 210, 211
Stephen, XV, 224, 260
Thomas, I, 425
PRITCHETT, William, XV, 309
PROCTOR, VI, 210
George, I, 85
PROPS, Adam, VII, 180(2)
Michael, VII,180(2),182
PROSSER, John, V, 88
Thomas, VIII 173(2), 174(3); XI, 399; XII, 374, 729; XV, 353
PROSYER, John, II, 159(3)
PROUDE, William, I, 82
PRUDDEN, James, XVI, 204
PRUNK, Henry, VII, 206
PRUNTY, David, XV, 270
John, XII, 661; XIV, 242; XV, 249
PRUSEY, Ambrose, I, 84
PRYAR, Richard, VII, 196
PRYOR, I, 288
Nicholas, VII, 203
Samuel, XII, 400
William, VII, 202, 203, 218
PUGH, Jacob, XV, 274
Samuel, XV, 267
Theophilus, IV, 529, 530(2); V, 371; XV, 444
PULLEN, John, XV,121; XVI, 329
PULLIAM, Drury, VII, 129
William, IV, 179; VI, 17
PULLON,† Loftus, VII, 189, 190
PULTNEY, John, VII, 21
PURCELL, David, VII, 653
Thomas, XV, 459
PURDIE, George, VIII, 173
John H., XVI, 140, 346
PUNDY, Jonathan, XV, 463

PURIFIE,* Thomas, I,133(2), 149, 150, 153, 170, 178, 187, 202
PURKINS, William, XIV, 311
PURNALL, John, XIII, 315; XIV, 390, 425
PURNELL, William, XV, 338; XVI, 60
PURSELL, Jonathan, XIII, 90
PURSLEY, James, XIII, 218
PURVIS, I, v(4), vi(2), vii, ix(3), xix, xx; II, iii (4), iv(3), 41(7), 42 (10), 43(5), 44(8), 45(10), 46(4), 47(2), 48(5), 49(3), 51(8), 52(3), 53(4), 54(5), 55, 56(2), 58, 61(5), 62, 63, 64, 65(4), 66, 67(2), 68(3), 70, 71 (4), 72(3), 73(2), 74(4), 76(3), 79, 85, 86, 89(2), 90(4), 91 (2), 92, 94, 97, 98, 111, 115, 121, 128(2), 129, 130(4), 136, 138 (3), 140, 141(2), 142, 143, 144, 145(2), 146, 147, 163, 164(7), 165 (7), 166, 169, 170(3),
181(2), 192(2), 195, 208, 211, 212 215(2), 216, 217(2) 220, 222, 227(2), 22 (2), 230, 232(3), 23 (3), 234, 235(2), 23 (2), 237, 241, 242 243, 244, 245(2), 246 247(5), 255(2), 260 265(2), 266, 267, 268 270, 278, 283(2), 29 301(2), 307, 308, 311 366, 394(2), 397, 398 399, 404, 411, 437 442, 444, 458, 473(4) 483, 486(2), 490; II 9(3), 14, 15, 222
John, III,544(4),545(4
PURYEAR, Thomas, XV, 223
PURZINS, William, VII, 195
PUTNEY, David, XIV, 410(2
Elizabeth, XIV, 410(2
PUTT, John, VII, 191, 198
PUTTECT, William, VII, 20 (2)
PYDURN, John, VII, 205, 20
PYLAND, James, I, 374, 378 506

Q

QUARLES, IV, 335, 383, 481; V, 142, 144; VI, 173, 176; VII, 78, 98, 323; IX,154, 160
Isaac, XII, 407
John, I, 84; IV, 267;
VII, 209; VIII, 585
X, 109(2)
Robert, XV, 31
Tunstall, XII, 682
QUICK, William, I, 85
QUINN, John, XIV, 308

R

RABLEY, Thomas, III, 562(3)
RADCLIFFE, John, I, 3
RADFORD, XV, 70
John, XIV, 311
RAE, James, VII, 663
Robert, VI, 282
RAGSDALE, Drury, XII, 407
John, VIII, 444
Peter, VII, 205, 209
Richard, VII, 206, 226
William, IV, 528; VI
209

RAILEY, Thomas, XIV, 265
RAINSEY,* Edward, II, 197
RALEIGH, Philip, XV, 233, 234
RALLS, George, XIII,580(3), 581
RALSTON, William, VII, 185
RAMSAY, Andrew, XIV, 167 (2)
Edward, II, 328,347,546, 547
James, VII, 180, 437; XIV, 334(3)
John, VII, 190, 193, 437; XIII, 322
Mary, XIII, 322
Patrick, VIII, 413(2)
William, VIII,550; XVI, 179
RAMSDEN, Millicent, I, 85
RAMSEY, Andrew, XII, 512 (2)
Bartholomew, VII, 203
Charles, VIII, 129
Edward, II, 249, 330
John, VII, 211
Josiah, VII, 210
Patrick, VII, 609
Richard, VII, 212
Thomas, I, 431; III, 566 (2)
RAMSHAWE, Thomas, I, 154
RAMSLEY, I, 414
RANCKIN, Robert, XII, 658
RAND, William, VII, 156(2), 157(3)
RANDALL, IX, 442
Abel, IX, 425
RANDEL, James, VII, 203
RANDOLPH, IV, 266, 334; XIV, 156
Beverley,† V, 112(3), 113(6); VI, 273; XII, 8; XIII, v
Brett, XIII, 293
David, XV, 55
David Meade, XVI, 90
Edmund, I, xxiii, xxiv, 238(2), 282(2), 288 (2), 322(2), 339(2), 352(2), 358(2), 369 (2), 429(2), 505(2),

516(2), 526(2); II, 9(2), 33(2), 149(2); IX, 103, 201; X, 318, 520(2); XI, 446; XII, 8(2), 639; XIII, 8, 630; XV, 69, 353; XVI, 34, 249, 335
Elizabeth (Lightfoot), V, 112, 113(4)
Henry, I, v, 424; II, iii, 34, 136, 148(2), 165, 201, 253, 466; VII, 203
Mary (Page), VIII, 152
John, I, 76, 121, 238, 282, 288, 322, 339, 352, 358, 369, 429, 505, 516, 526; II, 9, 33, 149; IV, 370, 371, 372(7), 373(4), 374 (6), 375(7); V, 64 (3),65; VII, 59, 83 (3), 175(3), 260(3), 350(3), 360, 361(2), 498(3), 598, 599; VIII, 146, 213, 369, 378
John, Junior, XV, 121, 269
Judith, XV, 121,127(2), 128
Peter, V, 564; VI, 281, 291, 307, 418; VII, 116, 276, 288, 354, 456, 568, 647; VIII, 115, 175, 272(2), 412; X, 446; XIII, 98; XV, 259
Peter, Junior, XVI, 410
Peyton, I, 121, 137, 147, 153, 238, 282, 288, 322, 339, 352, 358, 369, 429, 505, 516, 526; II, 9, 33, 149, 163, 170(2), 171, 172, 178, 179, 192(2), 193, 195, 208(2), 212, 215, 216, 217(2), 224, 229 (2), 232, 233(3), 234, 235(2), 236(2), 237, 241, 243, 244, 246, 247(2), 255(4), 261,

264, 265(2), 266, 267, 268, 270, 277, 283(2), 286, 293, 301, 308, 312, 326(2), 327, 329, 341(2), 366, 380, 397, 411, 433, 447(2), 458 (2); III, 9, 10, 11, 12, 13(8), 14, 15, 43(2), 44, 45, 47, 50(2), 52, 54(2), 56, 57, 58(3), 60(3), 62, 63, 66, 69, 70, 71, 72, 75, 78, 79, 82, 83, 99, 100, 102, 105, 115, 155, 158, 159 (3), 167; VI, 197(256, 437, 454, 524, 528, 529; VII, 13, 19, 39 (2), 49, 58, 59, 76, 82(5), 83, 84, 167(2), 175(4), 259(3), 260, 276, 288, 336, 360(4), 353, 360(3), 361, 466, 468, 498(4), 568, 647; VIII, 146, 149, 175, 210, 271, 346, 365, 378, 394, 463, 501, 576, 587, 648(2); IX, 7; X, 446(2)
Richard, IV, 181, 307; V, 64(3), 65(2), 321, 402(2), 403; VI, 281; VIII, 391, 412, 422, 656; IX, 70
Richard R., XVI, 268
Robert, XIII, 92
Ryland, VII, 592; XV, 390, 425
Samuel Fitz, XIV, 322
Thomas, IV, 307; VIII, 606; XV, 259
Thomas E., XIV, 406
Thomas Mann, VIII, 161, 162(4), 163, 422, 459; XV, 263(2), 264 (6), 265, 270, 427
Thomas Mann, Junior, XIV, 257
William, II, 13; III, 166, 481; IV, 307; V, 268 (2), 378(2); VI, 273, 281, 291; VII, 116,
120, 212, 288, 354, 456; VIII, 162, 412, 656; XI, 147
RANDOLS, Francis, VII, 196
RANKIN, Benjamin, XII, 361,* 371, 404; XIV, 153
James, XV, 227
Robert, XII, 608; XIII, 183
RANSDELL, Chilton, XV, 223
RANSOM,† Peter, I, 370, 373, 375(3)
RANSONE, Richard, XII, 371
RASCOW, VIII, 602, 603
RATCLIFFE, John, I, 81, 83
Richard, XVI, 177(4)
Silas, VII, 220
Thomas, XVI, 427
William, VII, 220
RAUSCH, John, XV, 362
RAVENSCROP, Thomas, VII, 212
RAWLINS, Anthony, VII, 206
Peter, VII, 206
RAY, VI, 17
John, VII, 212; VIII,131
Joseph, VII, 206; VIII, 129
Robert, IV, 113
Thomas, VII, 218
William, VII, 201
RAYMOND, Thomas, I, xxi
READ, George, I, 22, 36
Hankinson, VII, 214(2)
Henry, XIII, 299
Jacob, IX, 425
John K., XIII, 293; XV, 447
Joseph, I, 46
Thomas, XIV, 308; XV, 259; XVI, 346
READE, Benjamin, III, 59; V, 69(2), 70(4); VII, 484(2)
Clement, VI, 253, 277, 291; VII, 225(11), 227(3), 232, 306, 307 VIII, 141
Clement, Junior, VII, 307

30

Francis, VIII, 484(2)
George, I, 356, 421, 499,
505, 626; V, 72; VIII,
484
Gwyn, v, 70(2), 71(3),
72(2); VII, 139(2)
John, VI, 242; VII, 211,
402; VIII, 484(3)
Lucy (Gwynn), VIII,
484(2)
Margaret, XIII, 95, 96
(3)
Mildred, VIII, 484(3)
Robert, VII, 200; VIII,
484(2); XIII, 95(2),
96
Sarah, VIII, 483, 484
(2), 485(4), 486(3)
Thomas, VII, 206; VIII,
172, 484(9); XI, 273
READER, Benjamin, XIV, 242
Simon, XIV, 411
REAGER, Jacob, XIII, 91
REAH,* William, VII, 196
REAME, Alexander, VIII, 554
REAMS, Frederick, VII, 201
REBURN, Adam, VII, 187
Henry, VII, 193
John, VII, 188
REDCLUFFE, William, XV, 379
REDD, John, XIII, 297; XIV,
241, 316
REDDICK, Lemuel, V. 250
Mills, V, 200(2)
REDDINGS, John, II, 328
REDMAN, John, XIII, 165
REE, John, VII, 194
REED, II, 472
Andrew, XV, 44
Eldad, VII, 191
James, XVI, 162
John, XV, 120
Joseph, IX, 374
William, VII, 195
REEDER, Benjamin, XV, 31,
49; XVI, 330
REEKES, Stephen, I, 552
REEKS, Thomas, V, 369
REESE, Jacob, XV, 121
REEVES, Benjamin, VIII, 276
Josias, XV, 159
REGAN, John, VII, 216

Michael, Junior, VII, 21
REGAULT, Christopher, II,
302(2); III, 479(2)
REID, Alexander, VII, 129
Andrew, XVI, 403
Eve (—), XVI, 240(4)
George, XVI, 240(3)
James, XI, 139
John, XII, 719; XIV,
155; XV, 359
Nathan, XIV, 423
Robert, VIII, 549
Samuel, XIV, 270
REIGER, John, VII, 185
REINE, Charles, XIV, 331(3)
REITY, Francis, VII, 199
RELSBACK, John, VII, 23
REME, Daniel, VII, 185
REMI, Daniel, VII, 183
REMSEN, Henry, Junior, XI,
575
RENICK, William, XII, 282
RENNICK, Robert, VII, 190
(2)
RENNOCK, George, IX, 425
RENNOLDS, Robert, XIII, 171
RENO, Enoch, XV, 241
Lewis, VII, 24
RENT, Jacob, VII, 200
RENTFRO, James, VIII, 172,
173(2)
Joseph, VII, 211; VIII,
128(2), 172(2), 173
(2)
Moses, VII, 207
RENTFROE, James, VII, 208
Joseph, VII, 207, 208(2)
Stephen, VII, 208
REPLEY, XII, 221 ...
REVELL, Randall, I, 431
REVES, Robert, XV, 419
REYNOLDS, I, 87
Charles, I, 373
Henry, I, 83
John, VII, 326, 447;
XIV, 322, 406; XVI,
194
Richard,† I, 84; VI, 288;
VII, 156
William, XI, 473; XIV,
155, 308

RHEAH,* Archibald, VII, 196
Robert, VII, 196
RHODES, Clifton, VII, 222;
XIV, 255(3)
Robert, XII, 603; XIII,
87
RHOYDES, Rebecca, III, 59

RIBOT, Francis, III, 228
RICE, Allen, XVI, 334
David, XI, 273, 283
Dominick, II, 371, 379
Edward, VII, 218
George, VII, 215
James, VII, 202
John, VII, 25, 220; XVI.
77(2)
John II., XVI, 183
William, XVI, 432(4)
RICH, Robert, I, 86
RICHARDS, Gabriel, XIII, 325
Jacob, VII, 187
John, VII, 187, 657(3),
658; VIII, 132; IX,
305(2), 306(2); XIV,
257(2)
Mourning, VII, 151(4)
Richard, I, 154, 178
William,† XIV, 154,
264(2)
William Bird,‡ V, 396;
VIII, 446
RICHARDSON, Archibald, XII,
211; XIV, 308
Clapham, V, 196(3)
Daniel, VII, 206, 207
John, VII, 205(2)
John, Ar., XV, 353
Jonathan, VII, 205
Joseph, VII, 207
Joshua, VII, 205
Nathan, VIII, 208(2)
Randolph, X, 325
Samuel, XII. 682; XV,
339
William, XVI, 42, 431
(2), 432
RICHBOURG, Claude Philip de,
III, 328
RICHENS,§ John, II, 371, 378
RICHERSON, Joseph, XV, 189
RICHESON, Holt, XII, 774

(5); XIII, 628(2)
Nathan, VII, 226
RICHEY, Alexander, VII, 225
RICHMOND, John, XIV, 335
(3)
RICKETTS, John Thomas,
XV, 383
RICKLE, William, VII, 220
RICORDS, William, XIV, 280
(3)
RICTOR, John, VIII, 621(2)
RIDDELL,‖ Cornelius, VII,
406; VIII, 415
John, VII, 437
RIDDICK, Henry, IX, 466
Josiah, VIII, 471
Lemuel, VI, 16,227; VII,
154(3), 155(5), 156
(2), 515; VIII, 156
(3), 570, 660; XIV,
155; XVI, 110
Willis, VIII,156(3); IX,
466; XII, 211, 635;
XV, 223
RIDDLE, Susanna, X, 211(2)
William, XV, 383
RIDGE, William Short, VII,
218
RIDGLY, R., X, 552
RIDGWAY, Samuel, Junior,
VII, 204
RIDGWINE, Thomas, I, 82
RIDLEY, George, VII, 202
Peter, I, 289, 339, 343
Thomas, XIII, 297, 549
RIEVES, Nathaniel, XV, 176
RILEY, John, VII, 208
RIND, James, XV, 323; XVI,
249(2)
Mary, XVI, 240
Nicholas Brown Sea-
brook, XVI, 249(2)
RING, Joseph, V, 69
RINGS, Burtis, XV, 284
RINKER,¶ Jacob, XI, 57;
XIV, 419
RIPLEY, James, XV, 419
John, VI, 242(2)
RISING, Peter, XV, 420
RISK, James, VII, 102
RISPASS, Christopher, VI,242
RISQUE, James, XV, 44

RITCHIE, Archibald, VII,569;
VIII, 46(8), 47, 194
(5), 195
Robert, XVI, 376
Thomas, XVI, 194, 335
William, XIV, 154(2)
RITSON, Thomas, XI, 530
RITTENHOUSE, David, X, 521,
524, 528, 530, 531(2),
532, 533(2), 534(2),
535; XI, 355, 556
RIVES, Robert, XIII, 316(2);
XIV, 322; XV, 182

ROACH, Ashcroft, VII, 203
Mahlon, XV, 459
Millington, XIII,626(2)
ROADS, John, XVI, 233
ROANE, XI, 310
John, XIV, 266; XVI,
223(2)
John, Junior, XIV, 266
Spencer, XVI, 223(2)
Thomas, XIV, 399
William, VIII, 630(2),
631(5)
William H., XI, ii(3)
ROBB, James, XV, 189
ROBBINS, I, 374
John, I, 323, 359
ROBERDEAU, Daniel, I, 46
ROBERDS, William, VII, 22
ROBERSON, Barned, VII, 223
Zachariah, VII, 205
ROBERTS, Benjamin, XII, 391
Edward, XVI, 130
Humphrey, VII, 653
James, VII, 225, 227,
307; VIII, 417
James, Junior, VII, 305;
VIII, 130(2)
John, XIV, 322; XVI,
379
Jonathan, IV, 529(2)
Lewis, XIII, 227(3)
Michael, VIII, 173
Rachel, XIII, 227(2)
William, VII, 23(2),
402; VIII, 128; IX,
235; XII, 375
ROBERTSON, I, xiii, 5,513(3),
526, 527, 528; II, 9;

XII, 512
Alexander, XII, 400
Christopher, XIII, 541,
607(2), 608
Edward, XV, 334
George, VII, 191
James, VII, 190, 204;
XV, 228
John, VII, 205, 207;
VIII, 129
John, Junior, VII, 205
Patrick, XVI, 188(2)
Samuel, VII, 207
Walter, XI, 362(3), 363
(2)
William, I, ii(3); III,
431; VII, 214; XII,
6(2); VIII, ii; XV,
374, 436; XVI, 324
ROBINS, Anne, IV, 462, 463
(7)
Bowdoin, VII, 130
Christopher, IV,462(3),
464(4)
Elizabeth, IV, 462, 463
(7)
George, I, 86
John, IV, 461, 464(4),
465(2)
Mary, VIII, 222(2), 468
(2)
Obedience,* I, 149, 170,
187, 236, 283, 370,
408, 432, 499, 505,
526
Thomas, IV, 462(4),464
William, VIII, 462(2)
ROBINSON, VI, 17(2); XIII,
284; XIV, 154, 158
Alice, XI, 110(2)
Anne Washington, XI,
110
Arthur, I, 84
Benjamin, V, 303(2);
VIII, 216(2); XIV,
242; XVI, 225
Beverly, XVI, 223(2)
Braxton, XV, 338; XVI,
60
Christopher, III, 553,
554, 560(2); VI, 407;
VII, 570, 628

David, XII, 202
George, VII, 189, 190,
199(2)
Harry, XI, 110(5)
Henry, I, 84; VI, 291,
394
Isaac, XV, 262
James, VII, 218, 222;
XIV, 321, 322(3)
Jehu, I, 83
John, I, 85; IV, 235; V,
173, 321(2), 364; VI,
230, 324, 394, 414(3),
415(4), 416(5), 418,
437, 454, 460, 464,
467,468, 486, 523, 524,
528, 529, 530(2); VII,
13, 18, 33, 34(2), 48,
49(2), 58, 76, 77, 79,
83, 87, 118, 171, 178,
190, 195, 196, 209(2),
243, 247(3), 253, 256,
257, 259, 262, 263,
276, 288, 313, 327,
337, 352, 359, 371,
372(2), 373, 374, 382,
449, 452, 453, 454,
466, 467(2), 492, 497
(2), 501, 528, 568,
641, 647; VIII, 30, 33,
40, 145, 211(2), 212,
270, 271(5), 272(5),
273, 297, 349(5), 360
(3), 351, 455, 456(2),
460(2), 461, 463 464;
IX, 237; X, 446(2);
XII, 716; XV, 30,323;
XVI, 403
John, Junior, V, 64(3),
65(2), 402(2), 403,
407; VI, 195(3), 214,
248(2), 249
Jonathan, V, 74
Margaret, VI, 110(3),
111
Maximilian, V, 194(2);
XI, 110(2), 111
Peter, VII, 298,489; XV,
52
Samuel, VII, 210
Susannah, VII, 349,
350(2)

Thomas, VII, 191, 216;
XII, 407
William, V, 74; VII,569;
VIII, 131,220,221(3);
XI, 110(7), 111; XII,
110; XIII, 292
ROCK, XIII, 480
ROCKETT, X, 459, 474(2),
475; XI, 210, 235, 237
(4), 238(2); XII, 66,
67, 281(2), 581, 582;
XIII, 70, 84, 455, 479,
503, 573(2), 579(2)
RODES, John, Junior, XVI,
191
Matthew, XVI, 149
RODGERS, Edward, I, 78
James, VII, 200
John, VII, 226; XV, 188
(2)
Peter, XV, 291
RODNEY, Cæsar, I, 36
Roe, IV, 266, 335, 383, 387
(2); V, 137, 143, 145,
146; VI, 169(2), 174,
176, 177; VII, 79, 98,
100, 101; IX, 154,
161*, 489(2), 511,
513; X, 273, 356, 476
Henry, I, 84
ROGERS, XI, 310
Andrew, VII, 223
George, VII, 195
John, I, 289; XIII, 106,
216; XIV, 323; XV,
181(3)
Lewis, XIV, 267(2)
Nathaniel, XIV, 281
Peter, VIII, 130(2), 131
(4)
Richard, I, 84
Stephen, VII, 22
ROLEMAN, Jacob, VII,188(2)
ROLESTONE, Matthew, VII,
179, 180
William, VII, 179, 180,
181, 188
ROLFE, John, I, 111
Thomas, I, 327(3)
ROLLIN, Matthew, VII, 199
ROLLING, James, VIII, 552

Thomas, VIII, 552
ROLLINGS, Pemberton, X,135
ROLLINS, Mark, VII, 212
ROLMAN, Jacob, VII, 184;
VIII, 127
ROLSTON, Samuel, VII, 199
ROMNEY, I, 82
William, I, 90
RONALD, William, XII, 639;
XIII, 171, 293
ROOKINGS,* William, II, 370.
376 (3), 377, 547
ROOKWOOD, I, 83
ROOTES, John, VIII, 483, 484
(2), 485 (3), 486; X.
120 (2)
Philip, VII, 326,447,570
Sarah, X, 120 (2)
Sarah (Reade), VIII,
483, 484 (2), 485 (4),
486 (3)
Thomas, XIV, 268
Thomas Reade, VII,570;
XIV, 257
ROPER, VIII, 645
Eldridge, XVI, 427
ROSCOW, James, VIII, 301,
302 (4), 303
William, VIII, 301 (6),
302 (3), 303 (2)
Willis, VIII, 301
ROSCRANS, James, XIII, 195
(6), 196 (3)
ROSE, IX, 667; X, 370; XIII,
559
Alexander, VII,569; XI,
363
Charles, XII, 229, 665;
XV, 182 (2), 183
Daniel, XVI, 321 (4),
322 (4)
Duncan, XII, 420; XVI,
117
George, VII, 25
Henrietta (White),XVI,
321 (2), 322 (2)
Hugh,IX, 568; XII,229;
XIII, 315, 316
John, XII, 665; XIII.
315. 316; XV, 182(2),
183
Patrick, XII, 665; XIII.

315, 316; XV, 182(2),
183
Robert, VII, 325, 446;
VIII, 28. 636(2)
William. VII, 211
ROSEBURY, William, VIII,131
ROSECROUTS, Hezekiah, XIII.
170
ROSIN, John, VII, 24
ROSINCRANTZ, Hezekiah,
XIV, 411
ROSS, VIII, 423; XII, 71;
VII, 156, 316
Alexander, X, 139(4)
Andrew, VI, 282
David, X, 365; XII, 66
(2), 420, 682(2),683;
XIII, 480; XIV, 155
(5); XVI, 79, 95, 165,
167
George, I, 36
James, VII, 223
William, VII, 188, 222;
XIV, 336
ROSSELL, Stephen C., XVI,51
ROSSER, David, VII, 204, 208
ROTHERY, Daniel, VII, 435,
437; VIII, 269
Matthew, VII, 437
ROTS, David, XI, 438
ROUCE, Matthias, VII, 23
ROUSE, Louis, XIII, 616
ROUT, John, XIV, 153
ROUTLEDGE, Robert, XIV,
315(3), 316
Row, Thomas, I, 78
ROWE, Thomas, XIV, 152
William, XIII, 621
ROWEL, Samuel, V, 367
ROWLAND, Augustine, VII,
223
George, VII, 191
Thomas, XII, 202, 675
ROWLANDS, John, IX, 242
ROWLETT, William, XVI, 48
ROWLEY, William, VII, 221
ROWLSTON, I, 139, 140
ROWN, William, VII, 326.
447
ROWSIE, Edward, Junior,
XIII, 221

ROY, IV, 336, 382, 383, 386,
438; V, 14, 142, 144,
233, 287; VI, 18, 172,
175; VIII, 77, 97, 390;
IX, 153, 160, 488. 510;
X, 272, 355, 475; XI,
210, 235; XII, 258,
455; XIII, 479, 502
John, IV, 268
Mungo, X, 210; XII,
698; XIII, 287, 576
ROYAL, John, XIV, 390; XV,
187(2), 188, 259
Richard, VI, 277
William, XVI, 72
ROYALL, John, XIII, 293,
570, 627
John D., XVI, 410
William, XV, 380
ROYLEY, Pharoah, VII, 207
ROYSTER, XIV, 156
Thomas, XIII, 296
William, VII, 588
ROYSTON, V, 143, 145, 234;
VI, 174, 176, 226(2);
VII, 632; VIII, 79, 98,
100(3), 236, 322(2),
324, 508; IX, 164,159,
161, 332, 489, 511,
513(3); X, 273, 356,
475(2); XI, 211, 236,237,
278(2); XIII, 480,
504; XVI, 354,420(2)
John, IV, 113, 234, 235
(2), 236(2), 237(3),
439; V, 197(2), 198
ROZSEL, Stephen C., XVI,380

RUBLE, Jesse, XV, 215(3)
RUBSAMEN, Jacob, XI, 57,
449; XIII, 479
RUCKER, Ambrose, XIII,296,
315, 316; XIV, 389
Benjamin, XIII, 296;
XIV, 389
John, VII, 204
Peter, VII, 214
RUDD, Edward, XIII, 267;
XIV. 169
RUDDALL, Archibald, VII,215
RUDDLE, Isaac, XII, 677(3)
RUFFIN, Benjamin, XIII,297;

XIV, 254(2), 255
Edmund, XI, 57
George. XIV, 320; XV,
265; XVI, 214
James, XII, 407
John, V, 369(2),370(3);
VI, 239, 240, 507; VII,
569
Joseph, XVI, 140, 346
Robert, III, 537(2),538;
VI, 485; VII, 570,
602; VIII, 434(2)
RUFFNER, David, XV, 466;
XVI, 194
Joseph, XVI, 194
RULE, James, VII, 635
RUMNEY, William, I, 67, 77
RUMSEY, James, XI, 502(9)
RUNKLE, Jacob, VII, 186
RUNNALS, Stephen, VII, 206
RUPERT, II, 528
RUSH, Benjamin, I, 36
Charles, VII, 185
RUSHOUT, John, V, 559
RUSK, James, VII, 197
RUSSEL, XV, 234(2)
James, I, 83
John, I, 84; XVI, 159
Peter, VIII, 149
Robert, XII, 672
Samuel, VII, 212
William, I, 83; IV, 531;
VI, 18; XII, 664
RUSSELL, VIII, 209
Albert, XIII, 171; XV,
223
Andrew, XV, 426
John, VII, 129
Moses, XV, 260
William, VII, 22, 23,
227; XVI, 197
RUST, V, 143, 145; VI, 174,
176; VII, 532*; VIII,
79, 98, 101, 324; IX,
154, 161, 489, 511,
513; X, 273, 356, 475;
XI, 211, 236, 238;
XII, 64(3)
Benjamin, IV, 531(2);
VI, 18(2); VIII, 370
(2)
Peter, XVI, 158

RUTHERFORD, Robert, VII,
232, 236; IX, 247;
XII, 371
Thomas, VIII, 10, 124,
252; IX, 247, 576;
XV, 110; XVI, 100,
335
Van, XV, 99
William, VII, 218
RUTLAND, V, 559

RUTLEDGE, XV, 121
Edward, I, 36; X, 540
George. XV, 133, 435,
436
John, I, 23

RYAN, Nathan, XIII, 609(3)
RYLEY, Pharoah, VII, 205
RYON, Joseph, VII, 205

S

SACKLER, John, III, 552(2),
664
SACKVILLE, Richard, I, 81
SADLER, Matthew, II, 371
Rowland, I, 239
SAGE, Henry, VII, 226
ST. ALBANS, II, 623, 529,
539, 571, 576, 579,
581; IV, 515(2), 516
(2)
ST. CLAIR, Alexander, XII,
606, XIII, 174, 588,
609(3); XIV, 308;
XV, 44, 99; XV, 100
ST. JOHN, John, I, 86
William, I, 82
SALLARD, John, VII, 493
SALLEE, Isaac, XIV, 240,
328
SALLEY, John, VII, 198
SALLING, George Adam, VII,
203
SALMON, Christopher, I, 85
Henry, XIII, 616, 617
John, VIII, 131; XIV.
337(2)
SALTER, Nicholas, I, 83
SAMBACH, William, I, 84
SAMPLE, Moses, VII, 186
SAMPSON, Richard, XIII, 611
SANDERS, Briton, XV, 121
John, II, 548(2)
Robert, VII, 223
Stephen, XVI, 174
Susannah, V, 294
SANDFORD, Daniel, XI, 332
Joseph, XVI, 338, 403

SANDIDGE, John, XVI, 149,
318
Joseph, XIII, 608, 609
(2)
SANDRIDGE, XVI, 430
SANDWICH, II, 511
SANDYS, V, 559
Edwyn, I, 78, 82, 83,
90, 121, 122(2)
George,* I, 84, 111, 114,
128, 230
Henry, I, 83
Michael, I, 81, 90
Richard, I, 83
Samuel, I, 82
Thomas, I, 83
SANKEY, Richard, XI, 273
SAPPINGTON, John, XII, 603
SATTERFIELD, Benjamin, VII,
21
SATTERWHITE, William, VII,
220; VIII, 130, 131
SAUNDERS, Ann Swann, XI,
391; XIII, 481
David, XIV, 422; XV,95
George, VII, 21
Hubbard, XV, 52
John, XVI, 427
John H., XVI, 409(5),
410
Julius, XVI, 38
Peter, XIV, 316
Robert, XVI, 50, 197
Roger, I, 170, 187, 203
Samuel Hyde, XIV,
319(2), 408; XV, 130

(2), 167(4), 168;
XVI, 409
Thomas, VII, 218
SAUNDERSON, XVI, 425
Alexander, XVI, 165
SAVAGE, VIII, 222, 468, 470
Abraham, XV, 31
Anthony, II, 15
John, VIII, 222(2). 223
(2), 468, 469, 470
Littleton, XII, 364, 496
Mary (Robins), VIII,
222(2)
Nathaniel Littleton,*
VIII, 222(3) 223(4),
468(5), 469(8), 494
Patrick, VII, 196
Thomas, VIII, 222(3)
SAVIN, Robert, I, 139, 149,
203
SAWYER, III, 471; VI, 14
Francis, II, 364
SAWYERS, Alexander, VIII,
127
Robert, XIV, 327
Sampson, XV, 55
SAYER, David, VII, 196
Robert, XIII, 690
SAYERS, Alexander, VII, 179,
183; VIII, 129
David, VII, 197
Sampson, VII, 191
SAYEUR, Samuel, XIV, 426
SAYRE, I, 171

SCALES, Peter, XV, 160
SCARBOROUGH,† Edmund, I,
149, 154, 170, 187,
203, 239, 289, 340,
356, 370, 384(2),
529; II, 38, 122, 160,
161, 183, 184, 196(3),
203, 236
Edward, II, 168(3),250
William, II, 370,461,553
SCARBURG, Charles, II, 548,
549(4)
SCARBROUGH, Henry, VII, 634
(2), 635(3)
SCARLETT, Anne, VIII, 635
(2), 636, 637
SCARLOCK, Huncrest, VII,219

SCARPE, John, I, 86
SCHERER, Samuel, XV, 353
SCHURK, Lewis Cornelius,
XIII, 159
SCOBELL, I, 511
SCOGGINS, Micajah, VII, 225
SCOT, Bartholomew, VII, 131
(2)
David, VII, 213
George, I, 84
James, VII, 131
John, I, 78, 81, 90
Thomas, I, 87
SCOTCHMORE, Robert, I, 148,
179, 205
SCOTT, VI, 21; VIII, 544;
XIII, 175; XVI, 149
Alexander, VII, 630,
631(2), 632(2), 633
(2), 634(2); XV, 30,
121
Anderson, XII, 698;
XIV, 268
Andrew, XV, 262
Archibald, XIII, 588
Charles, IX, 71; XI,
309; XII, 580(2),581;
XIV, 390; XV, 121;
XVI, 246, 268
Daniel, V, 365
David, VII, 181; XII,
297, 522; XIII, 151;
XIV, 157(2); XV,
126(6), 163(3)
Elizabeth, XII, 220(3),
382
Exum, VI, 283
Francis, XIII, 315
Gustavus, XIII, 283;
XIV, 163
Jacob, XII, 83, 297;
XIV, 167
James, VII, 130(8),211,
427, 630, 631(4), 632
(3), 633(2); XII,
382(5); XIII, 306
(3); XIV, 265; XVI,
273(2)
James, Junior, VII, 630,
631, 632(6), 633(2),
634
James-Jordan, VII, 624

32

John, XIII, 315, 316 571
(3) ; XIV, 155
John B., XIII, 315; XV.
48(2), 67, 69, 120.
172, 380; XVI, 136,
183, 403
Joseph, VIII, 543; XIII,
297, 315
Reuben G., XII, 6(2)
Robert, VI, ii(2) ; VII.
213, 425(2), 426;
XIII, 212
Robert G., VIII, 2; X.
ii(2); XI, ii(5)
Thomas, XI, 273; XIII,
556; XV, 132; XVI.
400
William, XII, 220(2);
XIII, 297; XVI, 167
SCRIVENER, Joseph, VI, 241
Matthew, I, 83
SCRUGGS, Gross, VII, 205;
VIII, 585
Henry, VIII, 131
Valentine, XIV, 240,328
SCUDDER, Nathaniel, I, 46
SCURLOCK, Miel, VII, 50
SCURRY, John, XIII, 321
SCUTT, William, VII, 21

SEA, George, VIII, 275
SEABRIGHT, William, I, 83
SEABROOK, John, XV, 353;
XVI, 249(2)
SEALE, Anthony, X, 209
Anthony, Junior, IV.
179
SEALES, William, VII, 220
SEAMOUR, Edward, I, 78
SEARS, John, VII, 493
SEATON, VI, 16; XIV, 154
George, II, 533; IX.
145(2), 146(2)
Howson, XV, 216
James, VII, 24
SEAVEAR,* Valentine, VII.
213(2)
SEAWARD, Nicholas, VII, 449
SEAWELL, XV, 311
Henry, I, 179
SEBASTIAN, Benjamin, XIII.
91

SEED, Edward, VII, 22
SEEKFORD, Henry, I, 82
SEELY,† Thomas, I, 154, 169,
187
SECAR, Thomas, XIV, 399
SEIRL, Thomas, VII, 196
SELDEN, XIV, 157
Cary, VIII, 264
George, XIV, 428; XV.
176
Joseph, XVI, 35, 79, 90,
95
Miles, VIII, 369; XII,
383, 611, 729; XIII,
316; XVI, 79
Miles, Junior, XI, 309
Samuel, VIII, 627; IX,
72, 305; XIII, 204;
XVI, 40(2), 195(3)
William, VIII, 2
Wilson, XII, 404; XIV,
153
Wilson C., XV, 214
SELLACKE, Richard, I, 613
SELLER, John, VII, 185
SELLERS, John, XII, 595, 596
(2)
SELSER, Christiana, XIV, 257
Henry, VII, 215
SEMPLE, James, XVI, 50,197,
417(3)
Joanna, XVI, 417(4)
John, XIII, 283
John W., XIV, 268
Samuel, VII, 179, 180
SENSENEY, John, XIV, 323
Peter, XIV, 322
SEQUEYRA, Jon de, VII, 569
SETTLE, Isaac, VII, 25
SETTLINGTON, Robert, XVI,
169(2)
SEVIER, John, XV, 435, 436
SEWARD, VI, 449
Henry, VII, 515(2)
John, VII, 514(2)
Nicholas, VII,327; VIII,
30
William, VII, 230, 514
(3), 515, 516(2)
SEWELL, XII, 471; VI, 14,
492(2) ; VII, 582; XI,
187; XIV, 171

John, XV, 67
Thomas, XIII, 218, 219
William, VII, 22
SEXTON, Samuel, VII, 212
Thomas, VII, 206
SEYER, Thomas, I, 87
SEYMOUR, Abel, XVI, 51

SHACKLEFORD,* Benjamin,
XV, 175, 203
Clement, XVI, 419(2)
Elizabeth (Robins), IV,
464(2)
James, IV, 463(6), 464
John, XV, 53, 209
Lyne, XIV, 399
SHADDIN, Matthew, VII, 199
SHAFER, XIII, 71(2)
SHANKLIN, Edward, VII,181
John, VII, 180, 188(3)
Richard, VII, 181, 187
SHANNON, Thomas, XVI,403
William, VII, 186, 188;
VIII, 127; XIII, 211
(3)
SHARF, Benjamin, XIV, 314.
322†
Lincefield, XV, 223
William, I, 86; V, 565
SHARPE, Serit, I, 138
SHAVER, Paul, VII, 184
SHAW, William, VII, 184,
187
SHEARER, John, VII, 217
Thomas, XV, 425
SHEARMAN, Rawley, VIII, 64
SHEDDIN, Matthew, VII, 199
SHEFFIELD, Edmond, I, 81,90
SHELBY, Evan, IX, 555; X,
143(2), 144(3)
Isaac, XI, 283; XII, 231,
282, 396, 456; XIII,
184
SHELLEY, Henry, II, 815
SHELTON, I, 82; III, 472; V,
142, 144
Armistead, XV, 334
Clough, XII, 665; XV,
182(3)
Jesse, XI, 370, 371
Ralph, VII, 201
Robert, XIII, 610(3)

Samuel, XIV, 425
Wetherston, XVI, 149
William, XIII, 297
William II, XVI, 45
SHENK, Martin, XVI, 233
SHEPARD, XV, 312
Jacob, VIII, 131
Moses, XV, 274
Thomas, XV, 228
SHEPHARD, VII, 583
SHEPHEARD, Robert, I, 322,
339, 342
SHEPHERD,‡ IV, 267, 335,
383, 385; V, 142, 144;
VI, 173, 175, 492;
VIII, 78, 98, 324; IX,
154, 160, 488, 510;
X, 273, 356, 476; XI,
188, 211, 235; XII,
65(2),301,581; XIII,
479, 503; XIV, 172
Abraham, IX, 546; X,
197; XII, 717,718(3);
XIII, 481
David, XII, 661
John, I, 283
Matthew, I, 86
Richard, I, 85
Samuel, XIV, 2(3), 436;
XV, 471; XVI, 441
Solomon, IV, 529(3);
XI, 332
Thomas, VII, 600; VIII,
146, 147, 263
SKEPFARD, Elizabeth, XV.
273
John, I, 370, 379, 386
Philip, XV, 273
Thomas, I, 203
SHEPFERD, John, XV, 137
SHERALD, Joshua, VII, 22
SHERLEY, William, I, 85
SHERMAN, Roger, I, 22,36,46
SHERRARD, William, XIII,218
SHERRIL, Joshua, VII, 213
SHEVER, Paul, VII, 181
SHIDMORE, James, VII, 161,
188
John, VII, 181, 188
Joseph, VII, 181, 182
Randolph, XVI, 54

SHIELDS, Alexander, XVI,
403
John, VII, 181; XV, 228
Patrick, VIII, 130
Robert, VI, 242
Robert, Junior, V, 371
SHULL, John, VII, 180
SHILLING, George, III, 466
SHILLINGER, George, VII,186
SHINGLETON, John, VII, 213
SHIPLEY, Edward, VII, 224
Hugh, I, 85
Robert, VII, 206
Robert, Junior, VII, 206
SHIPMAN, Isaiah, VII, 184
Jonathan, XVI, 57
Josiah, VII, 161
SHIPTON, Thomas, I, 83, 85
SHIRLEY, Jarvis, VII, 216
Thomas, VII, 25
Walter, VII, 215
SHIVERS, Thomas, IV, 529
(2)
William, IV, 529
SHOCKOE,* IV, 334, 381(2),
385, 479(4) ; V, 142,
144, 191, 192; VI, 14,
169, 172, 176, 223,
226, 352; VII, 532,
533(3) ; VIII, 78, 98,
100(7), 101, 236,
322, 497(4) ; IX, 154,
169, 160, 332, 488,
510, 513(5) ; X, 273;
XI, 235, 237(4), 238
(3) ; XII, 66,67; XIII,
572, 573(2), 579(2) ;
XIV, 263(2)
SHOEMAKER, Daniel, VII, 21
George, VII, 218
John, XVI, 402
Simon, VII, 21, 218
William, VII, 203
SHOLTS, John, XV, 270
SHORE, Henry S., XVI, 79,
95, 335
John, XIII, 174; XV,
259, 265; XVI, 214,
268
Thomas, VII, 21; XIII,
42, 481
SHORT, Elizabeth, II, 155

— (Kerr), XI, 148(3)
William, XI, 148(4).
149; XI, 681, 682(2)
SHORTRIDGE, George, VII, 21
SHREWSBERRY, Nathaniel,
XVI, 179
William, XVI, 179
SHROPSHIRE, John, VII, 23
WilIam, VII, 23; XI,
345, 363
SHUGART, Michael, XV, 31.
65

SICKLEMORE, John, I, 83
SIDNEY,† John, I, 283, 340,
430, 501, 506, 508,
512, 529
SILLIVANT, John, VII, 220
SIM, Thomas, XV, 214
SIMM, XIV, 156
SIMMON, XIV, 156
SIMMONDS, Thomas, VII, 21
SIMMONS, VI, 19
Benjamin, VII, 230
Charles, VII, 208
John, IV, 363, 460; VI.
285, 286; XV, 264
(2), 255
Williams, VII, 205, 206,
219
SIMMS, Charles, X, 139(6),
140; XII, 393; XIII.
94, 312, 592
Richard, XVI, 225
William, VIII, 369
SIMON, Christian, XVI, 398
Joseph, XI, 277, 321,
322(3), 474(3), 475
(2) ; XII, 395(3), 396
SIMONS, Christian, XVI, 61
SIMPSON, XII,165; XV,243;
XVI, 422, 423
Benjamin, VII, 212
James, VII, 191, 194;
XVI, 241(2)
SOUTHY, VII, 391; IX, 125
SIMS, Charles, XV, 249
Drury, VII, 212
Jonathan, XIV, 336
Matthew, XIII, 648(2),
549
Thomas, XIV, 336

SIMSON, XVI, 275
George, VII, 21
Gilbert, Junior, VII, 21
(2)
SINCLAIR, Arthur, XI, 57
John, XIII, 566(4), 567
Peter, VII, 212
Wayman, X, 325
SINCLARE, John, VII, 21
SINCLEAR, Isaac, XV, 419
SINDER, Margaret, VII, 25
Mary, VII, 25
SINGLETON, Anthony, XIII,
176, 217, 599
James, XV,67,260; XVI.
252
Peter, VIII,570; XI,332
Robert, I, 83
Standley, VII, 24
SIPSEY, John, I, 179, 203
SITLER, Isaac, XIII, 315;
XV, 323
SITOLENTOWN, Andrew, VII,
198
SITTON, Christopher, VII,205
SIVERS, Jacob, VII, 182
Nicholas, VII, 184, 185

SKEDMORE, Joseph, VIII, 126
SKEEN, John, VII, 406
SKEGGS, John, XIII, 321
SKELLAREN, George, XI, 450
SKELTON, V, 173, 175
Elizabeth, VIII, 55, 56
James, I, 86; V, 286, 287
Reuben, VI, 300, 301,
302(4)
William, VII, 204
SKIDMORE, Thomas, XIV,256
SKILLERON, George, XI, 341
SKILLERN, George, VII, 190;
XII, 202
SKILLERS, George, XII, 674
SKINKER, XV, 17
John, VIII, 126; IX,575;
XI, 204, 363
Samuel, IV, 113
William, XV, 179(2)
SKINNER, John, VIII, 220,
221(2)
SKIPWITH, XIV, 166
Henry, XIV, 390

Peyton, XI, 344; XIV.
156; XV, 114
William, VII, 608

SLAUGHTER, X, 215
Charles, XV, 359
George, X, 293; XI, 470
John S., XV, 121
Lawrence, XIII, 215
Reuben, XIV, 312, 322
Robert, VII, 214; XIV,
418(2) ; XVI, 182
Robert, Junior, VII, 326
447; XI, 36; XV, 176
Thomas, VII, 213, 232,
306
William, VII, 213(2),
214; XV, 121
SLAVIN, John, XV, 53
SLAYTON, Daniel, VII, 224
SLEDD, John, XIII, 607, 608
SLEEDER, Simon, IV, 462
SLIMMER, Christian, IX, 585
SLINGESBY, I, 82
SLINGSBY, H., II, 511
SLINKER, Charles, VIII, 129
SLODSER, Lodowick, VII, 199
SLOE, Thomas, XIII, 183

SMALL, Andrew, III, 59
William, VII, 569
SMITH, I, 122; V, 142; VI,
173, 351, 493(3) ; VII,
584; XI, 188(2), 506;
XII, 52,301(2) ; XIII,
160; XIV, 172(2);
XV, 157(2), 210, 211,
269(2), 274, 312(3),
315
Abraham, VI, 181(4),
182, 183, 206
Alexander, XV, 130(3)
Ann, XVI, 403
Armistead, XIII, 197
Arthur, I, 289; III, 554;
VI, 223(3), 240, 274
(2), 275, 288, 308(3),
309(8), 310(8)
Augustine, IV, 235(2)
Augustine, I., XVI, 337
(2), 389(3)

Baldwin Matthews, VI,
18; VIII, 659
Byrd, Will, 685, 590
Charles, V. 287(3), 268
(2), 289(2), 290, 291;
VI, 317(2), 318; VII,
24, 130, 201, 493; XV,
121, 446
Charles, Junior, XII,
608; XIII, 88, 176(2)
Christopher, X, 209;
XV, 121, 240
Cleophas, I, 83
Daniel, VII, 187; IX,
422, 555, 561, 564;
XVI, 56
David, VII, 21, 181, 188
Dorothy, V. 289, 291,
317(2), 318
Edmond, I, 85
Edward, I, 87; XI, 511;
XIII, 315; XVI, 100,
232
Elizabeth, V, 289, 291;
VI, 317(4), 318
Elizabeth (——), 318
Elizabeth (—) (Neal),
XVI, 270(2), 271
Ezekiel, I, 86
Frances (Colston),VIII,
169(2)
Francis, IV, 117; VII,
201
Gasper, VII, 183, 184,
185
George, VI, 308,309(3);
VII, 206, 209; XVI,
149, 174
George William, (XIII,
222(3), 307; XV,323;
XVI, 95, 292, 335
Granville, XIII, 314:
XIV, 265; XVI, 330
Guy, VII, 585
Henry, VII, 180, 184;
XIV, 424; XV, 274
Jacob, V, 260; VII, 203
James, I, 36; VI, 308,
309; XIV, 394; XV,
37, 272; XVI, 158
Jane, VI, 309 (2)
Joel, VII, 212

John,* I, 3, 82, 83, 138,
141, 145, 178, 429,
431, 499, 500, 601,
503(2) ; II, 184; III,
560(2), 565(2); V,
397(2), 399(3); VI,
408(4), 409(3), 410;
VII, 180, 183, 189,
191, 200(3), 629(3),
635, 636, 637; VIII,
128, 129, 131,169(2),
663(2), 665(2); XII,
76,223.672,673; XIII,
171; XIV, 378; XV,
334; XVI, 62(2)
John, Junior, VII, 200;
XV, 121(2)
John A., XVI, 226
John Blair, XI, 272
Jonathan Bayard, I, 46
Joseph, XV, 30, 214
Joshua, VIII, 131
Josiah, VII, 437
Larkin, XII, 698; XIV,
268
Laurence, XV, 134
Lawrence,† II, 347, 434,
448, 449(4), 450(5),
451(2), 452(3), 453,
454, 545; III, 59, 565,
566; V, 69(4), 71(2),
289(2), 290, 291; VI,
317(2), 318, 407, 408
(4), 409(10), 410(4),
411(2), 412; VII, 204
Martin, XV, 121
Mary, VI, 408, 409
Mary (Colston), VII,
636, 637; VIII.169(2)
Mildred, V, 370
Moses, XV, 121
Nathaniel, VI, 400(2)
Nicholas, I, 513, 528; V,
194(2)
Obadiah, XV, 166
Othowell, I, 84
Peter, VIII, 127
Peyton, XII, 659
Phoebe, II, 36(2)
Richard, I, 85; VI, 308,
309

Robert, I, 85; II, 201,
225, 226, 518, 519,
529, 563, 568, 569;III,
643, 544(3), 557, 570;
V, 288(5), 289(2),
290(2), 291(4); VI,
316, 317(4), 318(2):
XI, 21(4), 22; XV,
134
Robert (Mrs.), V, 289
(2), 290, 291
Roger,* I, 111, 128, 137
Rowley, XIII, 48; XIV,
153
Samuel, I, 86; XVI, 58
Sarah, VI, 309(2), 317,
318
Thomas, I, 3(4), 67, 77,
78, 81, 90(2); VI,308,
309(3); VII, 62, 197,
224(2): XII, 420:
XIII, 567; XIV, 267
Toby, I, 239, 359; II,
36(3)
Valentine, 475
Willium, IV. 50; VII,
4(2), 21; XIII, 321;
XIV, 276(2); XV,
121; XVI, 149, 270
(2), 433(3)
SMITHERS, Gabriel, XVI, 379
SMITHEY, Benjamin, XVI,
67(2)
SMOOTE, William, I, 287
SMYTH, Adam, XI, 56, 338,
339; XIV, 274(2),
275(3)
Alexander, XIII, 583,
590: XIV, 275, 308
Richard, I, 196

SNALE, Elizabeth, XIII, 322
Thomas, XIII, 322
SNAPP, John, XI, 57
SNEAD, Thomas, I, 84
SNFZED, V, 114
SNELSON, John, VII, 130;
VIII, 391
SNICKER,† XII, 76, 77, 78,
375, 524; XV, 110,
298, 299; XVI, 51

Edward, XII, 404(2);
XIV, 153
SNICKERS, Edward, VIII,550
SNIDER, Christian, XVI, 403
SNIDO, Christian, XIII, 585
SNINGERS, Edward, VII, 217
SNODGRASS, James, VII, 199
John, VII, 196
SNOW, Henry, VII, 225
John, VII, 206
Thomas, XIII, 324

SOAME, Stephen, I, 81
SOAN, IV, 334; V, 14
John, IV, 266, 382, 385
SOANE,† Henry, I, 370, 373,
379, 386, 430, 627;
II, 16, 31, 32, 33, 38,
147
Joseph, I, 85
SOMERS, George, I, 57(2),58,
62(2), 6(32), 65, 66,
80, 82
SOMERVILLE, William, XVI,
340(3)
SOMMERVILLE, Joseph, XIV,
321
SOFIIIA, Princess, VI, 254,
257, 273, 379, 383,
386, 503, 504; VII,
132, 144, 150, 154,
246, 302, 304, 430,
614, 617, 619; VIII,
43, 168
SOUTH, Isaac, VII, 187
SOUTHALL, Turner,§ VIII,
656; X, 318; XI, 393,
450; XIII, 320(2):
XV, 353
SOUTHAMPTON, I, 76
SOUTHARD, William, VII, 21
SOUTHCOAT, Thomas, II, 249
SOUTHERLAND, George, III,
466
John, XIV, 267
SOUTHERLIN, John, XV, 124
SOUTHERNE, John, I, 125,
148, 154
William, I, 87
SOUTHING, III, 220
SOUTHWICK, John, I, 85
SOWELL, XII, 301

SPAICHT, Richard Dobbs, I,
22
SPALDEN,* Edward, VII, 203
SPANGLER, Anthony, XVI, 47
Frederick, XV, 132;
XVI, 56, 400
Philip, XV, 65; XVI, 29
SPARKS, I, 82
Charles, XIII, 218
SPARROW, Charles, I, 359,
373, 527
Steven, I, 87
SPEAD, James, VII, 225
SPEAKE,† Thomas, VII, 215
216; VIII, 415
SPEAKER, Benjamin, XV, 360
SPEAR, Thomas, XIII, 92
SPECKARD, Philip, XIII, 83
SPEED, Henry, XV, 114
James, XI. 283; XII,456
Joseph, XV, 52
Richard, XVI, 37(3)
SPENCE, V, 143; VI, 174;
VIII, 79
John, XVI, 174, 236
Patrick, IV, 267
Thomas, VII, 188; XIV,
409(2)
SPENCER, III, 219, 471
Catherine, VI, 242
Elizabeth, XI,391; XIII,
481
Francis W., XIV, 156
James, VII, 206
Jane, XVI, 389(2)
John, XIII, 218
Joseph, XIV, 428(2),
429; XV, 176(3)
Nehemiah, XIV, 428
Nicholas, II, viii(2),
225, 226, 250, 330,
563, 568, 569, 583;
III, 8, 41, 557, 566,
570
Samuel, XV, 182
Thomas, VII, 181
Vrian, I, 85
William, I, 203; XIV,
322
SPICEM, John, IV, 117(2)
SPIEGEL, Michael, XVI,37(2)

SPIERS, Alexander, VIII, 412
James, VI, 415, 416*
SPILLER, William, VII, 130;
XIII, 619, 620; XIV,
266
SPILMAN, Jacob, VII, 24
John, XV, 178(5)
Thomas,‡ XV, 120, 178
(2); XVI, 329
SPINDLE, Thomas, XVI, 225,
329
SPITY, John, VI, 508
SPLANE, William, VII, 24
SPOONER, George Wilson,
VIII, 44
SPOTSMAN,§ Lawrence, XIII,
155
SPOTSWOOD, Alexander, I, 3;
III, 8; IV, 5, 29, 60,
67, 68, 75, 76, 95, 117,
546, 547, 548(2), 549,
551, 552, 553, 555,
557, 558, 559, 560,
564, 565; VII, 323,
325, 326(2), 327(7),
328(2), 329, 330(3),
445(2), 446(2), 448
(3), 449(6), 450, 451
(3), 452(2); VIII, 27,
28, 29, 30, 31(3),
33(3); X, 470; XIV,
433
Anne, VII, 327(2), 449
(2); VIII, 30(2)
Anne Catherina, VII,
324, 325, 445, 447,
448(2); VIII, 28, 29
Dorothea, VII, 324, 325,
445, 447, 448; VIII,
28, 29
John, VI, 256; VII, 323,
324(4), 325(5), 326
(2), 327(8), 328(5),
329(5), 445(3), 446
(5), 447(6), 448(7),
449(6), 450(6), 451
(3); VIII, 27(2), 28
(4), 29(5), 30(7), 31
(6), 32(2), 33(3),
667, 668, 669
Mary, VII, 327(5), 329,
445, 446(2), 448, 449

(2), 451(2); VIII,
30(2)
Robert, VII, 324(2),
325, 326(2), 328(2),
445, 446(2), 448, 449,
450; VIII, 28(2), 29
(3), 31(2); XVI, 388
(2)
SPRAGIN, Thomas, VII, 219
(2)
SPRAGINS, Melchisideck,*
XV, 380; XVI, 401,
403
SPRANGER, Henry, I, 86
SPRATLEY, Thomas, XIII,612
SPRIGG, Osborne, XV, 465
Zachariah, XII, 599, 661
SPRINGER, Josiah, VII, 251
SPRINGHAM, Matthew, I, 84
SPRINGSTONE, Abraham,
XIV, 411
SPRINSON, Robert Hilde-
brand, I, 83
SPROTSMAN, Lawrence, XIII,
68, 176, 177
SPROUL, John, VII, 195
SPROUT, John, VII, 198
SPROWLE, Andrew,† VII,653;
XIII, 211, 219, 220(2)
Samuel, VII, 193
SPRY, Henry, I, 82
SPURLOCK, John, VII, 205
209
STACKHOUSE, William, VII,
21
STAFFORD, James, XVI, 158
Richard, I, 85; XII, 595
STAGG, Thomas, I, 375
STAINBLACK, Peter, XI, 723
STALKER, Rebekah,‡ VIII,
130, 172, 173(2)
STALLENGE, William, I, 84
STAMPS, William, VII, 475
STANARD, Beverly, VIII, 167
Larkin, XV, 348(4)
William, XIV, 322
STANDEFORD, David, XIII,
148
STANDERFIELD, James, VII,
211

STANHOPE, John, I, 81, 90
STANTON, Thomas, IV, 363
STAPER, Richard, I, 83
STAPLES, John, XIV, 241
William, XV, 49
STARK, Bolling, X, 572
STARKE,§ Belfield, XV, 122,
164, 165(2), 338, 365;
XVI, 60
Thomas, XV, 353
William, VIII, 289(2),
290(9), 291(2); XVI,
60
STARLING, William, XIII, 296
STARRINGTON, John, I, 102
STAUNTON, William, VIII,
129
STAYTON, Richard, VII, 607
(2); VII, 171(2)
STEADY, Robert, VII, 201
STEAGALL, Bottom, XVI, 56
(2)
STEALEY, John, XIV, 242,
272; XV, 249
STEALY, John, XVI, 235
STEARMAN, Richard, VII,216
STEED, Nathaniel, VII, 212
STEEL, IX, 421
Andrew, XI, 100
James, VII, 181, 190,
191; XIII, 554; XV,
270
John, XII, 521; XIII,
589
Robert, VII, 195; VIII,
129
Samuel, XIV, 266
Thomas, XV, 270
William, XI, 100; XV,
270
STEELE, James, VII, 198
John, XII, 676; XV, 66
Robert, VII, 193
Samuel, VII, 193
William, XII, 83
STEENBERGEN, William, XV,
383
STEENSON, James, VII, 198
STEGG, Thomas, I, 239
STEIGLE, Jacob, XV, 31
STEINBECK, Frederick, XVI,
51

STEPHEN, Adam, VI, 528;
VII, 493; IX, 569(2),
870(2); XI, 374(2)
STEPHENS, Adam, XVI, 28
  Frances, II, 322(4),
  323(7)
  George, I, 289, 370, 373
  Jehu, XIII, 590
  John, VII, 21
  Joseph, VII, 21
  Lewis, VII, 217, 234(2),
  235, 236; XV, 216(2)
  Richard, I, 129, 160, 178,
  187
  Samuel,* II, 322(10)
  William, VII, 222
STEPHENSON, Adam, VII,
  180, 181, 189
  David, XIII, 588
  Hugh, VII, 216
  James, VII, 183, 187;
  XV, 245; XVI, 47
  John, VII, 181, 187, 215,
  216; XVI, 209
  Thomas, VII, 187
  William, VII, 216
STEPTOE, James, XIV, 422;
  XVI, 100
STERN, Frederick, VIII, 127
STERNE, John, XVI, 266(2)
STERRETT, William, XV, 362
STEUART, Alexander, VII,191
  Charles, VII, 653
  David, VII, 195
  Robert, VII, 197
STEUBEN, Baron von, X, 376
  (2), 571, 573, 574;
  XII, 15
STEVENS, Edward, XI, 204;
  XV, 53, 209
  Richard, I, 153
  Thomas, XV, 459
STEVENSON, Adam, VII, 187,
  188
  James, VII, 187, 188,
  195, 197; XV, 249
  John, VII, 179, 180, 187,
  188, 193, 194
  Robert, VII, 197(2)
STEVISON, William, VII, 182
STEWARD, James, VII, 402

STEWARDSON, William, XVI,
  179
STEWART, Alexander, XIII,
  616
  Archibald, XI, 164; XV,
  44, 99
  Daniel, XV, 223
  David, VII, 197(2),
  475(2); XII, 393;
  XIII, 580
  Donald, XVI, 410
  Edward, XV, 53(2)
  Henry, XIII, 304, 305
  Hugh, XIII, 580
  James, VII, 195; VIII,
  129
  John, VII, 493; IX, 422;
  XI, 139; XIII, 304,
  305(4), 614(2); XV,
  44
  Robert, VI, 528; VII,
  216, 493
  Walter, VI, 528
  William, XIII, 93; XV,
  338
STIFF, Abraham, VII, 218
STILE, Humphrey, I, 86
  Persie, XIV, 155
STILL, John, VII, 184
STILT, John, VII, 185
STILWELL, Nicholas, I, 321
STINNETT, Benjamin, VII,
  203
  Benjamin, Junior, VII,
  203
STINSON, Thomas, VII, 193
STITH, I, 57, 110, 111, 119,
  121(2), 122, 138
  Griffin, VIII, 494, 661;
  XII, 364
  John, II, 364(5), 365;
  XIII, 322(3); XV,
  239(2), 240(2)
  Joseph, XV, 223, 234;
  XVI, 179
  Richard, VII, 227, IX,
  109(2); XI, 61; XII,
  605
  Thomas, XV, 52
STOAKES, Robert, II, 461, 550
STOCKDALE, Robert, VII, 217
STOCKEN, John, I, 86

*Samuell, Sammoell

133

STOCKLEY, Alexander, XII,
  636(5)
  Charles, VII, 64
  John, I, 86
STOCKTON, Richard, I, 36
  Samuel, VII, 203
  William, VII, 203
STODER, Christopher, VII,
  199
STOKE, John, I, 83
STOKELEY,* John, XV, 124,
  221, 223
STOKES, Christopher, I, 139,
  148
  Henry, VII, 224; XV,
  61
  John, XII, 492
  Robert, II, 370
  William, VII, 224; XV,
  338
STONE, XV, 229
  Hawkins, XIII, 283
  Henry, VIII, 126
  John, XVI, 401
  Jonathan, XV, 221
  Joshua, XV, 95, 160
  Marvel, XV, 315
  Thomas, I, 36; XII, 50
  William, VII, 200
  William S., XIII, 599;
  XVI, 47, 100
STONER, XII, 677
  Joseph, XV, 65; XVI,
  47
STONGER, John, XIII, 590
STONSAFER, Henry, VII, 213
STORMAKER, Valentine, XIII,
  171
STORNAKER, Jacob, XIV, 411
STORRS, XV, 353, 419; XVI,
  35, 79, 90, 95
STORY, James, VII, 214
STOTEN, Timothy, VII, 191
STOTT, Ebenezer, XVI, 100
STOUGHTON, Sam, I, 323, 340
STOVAL, Brett, XV, 160
STOVALL, George, VI,494(4);
  XIV, 156
  Joseph, XIV, 316; XV,
  210
  Thomas, XIII, 297
STOVER, Christian, XV, 379

Christopher, XV, 267
George, XV, 31(2)
Peter, VII, 474, 475
STRACHAN,† Alexander
  Glass, XIII, 42, 481;
  XIV, 320
STRACHEY, William, I, 86
STRADER, Christopher, XV,
  346
STRADLER, Stephen, VII, 215
STRANCE, Alexander, VII,
  223
STRATON, Joseph, XII, 398
STRATTON, Henry, XIII, 541,
  620(5)
  Joseph, I,148,179; XIV.
  266
  Zariah, XII, 637
STREATE, John, I, 86
STREBLING, Sarah, XV, 121
  Thomas, XV, 121
STREET, Anthony, XV, 61(2)
  Waddy, XVI, 346
  William, XIII, 611(2)
STREETER,‡ Edward, I, 405
  (2), 414
STRICKER, George, XII, 514;
  XIV, 410
  John, XV, 49
STRICKLER, Abraham, XV,49
  Benjamin, XI, 57
  Isaac, XVI, 233
STRIKER, Moses, VII, 406
STRINGER, John, I, 507, 512,
  529; II, 157; XII, 496
STRINGFELLOW, Henry, VII,
  23
STRIPLEY, VII, 479
STRITE, Christian, XVI, 29
STRODE, James, XIII, 297
  John, XIII, 143; XV,176
  Joseph, IX, 569
STROLE, Adolph, XIII, 91
STRONGARM, Richard, I, 83
STROTHER, Anthony, VI, 18
  (2); VII, 213
  Francis, VII, 22, 23, 213
  French, VII, 214; XI,
  36, 204; XII, 219,375;
  XIII, 143(4); XV. 53.
  176
  George F., XVI, 379

*Stockeley †Straghan ‡Stretter

134

James, XV, 223
Jeremiah, XVI, 379
John, VII, 22(2), 23
  (10), 213; XV, 30,121
Joseph, XIII, 143(7);
  XIV, 433
STROUD, Edward, VII, 217
STUART, VIII, 423; XIII, 42
  (2)
  Alexander, XV, 221;
  XVI, 34, 90, 336
  Archibald, XI, 341; XII,
  202, 676; XIII, 588;
  XV, 55, 66, 234, 446;
  XVI, 46, 94
  Benjamin, XIII, 554
  Charles, XVI, 158
  David, XIII, 99(2),100;
  XVI, 177, 395
  Eleanor (—) (Custis),
  XIII, 99(3)
  James, VII, 198; XVI,
  100
  John, VII, 198; XII,282;
  XIV, 257
  Robert, XIII, 554; XV,
  270
  William, XII, 685; XIII,
  137
STUBBLEFIELD, Robert, IV,
  142
STUBBS, Samuel, VII, 215
STURD, James, VII, 220 ·
  John, VII, 220
SUCKET, III, 472, 473
SULLIVAN, Cornelius, VII,
  188(2)
  Daniel, V, 243
  Daniel, Junior, V, 243
  (2)
  James, X, 293; XII, 225
  Margaret, IV, 528; V,
  243(5), 244(2)
SULLIVANT, Cornelius, VII,
  181
SUMMERS, Francis, VII, 217
  George, XVI, 225, 379
  John, VII, 21
  Simon, XV, 178
SUMMERVILLE, James, XIII,
  599

SUMNER, Bridget, V, 243
  Jethro, IV, 628; V, 200,
  202(2), 241, 242(5),
  243(2), 244(6); VII,
  493; VIII, 132
  Margaret (Sullivan),
  IV, 528; V, 243(5),
  244(2)
  Thomas, VIII, 471
SUNDERLAND, III, 41
SUSBERRY, Samuel, XIV, 266
SUTCLIFFE, Matthew, I, 78,
  82
SUTHARD, Stephen, VII, 215,
  216
SUTHERLAND, Alexander,
  VII, 197
SUTTLE, Martin, VII, 25
SUTTON, John, X, 372(2),
  373(2)
  Moses, XIV, 256
SWADLEY, Michael, VII, 192
SWAN, III, 470; V, 364; VI,
  14, 16; VIII, 263(4),
  370(2); XIII, 481;
  XIV, 155
  Thomas, I, 358
SWANN, XV, 221(2); XVI,
  70
  Elizabeth, VI, 446, 447
  James, XV, 191(2)
  John, XIV, 319
  Michael, XVI, 22
  Thomas, I, 406(2), 430,
  501, 547; II, 320, 428,
  589(2); III, 570*;
  XVI, 236
  Thompson, VI, 446(4),
  447(6), 448(2)
SWANSON, David, XVI, 419
  (3)
  Gabriel, XVI, 419(3)
  Jane, XVI, 419
  John, XVI, 419(3)
  John, Junior, XVI, 419
  (3)
  Joseph, XVI, 419(3)
SWANWICK, John, XI, 68
SWAVAGE, John, II, 250
SWEARINGEN, XIV, 153

*Swanne

135

Thomas, VI, 494; VIII,
  263, 415; IX, 546; X,
  197
Van, IX, 247; XII, 699,
  721; XIV, 157
SWEARINGHAM, Van, XIV,
  297(2)
SWEET, Benjamin, VII, 216
  Robert, I, 552
SWEPSON, Thomas, XV, 365;
  XVI, 110,135,185(2),
  346
SWIFT, Flower, XV, 30
  Jonathan, XIII, 174,175
SWIFTE, James, I, 84
SWINBURNE, II, 246
SWINDELL, Timothy, VII, 23
SWINEHERD,* IV, 266, 334,
  382, 385; V, 142, 144,
  146; VI, 172, 176, 177
SWINHOW, John, I, 85
SWINTON, Anna, XV, 189(3)
  George, XV, 189(4)
  James, XV, 189(4)
SWINYARD,† VII, 77, 80, 97,
  321, 323; IX, 488,
  510, 513(4)

SWISHER, John, XIII, 297
  Valentine, XII, 625
SWOPE,‡ Jacob, XVI, 94, 100
SYDENHAM, Jonathan, V,195,
  196
SYDNEY, Robert, I, 81, 90
SYDNOR, Epaphroditus, XV,
  120
  George, XIV, 420(2)
  Moore, XIV, 420(2)
  William, XIV, 420(5)
SYLVESTER, David, XV, 24
SYM, Benjamin, VI, 389, 390
  (2)
SYME, Andrew, XIV, 320
  John, VI, 291; VII, 130,
  485; VIII, 54(2), 55
  (9), 56(4), 57(3),
  391; IX, 70; XV, 363
  John M., XVI, 402(2)
  Mildred (Meriwether),
  VIII,55(3), 56, 57(2)
SYMMS, Benjamin, I, 252;
  XVI, 164(2), 165(2)
  James, VIII, 131

T

TABB, XII, 64
  John, VI, 227; VIII,264,
  506; IX, 49; X, 365;
  XI, 382
  Mary, VI, 242
  Philip, XIII, 137; XV,
  67
  Thomas, VII, 128, 232,
  568, 592; VIII, 115,
  276, 277, 412, 645
  William, VIII, 437
TABENOR, Thomas, I, 431
TACKETT, Nimrod, XVI, 31
  (2)
TAFF, John, VII, 64
TAIT, James, IX, 125, 311
TAITE, William, VII, 54, 228
TALBOT, III, 220, 472
  Charles, VII, 205, 206
  Isham, VIII, 585

James, VII, 206
John, VII, 204, 206,220;
  VIII, 130, 585
Matthew, VI, 382; VII,
  205, 206, 207
Thomas, VII, 437
TALBUTT, Thomas, VIII, 454
  (7), 455
TALIAFERRO, IV, 252; V, 133;
  VI, 17, 163; VIII, 90;
  IX,502; XI,226; XIII,
  495; XV, 164
  Betty Thornton, IX,573,
  574(3), 575(2)
  Charles, XVI, 429
  Francis, IX, 575
  John, IV, 176,235; VIII,
  626; IX, 575; X, 370
  John, Junior, VII, 626;
  IX, 673, 574(2), 575

*Swinherd †Swineyard ‡Swoope

136

35

Lawrence, XIV, 244,
  245 (2)
Richard, V, 288, 289 (4)
Walker, VIII, 390, 489,
  494, 580, 669
William, V, 88
TALLEY, Elkanah, XV, 67
  Henry, Junior, VII, 226
TANDY, Moses, XIII, 622
  Smyth, XII,229 (2),230;
  XIII, 316
TANKERSLEY, VI, 17
TANKERVILLE, IX, 585; XIV,
  153
TANNER, VII, 152; XV,63 (2)
  Branch, VII, 201
  Dorothy, XIV, 333 (3)
  Jacob, XIV, 333
  John, I, 86
  Margaret (Bland), VI,
    304 (4), 305, 306
  Thomas, VI, 304
TAPP, Vincent, XV, 183 (2)
  William, VII, 22; XV,
    178; XVI, 329
TAPSCOTT, Henry, VII, 50 (6)
TARPLEY, John, VII, 54
TARRANT, John, VIII, 128
  Mary, XIII, 102 (3)
TASKER, Benjamin, V, 292
  (2)
TATE, XVI, 189
  Charles, XVI, 42 (2)
  David, XIII, 66
  Edmund, XVI, 407 (4)
  George, XVI, 185
  Henry, VII, 211
  James, XVI, 273
  John, XIII, 589; XV, 30
  Lewis, I, 84
  Magnus, VII, 216
  Magnus, Junior, XV,291
  Nathan, VII, 206, 209
  William, VII, 206, 209;
    XIII, 544, 590; XIV,
    275 (2) ;   XV,   426;
    XVI, 32, 110
  Zenus, VII, 222
TATHAM, VIII, 320 (3), 324
  Ayres, XVI, 231 (5)
  Edward, XV, 95
  Tabitha, XVI, 231 (5)

William, XIII, 318 (2)
TATUM, Edward, VII, 212;
  XV, 185 (3), 186
  Nathaniel, VII, 211
TAUCETT, Joseph, VII, 216
TAVENER, Thomas, XVI, 209
TAVERNER, John, I, 64
TAYLER, Philip, I, 239
  William, I, 239, 339,348
TAYLOE, John, IV, 28, 367,
  378; VII, 288, 427,
  431, 568
  William, VIII, 452, 453
    (5)
TAYLOR, VI,17; X.293; XIV,
  154, 156; XV, 155
  Benjamin, XIII, 616 (2)
  Bennett, XVI, 35
  Bushrod, XV, 121, 383
  Charles, IV, 548; VIII,
    589; XVI, 217
  Creed, XV, 121,234,435,
    436; XVI, 268, 271,
    335, 574
  Daniel, V, 117
  Edmund, X, 135, 288;
    XI,283; XII,225; XV,
    155
  Etheldred, VI, 285, 451
  Frances, V, 216
  George, I, 36; III, 21
    (2) ; VII, 202; VIII,
    167, 281, 282,601; IX,
    574; XII,219(3); XV,
    89
  George Keith, XIV, 320;
    XV, 66, 265; XVI,
    268
  Henry, VII, 21; VIII,
    589, 660
  James, IV, 514 (2) ; VII,
    225, 435, 437; VIII,
    269, 390, 601; XII,
    375; XIII, 599; XV,
    447; XVI, 157
  James, Junior, IX, 574
  Jesse, XIII, 94,174; XV,
    221
  John, II, 370, 378; III,
    181, 202; VII, 216;
    XII, 386, 698; XIII,
    8, 171, 173, 230 (3),

297, 549, 576; XIV,
  332(2) ; XV, 69; XVI,
  157
  John McCaulas, XVI,
    217
  Martha, IV, 514
  Mary (Moorman), XII,
    614
  Philip, I, 284
  Richard, XIV, 24, 205;
    XII, 225, 231, 397;
    XIII, 615(2); XIV,
    243
  Richard Squire, XIII,
    73; XV, 353
  Robert, XIII, 599
  Simon, VIII, 624; XV,
    291
  Skelton, XVI, 45
  Thomas, I, 323; II, 15;
    XIV, 243
  Timothy, XVI, 51
  William, I, 85, 372, 408;
    VII, 44, 130, 196;
    VIII, 141, 391, 444;
    XII, 395, 676
TAZEWELL, Henry, IX, 68
  (2) ; XI, 405; XIII, 8,
  131; XIV, 432
  John, VIII, 378, 662,
    665(2), 666(5); IX,
    70, 175, 201
  Littleton W., XVI, 50,
    56, 100, 197
  Sophia (Harmanson),
    VIII, 666, 666 (2)
  William, VIII, 665(2),
    666 (2)

TEA, William, XV, 309
TEACKLE,* John, XII, 402;
  XIII, 233 (2)
TEAGUE, VIII, 659
TEAS, Matthias, VIII, 126
TEASE, Stephen, XV, 267
TEAZE, XVI, 78
TEBBS, John, XIII, 182
  Foushee,† VII, 24, 427;
    VIII, 158, 489
  William, VII, 229; XII,
    604
  Willoughby, XII, 373,

684(2); XIV, 394;
  XV, 37
TEDDER, Edward Allen, I, 63
TEIBOLT, Michael, VIII, 127
TELFAIR, Edward, I, 46
TELLINCHASTE, Nicholas P.,
  XVI, 159
TEMPLE, VI, 16; XI, 310;
  XII, 405
  Anne, XIII, 216, 217
  Benjamin, XII, 407,698;
    XIII, 73, 215 (4), 216
    (3), 217(2), 218, 619
    (2), 622; XIV, 266;
    XV, 70
  John, XIV, 243
  Joseph, XIV, 268
  Liston, XIV, 243
  Samuel, XIII, 73; XIV,
    268
TEMPLEMAN, Samuel, XIV,
  409(2)
TEMPLIN, Tarab, XII, 676
TENCHER, William, VII, 195
TENNANT, XIII,. 558
TERLINGTON, James, XVI,
  204, 250 (3)
TERREL, Edmund, XV, 346
  (3)
  Richard, XII, 282
  Richmond, XII, 383
TERRELL, Henry, VIII, 466
  (2), 467(2)
  Peter, VIII, 466(2), 467
    (2)
  Richard, XII, 397
TERRETT, William H., XVI,
  225
TERRIER, John, VIII, 132
TERRILL, Micajah, X, 446
  Samuel, XV, 121
TERRY, George, XIV, 241
  Nathaniel, VII, 220, 300,
    307; XIII, 278; XIV,
    156
  Stephen, VIII, 130
  William, XIII, 104, 193,
    278; XV, 48(2), 172,
    380; XVI, 38
THACKER, Anne, VI, 314(2),
  315(4) ; VII, 843

Chichley-Corbin, III.431
  Edwin, VI, 314, 316;
    VII, 343 (3)
  Edwin, Junior, VI, 314
    (2)
  Elizabeth, VI, 314(5),
    315 (3) ; VII, 343 (2)
  Frances, VI, 314(4),
    315(2) ; VII, 343(5),
    344(5)
  Sarah, VI, 314, 315 (3) ;
    VII, 343
THANAS, David, Junior, VII,
  21
THARMAN, Thomas, VII, 207
THARP, William, XV, 54
THATCHER, Stephen, VIII,
  132
THERIATE, Dominick, II, 302
  (2) ; III, 479(2)
THERIC, Francis, XIII, 315
THIRMAN, Thomas, VII, 210
THOMAS, VIII, 440
  Charles, XV, 210
  Cornelius, VII, 203;
    VIII, 44, 555 (2)
  Daniel, VII, 21
  George, VII, 207, 569;
    XV, 49
  Gideon, VII, 203
  Isaac, VII, 216
  James, VII, 217
  John, V, 74; VII,22,205,
    222; XIII, 326; XIV,
    422 (3)
  Lewis, VII, 129
  Robert, VII, 222
  Rowland, XV, 388 (3)
  William, I, 373; XIV,
    276 (2)
THOMPSON, I, 142; X, 447
  Abraham, VII, 199, 209
  Alexander, VII, 190, 196
  Archibald, VII, 220
  Benjamin, XVI, 161
  Elizabeth, VI, 446, 447;
    XIII, 225(3)
  Foster, XIII, 225 (3)
  George, I, 133; XII, 682;
    XIII, 225(4)
  Israel, VIII, 550; XII,
    75, 600

James, XII, 118
  Jane, XV, 223
  John, VII, 195, 208, 223,
    326, 447; XIII, 143,
    225 ; XV, 155, 168 (2),
    189, 236(2), 419
  Jonah, XIV, 387; XV,89
  Joseph, XIII, 225 (3)
  Lucy, XIII, 225 (2)
  Moses, VII, 191
  Philip Rootes, XIV, 245;
    XV, 175
  Robert, VII, 191, 196;
    XV, 284
  Rodes, XIII, 170
  Roger, XIII, 132, 224,
    225
  Samuel, XIII, 585
  Sarah, XIII, 225 (3)
  Thomas, VII, 437
  Thomas McKean, XV,
    169
  Waddy, XI, 508
  William, VII, 446, 447
    (2),448(2) ; VII,194,
    200; XIII, 278, 554;
    XVI, 403
  William, Junior, XIII,
    104
THOMSON, I, 139
  Abraham, VIII, 129
  Adam, VII, 226
  Charles, I, 26, 36; X,
    563; XI, 547, 561,
    575 (3)
  George, X. 112, 288
  Henry, XV. 49
  Hermon, VII, 201 (2)
  James, VII, 187,188 (2) ;
    XV, 270
  John, VII, 191
  Richard, II, 371
  Robert, VII, 196
  William, XIII, 95
THORNE,* Samuel, I, 111
  Octavian, I, 85
THORNBURY, Thomas, I, 379
THORNHILL, William, VII,
  214
THORNMAN, Obadiah, VII,
  131

THORNTON, XII, 580, 581;
  XIII, 481, 504; XV,
  282; XVI, 225,233 (3)
  Anthony, VIII, 580
  Anthony, Junior, X, 210
  Betty, IX, 673(2), 674
    (5), 675(2)
  Edward, VII, 131
  Francis, IV, 378, 531;
    V, 198(2), 199(2);
    VI, 18; IX, 673; X,
    370; XIII, 280, 281
    (3), 282; XIV, 154
    (2)
  John, VII, 447(3) ; IX,
    673(4), 574, 575(2) ;
    XIII, 143; XV, 121,
    242
  Lucy, IX, 573
  Mary, IX, 573, 574 (2)
    575(2)
  Matthew, I, 26
  Mildred, IX, 573(2)
  Presley, VII, 51(5), 427
    431, 568; X, 446 (2);
    XI, 316
  Reuben, IX, 573(2)
  Robert, I, 85
  Rowland, V, 288(2)
  Seth, VIII, 601
  William, IV, 378, 438;
    V, 189; XV, 121
  THORP, Benjamin, XIV, 322
    Lewis, XV, 347
  THORPE, George, I, 111
    Joseph,* V, 369(2), 370
    Otho, II, 407
  THOROUGHGOOD,† Adam, I,
    133, 139, 140, 148,
    170, 179, 187; II, 250
    John, XI, 270
    Lemuel, XI, 270
  THRAILKILL, Christopher,
    VII, 326, 447
  THRELKELD, Elijah, XIII,585
  THRIFT, Robert, VII, 227
  THROCKMORTON,‡ Mordecai,
    V, 396; VIII, 446
    Robert, VIII, 435
    Thomas, XV, 276
  TREOGMOSTON, Henry, I, 138
  THRUSTON, Buckner, VII,

91; XV, 234
  Charles Minn,§ IX, 247;
    X,135; XIV,378; XV,
    339
  James, VII, 215
  John, XIII, 299
THURLOE, I, xi
THURSTON, Plummer, XII,
  605
THWEAT, Archibald, XVI,
  160
  Giles, XV, 380
  James, VII, 225
  John James, XVI, 214

TIBALLS, William, II, 554(2),
  555 (2)
TIBBS, William, VII, 223
TICE, Matthew, VII, 184
  Matthias, VII, 185
TIDBALL, Joseph, XIII, 315;
  XVI, 232
TIDWELL, Richard, III, 415
TIFFIN, Edward, XV, 110
TILDEN,‖ John B., XV, 216,
  224
TILLETT, James, VII, 21
  Samuel, VII, 21
TILLINGHAST, Nicholas P.,
  XVI, 412
TILLIT, John, III, 210
TILLY, Thomas, VII, 306
TILMAN, John, VII, 211, 212
  Roger, VII, 212
TIMBERLAKE, Benjamin, VII,
  129
  Henry, VII, 493; XV,
    353
TIMONS, Edward, VII, 216
TINDAL, III, 472(2); VI, 16
  (2)
  Benjamin, XIV, 240
TINDALL, Thomas, I, 552
TINKER, John, VII, 209
TINLEY, John, VII, 196
TINSLEY, David, XIII, 296
  Thomas, VII, 130; XII,
    375; XIII, 73; XV, 70,
    353
  Thomas, Junior, VII,
    129, 130
TIPTON, John, XI, 57

TITHE, Richard, VII, 204
TITUS, II, 511

TOAST, James, VII, 192
TODD, IV, 267(2), 335, 383,
385, 387; V, 137, 142,
144, 364; VI, 17, 160,
173, 176; VIII, 78,
98, 100, 324, 634;
IX, 154, 160, 488, 510,
513; X, 273, 356, 475;
XI, 211, 235, 237, 238;
XII, 664, 698; XIII,
479, 503, 577, 578(2);
XIV, 268; XV,156(2)
Bernard, V, 395, 396
Belty, VIII, 57
Christopher, V, 395
Dorothy, VIII, 57
Harry, VIII, 633, 634
Jane, XII, 369(2), 370,
628
John, IX, 317(2); X,
288; XI, 100, 273;
XII, 369(4), 370(4),
628(4); XIII,231(5);
XVI, 46
John, Junior, X, 293
Levi,* X, 288; XII, 725,
726; XIII, 313(2)
Martha (Vicaris), VIII,
632(2)
Mary Owen, XII,369(3)
370
Philip, V, 395(2); VII,
483, 484; VIII,632(2)
Richard, V, 395(4);
VIII, 57(2), 58(5),
59(2), 632(2)
Robert, VI, 242(2);
VIII, 454; XI, 335,
336; XII, 369
Samuel, VII, 195
Thomas, V, 395(2),
396(5), 397(2); VII,
483, 484(3), 485(2);
VIII, 57, 58, 446, 631,
632(2), 633, 634(4)
William, V, 395(3), 396
(3); VII, 483,484(3),
485; VIII, 57, 59(2),
631, 632(9), 633(5),

*Levy   †Olliver   ‡Towns   §Townesend

141

634(2); IX, 568; X,
103(4); XIII, 275
TOLBERT, Hugh, XV, 270
TOLFORD, David, VII, 191
Robert, VII, 191
TOMERLIN, Moses, VII, 212
TOMKIES, Charles, IV, 457,
458(8)
Francis, VIII, 435
TOMKINS, Christopher, VII,
130
Harry, VII, 130(2)
TOMLINSON, Joseph, XV,
124, 363(3), 463(2)
T O M P K I N S, Christopher,
XIV, 243
TOMSON, Richard, II, 379
TONCRAY, John, XVI, 273,
390
TONEY, John, XV, 49
TOOL, Richard, XIV, 333
Sarah, XIV, 333(3)
TORRINGTON, V, 559
TOTTOPOTOMOY, I, 380(3),
403
TOWERS, George, XVI, 82
TOWLER, Charles, I, 84
TOWLES, XI, 310
Henry, XII, 215
Oliver,† V, 289(2); VII,
214; XI, 219
Thomas, XI, 204
TOWNES,‡ XV, 32
Henry, XVI, 54
John, XV, 30, 32(2)
Joseph, XV, 114
Richard, XII, 623(2),
624(6), 625; XIII,
106, 108(2), 196, 622
(2); XIV, 417
TOWNLEY, Alice, VIII, 630
(2)
Lawrence, VIII, 630
Sarah, VIII, 630
TOWNS, Joel, VII, 227
Stephen, VII, 206
TOWNSEND, Henry, VII, 218
John, I, 82
Richard,§ 138, 239, 282,
287, 288; II, 319
William, VII, 226
TOWNSHEND, John, VII, 181

142

TRADEN, Arthur, VII, 181,186
TRAHORNE, John, I, 148
TRAMMELL, William, VII, 21,
217
TRAVERSE, Rawleigh, II, 205,
260
William, II, 309, 330,
420, 428
TRAVIS, Champion, IX, 71,
149; XVI, 60, 107
Edward, I, 283
Edward Champion, VII,
570; VIII, 171(2)
TREMBLE, Robert, VII, 179,
180
TREE, Goodman, I, 140
Richard, I, 138, 179
TRENT, XII, 706; XIII, 156,
273, 479, 503, 571,
572, 573(2), 579(2)
Alexander, VII, 592;
VIII, 412, 422, 603;
XII, 706(3); XIII,
156(2), 274, 479; XV,
30
Alexander, Junior, XII,
683
Henry, IX, 233; XIV,
155
Obadiah II., XV, 137
Peterfield,† VIII, 422;
XII, 706(2); XIII,
156(2), 274, 479
William, XIII, 630
TRETHEWAY, John, IV, 516
(3), 517, 518(3)
TREVILIAN, Stephen, XV, 155
TREVOR, II, 511
John, I, 67, 77, 82, 90
TRIBBY, Joseph, XV, 459
TRIGG, Daniel, XIV, 275(2),
327; XVI, 217
John, XIII, 105
Stephen, X, 288, 293;
XVI, 53
William, VIII, 585; XV,
348
TRIMBLE, John, VII,190,192;
XI, 164
Robert, VII,181,184(2),
187, 188
Walter, VII, 197

*Peter Field

TRINE, William, VII, 829(3)
TRIPLETT, Daniel, XIV, 245,
308
Hedgman, XVI, 330
Thomas, VII, 21
TRIPPLITT, VI, 18
TRIST, B., XV, 271
TROTTER, James, XII,725,726
TROUT, Daniel, XV, 65
Henry, XII, 672, 673
TRUEHEART, Daniel, XII, 383
William, XV, 353
TRUSLER, Peter, VII, 186
TAUSSELL, John, I, 359, 386
TAUSTON, Thomas, I, 85
TRYAL, David, XV, 162

TUBEUF, Alexander de, XIII,
317(2); XV, 184, 417
(2)
Francis, XV, 184, 417
(2)
Peter Francis, XV, 184
(3), 417(3)
TUCKER, I, vii(2); IV, 528;
VII, 437; XIII, 145
Daniel, I, 84
George, XVI, 34, 50, 197
Henry St. George, XVI,
379, 423
James, XVI, 130
Johanna (Corbin), VII,
459
John, VII, 435, 437;
VIII, 269
Robert, VI, 227, 242;
VII, 435, 437, 459,
460, 569; VIII, 269;
IX, 465; XIII, 211
(2); XVI, 280
St. George, VIII, 8, 131;
XVI, 50
William, I, 129, 145, 153,
170, 187, 202; XIV,
420(3)
Wood, XV, 213, 564
Wright, XV, 52
TUDMAN, Elizabeth, II, 159
(5)
TUGGLE, Lodowick, XII, 659
TULEY, Charles, VII, 203
Christian, VII, 198

37

TUMMENS, Edward, VII, 215
TUNSTALL,* Edmund, XV,
334
Richard, V, 185, 396;
VIII, 446
Richard, Junior, VIII,
633; X, 103
Thomas, VIII,208; XIV,
241, 287
William, XV, 334; XVI,
82, 338
TUPPER, Ansylum, XIV, 337
(3)
TURBERVILLE, George, IV,
307; VIII, 465(2)
John, XI, 369; XII, 83;
XIV, 153; XV,177(2)
TURK, III, 472; VI, 16; XIV,
154
James, VII, 190
TURLEY, Sampson, VII, 21
TURNBULL, Charles, VI, 242;
X, 446(2)
George, VII, 602; XIII,
586
Robert, XIII, 301(6),
302(7); XIV, 320
Sarah (Buchanan),
XIII, 301(6), 302(6)
William, XIII, 585
TURNER, I, 82; VI, 169; VIII,
98, 324; IX, 154, 160,
488, 510
Anthony, VII, 216
Francis, XIII, 582
Harry, V, 194(2)
Henry, XVI, 423
Hezekiah, XV, 339
James, VII, 207; XI,
172; XIV, 266
John, II, 370, 376(2),
377, 547; VI, 242;
XV, 182
John Blunt, XV, 122,
176
Person, XV, 338; XVI,
50, 136
Reuben, XIV, 266
Richard, I, 83; VIII, 131
Stokeley, XVI, 52
Thomas, IV, 377; V,142,
144, 194(2), 289(2),

†Tunstal   †Tweddy, Twiddy

143

303(2); VI, 178, 175,
282, 394; VII, 159,
160(2),161(2); VIII,
78, 216(2); IX, 526;
XVI, 60
Zephaniah, XVI, 225
TURNEY, Richard, II, 461
TURPIN, Horatio, XIV, 319
Philip, XI, 316; XII,617
618(3)
Thomas, VIII, 603
TUTT, Charles, XVI, 226
James, VIII, 439(2);
XII, 376
Richard, VIII, 438(2);
439
William, VII, 213
TUTTIE, IV, 373, 374
TUTTY, VIII, 461

TWEEDY,† William, VII, 205,
208, 209
TWIFORD, James, XII,636(3)
Robert, XIII, 195(6),
196(3)
TWIMAN, William, VII, 23
TWINING, Nathaniel, XI, 369
(2), 396(5), 468(4);
XIII, 174
TYCE, Matthias, VII, 182
TYGER, IX,262; XI,366; XII,
393, 394, 404; XIV,
256(2), 408, 411(3);
XV, 49, 166(2)
TYLER, VII, 589; X, 543
Charles, Junior, XVI,
395
Daniel, XIII, 607
Elizabeth, XII, 208
George, XV, 180
George G., XVI, 379
Henry, III, 285, 428,
431; V, 369; VI, 239
(2); 240; XI, 320(2)
Isaac, XIV, 322
John, IX, 131; XI, 147;
XII, 207(2), 208(4);
XV, 223
Joseph, XII, 208(5)
Samuel, XVI, 50

William, VII, 299; XV,
121, 180; XVI, 168

TYNE, John, V, 370
TYRRELL, Francis, I, 84

U

UMBLE, Gunrod, VII, 186
Martin, VII, 187
Ury, VII, 187

UNDERHILL,* John, II, 13
Thomas, VIII, 661
UNDERWOOD, VI, 323, 430
Bedles, V, 368
William,† I, 374; VII,
214

UPCHURCH, John, VII, 212
William, VII, 212
UPSHAW, Forest, VII, 214
James, X, 210; XIII,541

James, Junior, XIII,
222(3), 307, 607(2),
608
UPSHUR, Abel, XII, 364
Littleton, XIII, 290
UPTON, John, I, 145, 149,
169, 187, 203, 236,
309, 340‡; VI, 449

URQUHART, William, XIII,
173

UTIE,§ John, I, 129, 138, 148,
150, 153, 202

V

VAIDEN, Isaac, XVI, 427
Joseph, XII, 383
VALENDINGRAM, George,
VII, 218
VALENTINE, Edward, XVI,
40
John, VII, 221
VANSEVER, Peter, VIII, 130
(2), 172, 173(2)
Peter, Junior, VIII, 172,
173(2)
VANBIBBER, James, XV, 379,
420
John, XIV, 312, 322
VANBUSKIRK, Lawrence,
XIV, 280
VANCE, Andrew, VII, 216,
217
James D., XV, 224
John, VII, 191, 215, 216,
217
Patrick, VII, 209
Samuel, VII, 216, 217;
VIII, 129; XIV, 266;
XVI, 72

Thomas, VII, 198
VANDEVIER, Lawrence, XIII,
174
VANDOVEAGE, Henry Fay-
son, II, 302(2); III,
479(2)
VANDYKE, Nicholas, I, 46
VANIMON, Peter, VII, 184
VANLANDIGHAM, Michael, II,
308(2); III, 479(2)
VANLANDINGHAM, Benjamin,
VII, 22
VANMETER, Daniel, XV, 245
Garrel, IX, 425
Henry, VII, 25(3), 216
(2)
Solomon, XII, 672, 673
VANSTAPHURST, Jacob, VI,
61(4)
Nicholas, XV, 61(4)
VAN SCARBRUM, Abraham, I,
382
VARDEMAN, John, VII, 206
VASS, Henry, XIII, 108(4)
Reuben, VII, 493

*Vaderhill   †Vaderwood   ‡Vpton, Utye

144

VASSAL, John, I, 85
VATERS, William, XVI, 38
VAUGHAN, Asa, XVI, 410
  Edward, I, 86
  James, VII, 226; XVI, 129, 312(2)
  John S., XV, 380
  Thomas, XIII, 549; XV, 136(5)
  William, VII, 221
VAUGHN, Abraham, VII, 224
VAUHAN, John, II, 16
VAUHOB, Joseph, VII, 192

VEAL, Daniel, VII, 653(2)
  George, VII, 653
  Thomas, VII, 652, 653
VEITCH, Henson, XVI, 51
VENABLE, Abraham,* V, 116(2); XV, 99
  Abraham B., XVI, 335
  Agnes (Moorman), XII, 614
  Charles, VI, 318
  Elizabeth (Smith), VI, 318
  James, XI, 272
  Nathaniel, XI, 272
  Richard N., XIV, 390; XV, 69; XVI, 110
  Samuel Woodson, XI,

273; XVI, 183
VENEMAN, Peter, VII, 182
VENN, Arthur, I, 84
  Richard, I, 87
VERE, Horatio, I, 81, 90
VERNON, James, VII, 223
VERNOR, John, VII, 224
VERSER, Daniel, XVI, 410
VERTUE, Christopher, I, 86
VESTAL, VIII, 550, 551; XII, 75, 77, 78, 376†; XV, 110, 111, 298, 299
  John, VIII, 550

VICARIE, Martha, VIII, 632 (2)
VICCARY, V, 255
VICK, Josiah, XIII, 289
VICTOR, John, IX, 576
VINCENT, Henry, I, 96
VINCKLER, Abraham, III,479 (2)
VINCLER, Abraham, II, 447 (3)
VIVION, Charles, XV, 135(3)

VOSS, Ephraim, VII, 290
  Robert Brooke, XIV,246
VOWELL, Thomas, XV, 260; XVI, 337
VOWLES, Henry, XV, 43

W

WABREANER, Jones, VIII,199
WADDELL, William, XIV, 424
WADDY, VI, 177; VIII, 323, 508(2); IX, 332(2), 488, 511, 513; X, 477 (2)
  Anthony, VI, 175; VIII, 79, 98
  Samuel, VII, 222
WADE, XIV, 153, 157
  Edmund, V, 250; VI, 19
  Edward, VI, 393
  Hampton, XVI, 246
  Henry, VII, 223
  James, XIV,333(2),334, 390

John, VII, 219, 220
Nathaniel, I, 85
Robert, VI, 375; VII, 219(3); VIII, 130, 131(2)
Robert, Junior, VII,307; VIII, 131
William, I, 67, 77, 81, 90
WANLOW‡
WAGAMAN,§ Henry, II, 302 (2); III, 479(2)
WAGENER, Peter, VI, 396(4), 397(2)
WAGER, William, VI, 242; VII, 569

WAGGAMAN, Ephraim, VII, 64, 131
WAGGENER, Andrew, XIII, 297
WAGGONER, Thomas, VI, 528
WAGONER, Lodowick, VII,187
WAGSTAFF, Francis, VII, 300
WAHANGANOCHE, II, 149 (3), 150(4), 154(3), 155
WAINWRIGHT,* IV, 266, 382, 385, 387; V, 136, 142, 144; VI, 169, 173, 175
WAITE, William, VIII, 625
WAKEFIELD, Charles, VII, 203
  Henry, VII, 204
  William, VII, 204
WALDEN, Charles, XV, 233, 234
  Theophilus, I, 81
WALDOE, I, 83
WALDROP, Michael, III, 466
WALKE, Anthony, VII, 437; VIII, 570; XIII, 613 (3)
  Anthony, Junior, VI, 227; VIII, 156(3); XIII, 613(2)
  Thomas, XIV, 419(4)
WALKER, II, 510; III, 472; VIII, 226; XIII, 258 (3); XV, 246(2), 435, 436(2); XVI, 244, 389(2)
  Alexander, VII, 193, 196(2)
  Baylor, VIII, 78
  Catharine, VI, 174
  Edmund, IV, 539
  Edward, XIII, 609(2)
  Francis, XIII, 87, 159, 175; XV, 271, 427; XVI, 309
  George, I, 85; VI, 291; VIII, 472(5)
  Henry, VII, 602; XI,260
  Hugh, VIII, 420
  Jacob, VI, 227
  John, I, 283, 323, 359, 422, 427, 499, 505, 512, 526; II, 153; IV,

462; V, 142; VI, 173; VII, 161; VIII, 149, 477; XII, 207(2), 717; XV, 342(2)
John M., XVI, 423 ·
Joseph, XI, 164
Merry, XV, 223
Mildred (——) (Meriwether), VIII, 55(2)
Peter, I, 386
Richard, VII, 51
Robert, XV, 419
Thomas, I, 83; II, 197, 198, 205, 250; III, 566 (2); VII, 116, 200, 222†, 354, 568; VIII, 10, 55(3), 56(2), 60, 115, 124, 127, 128, 149, 252, 367, 477; IX, 95, 555, 561, 564; X, 211(2); XIII, 159; XIV, 326(2); XVI, 309
Thomas Reynolds, VIII, 539
William, VII, 199, 210; XII, 717
WALKLASK, III, 568
WALKINS, Henry, VII, 229 (3)
WALKLETT, George, II, 372
  Gregory, II, 384, 461
WALKUP, Arthur, XV, 216
WALL, Charles, VII, 211; XVI, 43
  Charles F., XVI, 42, 43
  Daniel, VII, 211
  David, XVI, 42(4), 43 (2)
  George, VII, 212
  Jacob, VII, 23
  James, XI, 333
  John, XVI, 42
  Michael, XVI, 60
  Robert, VII, 211
  William, VII, 22, 213
  Zachariah, XIV, 277
WALLACE, Caleb, XI, 164, 283; XII, 391, 664
  James, VII, 193
  John, VII, 203
  Peter, VII, 189

WALLEN, Thomas, XIII, 544
WALLER, V, 233(3); VI, 16 (2), 173(2), 176, 224; VIII, 78, 98, 323, 508; XIV, 154
  Benjamin, V, 321, 402, 403(2); VI, 197, 230, 413, 414(3), 415(2), 416(3), 418, 437, 454, 524, 529; VII, 13, 39 (2), 54(2), 76, 83(3), 84, 175(3), 259, 260 (2), 276, 316(3), 353, 360(2), 361, 466, 468, 498(3), 570, 647; VIII, 213, 378, 461, 578, 628(2); IX, 70; X, 101
  Edmond, II, 511
  Edward, XII, 361; XIII, 88, 176(2)
  George, XIII, 297; XIV, 316
  George, Junior, XV, 210
  John, I, 63; IV, 235; XIV, 241
  Robert, VII, 435, 437; VIII, 269
  Thomas, VII, 226
  William, V, 198(2), 303(2); VII, 216(2)
WALLING, Edward, XIII, 218
WALLINGFORD, XV, 271
WALLINGS, George, II, 197
WALLIS, XIV, 153
  Thomas, V, 364; VI, 19
WALLOP, John, V, 83, 84(5), 85(4)
  Skinner, IV, 548(3)
  Sarah, V, 84(2)
WALSH, John, XVI, 321(2)
WALTNALL, Christopher, XV, 31
WALTROE, Henrietta, VIII, 627, 628(5), 629(3)
  Nathaniel, V, 564; VIII, 627(2), 628(2), 629
WALTON, XIII, 77
  Edward, III, 586
  George, I, 36
  George, Junior, VII, 212
  John, I, 46

Matthew, XII,676; XIII, 41(2), 42
Thomas, VI, 310; VII, 212
WAMACK, Charles, XV, 380
WANGHOP, Elizabeth, VII, 51, 52
WARD, VI, 504; XII, 723
  Benjamin, XVI, 410
  George, XIII, 217
  James, VII, 196
  James, Junior, VII, 196
  Jeremiah, XV, 379
  John, VII, 192(2), 193, 210, 223; IX, 585(2); XIII, 151; XIV, 157 (2), 266; XV, 55, 97, 377(2)
  Josep, VII, 196
  Richard, VII, 224, 227
  Robert, XVI, 410
  Seth, VII, 271, 412
  Sylvester, XIII, 170, 217(2), 218
  Wells, VII, 220
  William, VII, 193, 196, 197; XI, 139; XII, 659; XIII, 183, 583; XIV, 417(2); XV, 96, 97
WARDEN, William, XV, 274
WARDLAW, James, VII, 196
  John, VII, 195
  Robert, XIV, 266,'267; XV, 427
WARE, Frederick, XV, 179
  George, VII, 242
  James, XV, 343
  Peter H., XV, 31
WAREHAM, John, I, 179, 203
WARFIELD, Walter, XIII, 171
WARMAN, Francis, XIII, 230(4)
WARNER, Augustine, I, 507, 526; II, 340, 401, 546, 569; III, 670; VIII, 484, 630, 631
  Austin, I, 370
  George, VIII, 484(2)
  Mildred (Reade), VIII, 484(3)
  Robert, VIII, 484(3)

WARR, Thomas, I, 67, 77; II, 565
WARREN, Benjamin, V, 367, 368(2)
  John, V, 367; VII, 226; 'VIII, 270; XVI, 249 (3), 250(2)
  Michael, XIII,152; XIV, 166
  Peter, VI, 240; VIII, 661
  Robert, V, 370
  Thomas, I, 283, 514(2); II, 197, 205, 249; VI, 240; XII, 608
WARSHAM, William, XV, 31
WARWICK, IX, 554
  Abraham, XII, 665; XV, 182
  Anthony, VIII, 643
  Jacob, XVI, 161
  William, XVI, 100
WASH, Susannah, VIII, 132
WASHINGTON, XIV, 154
  Anne (Thacker), VI, 314, 315(4)
  Augustine, VI, 513, 514(3), 515(6), 516 (2)
  Bailey,* VII, 494, 670; XIII, 585
  Bushrod, I, vii; XIII, 94; XIV, 360; XV, 66, 69; XVI, 236
  Charles, VIII, 220, 221 (2); XII, 370(2)
  Corbin, XV, 177
  Edward, VI, 396, 397; XVI, 48
  George, I, 22, 24, 25; II, 518; V, 143; VI, iv (2), 17,174, 528; VII, 558, 669; VIII, 10, 43, 216(2), 640(2); IX, 345, 347, 445, 449; X, 575, 577, 581, 582; XI, 525(2), 526, 552 (3); XII, 42(3), 43 (2), 44(2),393; XIII, 100(2),152,610; XIV, 334(2), 435(2); XV, 44; XVI, 20;
  George S., XV, 291

Gray, XV, 240
  Henry, VI, 314(2), 315 (5); XV, 179, 282; XVI, 168
  John, II, 250, 309, 330; IV, 378; IX, 526
  John Augustine, VIII, 640, 641; XII, 371
  Lawrence, VII,494; XIV, 153
  Lawrence A., XV, 465
  Martha, XV, 267
  Mildred (Thornton),IX, 573
  Samuel, VI, 614(3), 515(4), 516(3); VIII, 624; IX, 247, 374, 573, 574; XV, 110,196
  Thomas, XV, 240
  Thornton, IX, 573, 574 (2), 575(3); XII, 371
  Warner, VIII, 624; IX, 247
  Washington, J., XV, 180
  William, XIII, 220
WATCHINGBAYLE, Robert, I, 171
WATERHOUSE, Edward, I, 82
WATERMAN, Asher, XV, 99, 132; XVI, 49, 56, 400
WATERS, Edward, I, 131(2), 132, 133(2)
  Obedience, VIII, 471
  Sarah, VIII, 471(2), 472(2), 473
  Thomas, VIII, 471
  William, I, 386, 407, 408, 529; VII, 83, 569; VIII, 470(2), 471(3), 473(3)
WATERSON, John, IV, 268
WATKINS, XII, 52; XIV, 153, 166(2)
  Abner, XV, 30
  Benjamin, VII, 408; VIII, 421; IX, 70
  Claiborne, XV, 426
  Evan, V, 260; VI, 19; VII, 217
  Francis, XI, 272
  George, IX, 334
  Henry, I, 129; V, 369

Joel, XI, 250, 272, 333; XIII, 565; XV, 120
John, VI, 240; VIII,618; XI, 57; XIV, 154
John D., XV, 272; XVI, 427
Joseph, XIII, 296
Robert, V, 368(3); XV,. 263(3), 350
Thomas, VIII,149; XIII, 193, 275, 553; XV,380
WATSON, XIV, 273
Abraham,* I, 373, 379, 386
John, XIII, 555; XV, 271; XVI, 149, 318
Joseph, XII, 625, 626
Josiah, XII, 393; XIII, 94, 174, 175, 592
Matthew, VII, 224
Robert, VII, 21
Thomas, I, 83
WATT, XIV, 241; XV, 76
WATTBROKE, Joseph, VII,217
WATTEY, William, I, 84
WATTS, VI, 352
Charles, XV, 419
Edward, VII, 179, 210 (2)
George, VII, 180, 183, 188, 210(2)
John, I, 82, 90; VI, 352; VII, 207, 210; VIII, 79, 391; XIV, 422
Mary, XV, 457(8)
Thomas, X, 325
William, XV, 457(2)
WAUGH, Abner, XVI, 156, 167(2)
Alexander, XVI, 395
Charles S., XVI, 162
James, XVI, 333
Richard, XI, 36
WAUGHOP, John, VI, 175
WAUGHUB, Joseph, VII, 199
WAYLES, John, VIII, 149
WAYLT, John, XVI, 94
WAYNAM, Thomas, I, 82
WAYNE, Anthony, X, 576
WATT, John, XVI, 100

WEALE, John, I, 236

WEATHERALL, George, VII, 22
John, XIV, 336
WEATUERLY, James, XVI, 422
WEATHERS, Cain, XV, 120
James, XV, 120
George, XVI, 429(2)
WEAVER, Matthias, VII, 23
Tilman, VII, 230
WEB, Thomas, I, 84
WEBB, VI, 16
Conrad, XVI, 309
Edmund, XIII, 321(2)
Edward, I, 84; III, 95
Foster, Junior, XII, 280
George, V, 321; VIII, 434(2); IX, 149, 286 (2), 287(2), 366, 481 (3); XIV, 154
Giles, I, 430, 506, 509, 528
James, VIII, 570
John, IV, 628; XIV, 406
Richard, I, 86
Stephen, I, 239, 283
Thomas, I, 83; XII, 296
Wingfeild, I, 386
WEBE, Sandya, I, 84
WEBBER, II, 472
WEBSTER, Dep., I, 384
John, XV, 249, 274
Peter, VII, 201
Richard, I, 430, 501
Roger, I, 178
William, I, 84
WEDDICK, Henry, II, 302(2); III, 479(2)
WEEDON, George, IV, 377; XI, 310; XII, 210
WEEKES, Robert, II, 371
WEEKS, V, 250
Abraham, III, 553, 554
WEEMS, Thomas, VII, 193
WEESE, Adam, VII, 182
WEIR, II, 254
Edward, VII, 203
George, XIII, 175, 818
WEISEGER, Joseph, XIII, 699
WELBURNE, Francis, VII,131
WELBY, William, I, 86
WELCH, Edward, I, 85

*Watson
149

John, XV, 166
Joshua, VII, 24
Nicholas, VII, 208
WELD, Humphrey, I, 81, 90
WELDON, Daniel, VI,375(2); XIV, 155
WELL, XII, 723
WELLDY, David, I, 513
WELLS, Absolum, XII, 721
Alexander, XV, 119(2); XVI, 179(2), 180
Bezaleel, XVI, 246
Bezwell, XV, 169
Charles, XV, 169
John, XV, 31
Richard, I, 340; XV,167
Thomas, I, 86
WENTWORTH, John, Junior, I, 46
WENINGER, Augustus, XVI, 235
WEST, I, 547(2)
Alice, I, 551
Abram, VII, 201
Anne, VI, 321, 428
Charles, VII, 488(3), 490(2),490(2); VIII, 426(2)
Edward, X, 196
Eleazer, XIV, 428; XV, 176
Francis, I, 4(3), 61,111, 128, 145, 153, 178, 202; V, 117, 297(4), 298(4), 299(3); VII, 64, 296, 486, 498; VIII, 454(2)
Henry, II, 647
Hugh, V, 104, 364; VI, 19; XIV, 153
John, I, 4(3), 84, 138, 148, 153, 178, 223, 288, 322, 339, 371, 380, 438, 426, 432, 504, 547(2); II, 319, 330, 438, 545, 546, 647, 548; III, 21(2); V, 297, 298(2), 299 (2); VI, 321(2), 322, 323(3), 324(2), 428 (3), 429(3), 430(2), 431, 432; VII, 488(3),

480; VIII, 286
Katharine, I, 84
Martha, V, 298(2)
Nathaniel, V, 297(2), 298, 299; VI, 321, 322(2), 428(3), 429 (8), 430, 431, 432; VIII, 224
Philip, XIII, 612
Roger, XIII, 592; XIV, 387; XV, 177; XVI, 337
Sibel, VII, 605
Thomas, I,* 81, 90; V, 297(7), 298, 299; VI, 321, 428, 429(2); VII, 21, 488(2); XIII, 98, 176(2); XVI, 163
Unity, VI, 322(3), 323 (2), 428, 429(7), 430; VIII, 224(4), 225, 227(3)
William, II, 370,376(2), 377, 547; VII, 22, 236
WESTBROOKE, Henry, XI, 150(2)
WESTERHOUSE, William, I, 499
WESTFALL, Cornelius, XIV, 411(2)
Jacob, XIII, 170
Jacob, Junior, XII, 639
James, XII, 661; XIII, 170
WESTROPP, John, I, 283
WESTROW, John, I, 85
WESTWOOD, Humfrey, I, 84
William, VII, 227,242(2)
Worlich, VIII, 659; IX, 466; XII, 97; XIV, 308, 323
WETHERALL, Robert, I, 370, 373
WETWOOD, Randal, I, 85
WEYE, John, I, 506; II, 197, 198, 250
WEYNMAN, Ferdinando, I,82
WEYRE, John, I, 530
WHALEY, James, III, 425,428
Mary, IV, 372
. Thomas, II, 370, 876,

*Lewarr
150

377, 461
WHARTON, VII, 24
WHARTON, Dabney M., XVI, 409
George, I, 81
John, XI, 36
Joshua, VII, 224
Samuel, XVI, 48(2)
WHEATLIFF, David, I, 390
WHEELER, James, XV, 30
John, XIII, 320(2)
Lettice, XI, 145(2)
Luke, XVI, 46
Maurice, XI, 145(2)
Nevett, II, 552
Rowland, X, 325
Thomas, I, 85
WHIDDEN, XV, 452
WHIPPLE, William, I, 36
WHISTLER, Francis, I, 85
WHITAKERS, Jabez, I, 129
WHITE, XVI, 422, 429(2)
Alexander, IX,247; XII, 371; XIV, 270; XV, 110, 249
Archibald, VII, 130(8), 131, 435, 437; VIII, 269
Chapman, XVI, 149(2)
Charles, V, 367, 368
Cornous, VII, 186
Daniel, V, 195
Francis, XVI, 193(2), 209
George, XIII, 297
Henrietta, XVI, 321
Isaac, VII, 216
James, I, 84; VII, 203; XV, 426; XVI, 32,110
John, XIII, 624(5); XIV, 265; XV. 44, 334; XVI, 31, 215(3)
Josiah, XV, 459
Leonard, I, 85
Rawley, XV, 334; XVI, 338, 401
Richard, II, 153; XV,30, 426
Robert, XV, 387
Robert, Junior, XVI, 62
Sarah, VI, 242
Thomas, I, 84; XV, 223

*Whitton
151

William, II, 330; IV, 93; VI, 242; VII, 216,226, 479; XI,58,332; XIV, 308, 322; XV, 23, 270, 334, 447; XVI, 329
WUITEHEAD, VI, 323, 430
WHITEING, Henry, III, 553, 554
WHITEMAN, Hezekiah, XII, 595
WHITESIDE, Moses, VII, 195
William, VII, 194, 203
WHITESITE, William, VII,206
WHITING, VI, 17
Beverley, V, 321, 399, 402, 403(2); VI, 197, 407
Elizabeth, XIII, 136(2), 137(2), 139(3), 140 (4), 141
Francis, VI, 243; VIII, 435, 485; X, 121; XII, 685; XIII, 92, 204; XV, 67
John, X, 121; XIII, 136, 140(2), 141(3)
Matthew, VIII, 494,664; XV, 180
Peter, VII, 569
Peter Beverly, XIII, 137
Peter P., XV, 67
Thomas, VI, 243, 411 (3); VII, 289, 569; VIII, 485; IX, 149; X, 121(3); XV, 67
WHITLEY, Jonathan, VII,195
Robert, XV, 270
Thomas, I, 84
WHITLOCK, Charles, XVI, 140
John, XIII, 218
Thomas, XVI, 174
William, XIV, 320
WHITLOCKE, Charles, XVI, 346
WHITMAN, Matthew, XV, 274
WHITMORE, George, I, 87
WHITSEL, Jacob, XV, 463
WHITSON,* John, II, 370, 461, 553
WHITT, Mary, XIII, 616

WHITTAKER,* William, I,358, 370, 373, 379, 386, 422, 506, 512
WHITTBY,† William, I, 370, 373, 375, 378, 379, 383, 385, 386, 407
WHITTEZ, Abraham, VIII. 131
WHITTINGHAM, John, I, 86
Thomas, I, 86
WHITTY, John, II, 36(2), 37
WHITWORTH, William, XV, 201
WHYTE, James, XII, 366(4)
WIATT, John, XIII, 296
WICKHAM, John, I, vii; XIV, 360; XVI, 34, 335
WICKWIRE, John, XII, 404; XIV, 157
WIDDOWES, Richard, I, 84
WIDENER, Jacob, XV, 274
WIDGEON, Thomas, VIII, 661
WIECK, Jacob, VII, 184
Joseph, VII, 184
WIFFIN, Richard, I, 84
WIGGINS, Edward, II, 328
WIGGINTON, Richard Y., XV, 53, 209
WIGMORE, Richard, I, 82
WILCOCKS, Elizabeth, III, 167(2)
WILCOX, John, I, 414, 421
WILDER, John, XVI, 62, 100
WILEY, Allen, VII, 214; XII, 672, 673
John, XIV, 390; XV, 30
WILKES, Burwell, XV, 240
Edward, I, 85
WILKIN, Joseph, VI, 13
WILKINS, James, X, 124
John, XIII, 617(3)
Joseph, XV, 176; XVI, 50
Nathaniel, XIII, 617
Thomas, V, 111; VII, 52
William W., XV, 122, 176; XVI, 60
WILKINSON, IV, 381, 383, 419; VII, 324, 426 (2); IX, 400; XI, 211, 235, 238

James, XII, 282, 369, 390(2), 391(3), 697 (2), 635; XIII, 91, 173, 272, 289, 297, 549
John, I, 203
Nathaniel, XI, 399; XII, 280, 375(1); XIII, 229; XIV, 266
William, VI, 174, 176; VII, 78, 98, 100
WILKS, Francis, VII, 222
John, X, 325
WILLCOX, John, I, 129, 431
WILLESTON, Hugh, I, 64
WILLEY, John, VII, 191(2)
Robert, VII, 191, 195
WILLHOIT, John, VII, 22
WILLIAM, I, 430
WILLIAM & MARY, III,42(2), 43, 62, 81, 98(2), 106 (3), 119, 124, 126, 137(4), 171(2), 360; IV, 143, 164, 429; V, 304; VI, 92, 132
WILLIAM III, III, 137(6), 166(2), 168, 169, 176, 200, 214(2), 216, 218, 422, 505; VII, 320,321
WILLIAMS, III, 471; IV, 335, 383, 385; V, 142, 144, 191(2); VI, 18, 173, 174, 176; VII, 78, 98, 425 (3), 550,551,597; IX, 154, 160, 488, 510; XIV, 153(2), 164
Aaron, VII, 223
Abner, XV, 270
Benjamin, VII, 218
Catharine, VI, 239
Charles, XIII, 218
Daniel, VII, 624
David, VII, 216; XIII, 607
David G., XVI, 410
Elisha, XVI, 161
Elizabeth, XIII, 610
Henry, XVI, 149(2),318
Isaac, XIII, 48; XIV, 157, 428; XV, 223,224
Isaac Hite, XV, 67

*Whittakers, Whitaker, WhitLacre
39
152
†Whittbye, Whilby, Whitbey

James, XIII, 218; XIV, 421
James M., XV, 95, 160, 334
Jesse, VIII, 403
John, I, 46; II, 473; VII, 21, 193, 198, 220, 224 (2); XII, 595; XIII, 610(2); XIV, 241, 394; XV, 37, 270
John C., XV, 210
Josiah, XV, 233, 234
Lewis, IV, 528
Mary, XI, 65(2)
Philip, III, 219(2), 471 (2); XIV, 421
Remembrance, VII, 216
Robert, XI,65(9); XIII, 275
Thomas, VI, 242; VII, 224, 226; XII, 690; XIII, 162, 174, 216
William, I, 36; VII, 203, 306, 326, 447
William C., VII, 421; XV, 175, 176; XVI, 194
WILLIAMSON, II, 528
Bazil, XV, 271
George, IV, 535
Hugh, I, 22
John, XII,381(4); XVI, 359(3)
Joseph, XI, 373
Nathan, VII, 21
Person, XV, 338
Richard, I, 82, 90
Robert, II, 197, 205, 249; XIV, 315
Samuel, XIII, 320
Thomas, VII, 624; X, 124; XIV, 332(4)
WILLIS, V, 250, 559; VI, 15; VII, 441, 625; XII, 583(2), 586(2); XIV, 155; XV, 30, 32, 99 (2), 297(2)
Edward, XVI, 38
Francis, I, 371, 374, 421, 427, 499, 507, 512, 514, 530, 552; II, 330; IV, 267; V, 278, 279.

390; VIII, 663
Francis, Junior, V, 399; VII, 569
George, XV, 164(2), 188(4)
Henry, IV, 235, 461, 463(2), 464(6), 465; V, 198(5), 199(3), 398(4); VII, 315(2), 650; VIII, 663(2)
John, V, 398
Joseph, VIII, 130, 172, 173(2)
Lewis, VIII, 220,221(2)
Mary, VIII, 663(2)
Robert Carter, IX, 569
Thomas, VI, 242
WILLISON, James, XII, 364
WILLITTS, John, XVI, 330
WILLOCK, James, VII, 222
WILLOUGHBY, VI, 493
Andrew, IX, 555
John, VII, 437
Thomas,* I, 133, 149, 150, 154, 170, 179, 187, 288, 321, 322
WILLOWBY, III, 220(2)
WILLS, Absalom, XIV, 157
Charles, XII, 599
Edmund, XVI, 410
Emanuel, XV, 205
James, XIII, 173, 300; XV, 205
John Scasbrooke, IX.70, 125; XII, 201; XIII, 173, 300; XIV, 418
Mills, XIII, 567
William, XV, 213, 364; XVI, 62
Willis, XV, 182
WILLSON, William, XV, 44
WILMER, Andrew, I, 85
Clement, I, 85
George, I, 85
WILMOT, Charles, I, 82
WILMOUTH, Thomas, VII,186
WILSEY, Joseph, XIII, 194 (2), 196(5), 196(3)
WILSFORD, Thomas, II, 370, 375(2), 377; III, 567
WILSON, XII, 118
Alexander, XVI, 53

* Willoby, Willowby, Willoughbye

153

Benjamin, VII, 24; XII, 394, 583, 586, 639; XIV, 242; XV, 243
Benjamin, Junior, XVI, 181(3)
Charles, VII, 191; XII, 637; XVI, 410
David, VI, 242; XV, 216
Felix, I, 85
George, VII, 191; VIII, 275; XIII, 42, 284, 481; XIV, 158
Goodridge, XVI, 183
Hugh, VII, 186; XV,379
James, I, 23, 36; II, 370, 375(2), 377, 546(2); VII, 192, 195, 196; XIV, 240
John, VII, 182, 192, 197, 200, 201; VII, 546, 570; XI, 164, 260; XII, 639; XIII, 170, 193, 275; XIV, 266, 267; XV, 49, 221, 224, 444; XVI, 52
Joseph, X, 325
Josiah, VII, 197
Matthew, XII,675; XVI, 46
Nathaniel, XVI, 136,346
Peter, VII, 218, 219(2)
Richard, VII, 180(3), 185
Robert, XVI, 304
Samuel, VII, 190, 226; XIII, 216
Solomon, XI, 630
Stephen, VII, 190, 199
Stephen R., XV, 176; XVI, 209
Thomas, I, 83; VII, 187, 193, 199; XV, 114; XVI, 324(3)
William, III, 59; VII, 164(2), 187, 190, 216, 217; XI, 165; XIII, 588, 592; XV, 375; XV, 274,284,291,442; XVI, 46, 403
Willis, XII, 586; XIII, 159*, 171, 175, 204, 599, 614; XV, 23, 30

WIMBISH, James, VII, 229
John, XVI, 401(2)
William, XV, 334
WIMBUSH, William, XVI, 52
WINCH, Samuel, I, 86
WINCHE, Humphrey, II, 511
WINCHESTER, Stephen, XVI, 100
WINDHAM, Edward, I, 236, 239
WINE, James, VII, 210
WINFREY, VII, 489
WINGFIELD, Charles, XVI,68
Edward Maria, I, 3, 67, 58, 62(2), 63(2), 65, 66, 83
Joseph, XVI, 68
Owen, VII, 215
WINGOE, Susanna, XVI, 408 (5)
WININGTON, Francis, II, 529, 531
WINN, XIV, 260, 267
John, IX, 61
Minor, XV, 30
Thomas, VIII, 645
WINNE, John, VII, 201
WINSLOW, Benjamin, XV, 388(4), 389
Beverley, XIII, 375
WINSOR, Olney, XIII, 176
WINSTON, Anthony, XV, 120
Edmund, X, 459
James, XV, 121, 240
John, XII, 375; XIII, 73
Peter, XII, 620(2)
William, VII, 55, 56, 131; XIII, 626, 627; XIV, 268; XV, 155
William, Junior, VI, 291; XIV, 243
William C., XIII, 73
William Overton, XIII, 623, 624(4), 625
WINTER, William, I, 82
WINTERTON, John, XII, 625
WIRRAL, Hugh, I, 82
WIET, William, I, v; XV,323; XVI, 335(2), 374
WISE, XIII, 629
John, III, 564; VII, 200; XIII, 233(2)

* Willson

154

Nicholas, II, 472; III, 59
Tully Robinson, VIII, 391
WISEDOM, John, II, 555
WISHART, Thomas, XII, 211
Thomas, Junior, XV, 23
William, XI, 270
WITCHER, William, IX, 568; XII, 659; XV, 97
WITHERHEAD, John, VII, 214
WITHERS, VII, 514
Edmund, VI, 514
John, VI, 513, 514(2), 515, 516(2)
Sarah, VI, 513, 514(2), 516(2)
Thomas, VI, 513,514(2)
William, VI, 513(3), 514(5), 515(6), 516 (2)
WITHERSPOON, John, I, 36,46
WITHLAW, John, VII, 198
WITTON, James, XV, 270
Richard, VI, 276(2), 507; VII, 232
Thomas, XV, 270
WITTS, Charles, VIII, 130, 172, 173(2)
WIZER, John, VII, 184

WOODROW, Alexander, XI, 150 (4), 151(3); XII, 220 (5); XV, 129(2), 130
Andrew, XI, 150(2), 151(3); XIII,90; XV, 129(6), 130(2)
WOITLAW, James, VII, 197
John, VII, 197
WOLCOTT, Oliver, I, 36, 46
WOLF, Lewis, XV, 224
WOLFE, Lewis, XVI, 52
WOLLIN, Thomas, VII, 220
WOLLY, Francis, I, 82
WOLSTENHOLME, John, I, 83, 90
WOMACK, Abraham, VII,227
Allen, XV, 334
Jacob, VII, 224, 227
William, V, 369; XVI, 401
WOMBLE, Matthew, XII, 201 (3)

WOOD, VII, 141, 402; VIII, 300
Abraham, I, 283, 289, 322, 326(3), 377, 386, 421, 426(3), 427, 432, 505, 526
James, VI,268,269; VII, 232, 235(2), 236; VIII, 124, 252; XI, 310; XII, 639; XV, 66, 309
John, XII, 202, 675; XIII, 171; XVI, 46
Leighton, Junior, XV, 185
Nehmiah, XV, 228(2)
Percivell,* I, 154, 179
Robert, XII, 612; XIV, 157
Thomas, I, 83, 84, 85; VII, 611(3), 612(2); IX, 124
Valentine, VIII, 149
William, V, 186; VII, 201; XIII, 182; XVI, 149(3)
William, Junior, XV, 30
WOODAL, John, I, 84
WOODARD, John, VII, 210
Richard, VII, 210(2)
William, VII, 210
WOODCOCK, John Sherman, XII, 625; XIV, 334; XV, 216, 224
WOODDIE, William, VII, 209
WOODE, Abraham, I, 373
WOODFORD, Mary (Thornton), IX, 573, 574(2), 575(3)
John T., XVI, 157
William, IV, 377; VII, 493; VIII, 601; IX, 573, 574(2), 575
WOODHOUSE, I, 83; II, 12
David, I, 83
Henry, I, 82, 340, 370
Thomas, I, 425
WOODING, Robert, VII, 219 (2); XIII, 173
Thomas H., XV, 334; XVI, 52, 401
WOODLIEF, Peter, XV, 265

* Percivall

155

WOODLIFE, I, 373
WOODLIFFE, John, I, 86
WOODON, George, VII, 493
WOODROOF, David, XIV, 389
WOODROUGH, David, XIII, 296
WOODROW, Andrew, XV,260; XVI, 162
WOODS, II, 328; XVI, 410
Andrew, VIII, 552; XII, 514; XIV, 424; XV, 124
Archibald, XII,603,639; XIII, 87; XIV, 424
Jeremiah, XV, 463
John, VII, 181, 203
Joshua, XV, 203
Josiah, XV, 50; XVI, 45
Michael, Junior, VII,203
Robert, XIII, 283(3); XIV, 158(2), 424
Samuel, VII, 203
William, VII, 183, 185, 202, 203(2); XIV, 330; XVI, 149
WOODSON, VII, 224; XV, 462 (2); XVI, 233(2)
Blake B., XV, 121
Charles, VI, 223, 352, 375(2); VIII, 76; XIV, 155
Drury, XVI, 229(3)
Frederick, XIII, 293; XIV, 319
George, XV, 167
John, III, 60; VIII, 459; XIII, 156(2), 166, 171, 481(2), 504; XV, 185; XVI, 246
Joseph, XVI, 268(3)
Matthew, XIV, 155
Michael, XIII, 218
Miller, XV, 30
Obadiah, VII, 204
Philip, XVI, 340(4)
Samuel,XIII, 296; XIV, 155; XVI, 309, 330
Stephen, IV, 342; VI, 14
Tarleton,* VI, 375(2), 376; XIII, 293; XIV, 165; XVI, 266(2)
Tucker, V, 190; VI, 15

Wade, XIII, 298
WOODWARD, Christopher, I, 138
George, IV, 393(2)
Henry, VI, 528; VII,493
Isaac, VII, 211
John, VII, 211
Richard, VII, 207, 210 (2)
Samuel, VII, 208
Susanna, XIII, 611
Thomas, I, 375
William, VII, 211
WOOLBRIDGE, Daniel, XI,391; XIII, 481
WOOLER, Edward, I, 84
WOOLF,† Reece, XVI, 54, 158
WOOLFOLK, John, XII, 623 (2), 624(6), 625; XIII, 106, 108(2), 196, 622(2); XIV,417
Paul, XIV, 243
WOOLSEY, John, VII, 212
WOOTEN, William, XIII, 566
WORBRIGH, William, I, 283
WORLEIGH, George, I, 236
WORLICH,† William, I, 359, 386, 529; II, 157
WORMAN, Francis, XII, 639
WORMLEY,§ Agatha, V, 86, 89
Charles, I, 235
Christopher,|| I, 238; II, 329; III, 545, 550
Elizabeth, V, 86(2), 89; VIII, 452(2), 453(2)
John, V, 85, 86(2), 87, 88(3), 89; VII, 628 (5), 629, 630; VIII, 162, 210(2), 231, 452 (6), 453(4), 637, 638; XI, 316(2)
Judith, V, 86, 89; VIII, 162(2)
Ralph, I, 359; II, 473, 544, 551(2), 553, 554, 564, 569(2); III, 59 (2), 545, 550, 567, 570; V, 85, 86(5), 87 (12), 88(4), 89; 576; VI, 17, 19, 291, 407, 411(3); VII, 628(4),

*Tarleton †Wolf ‡Worlich, Worleich ||X'pofer, Xpber §Wormley

156

629(5), 630; VIII,
161, 163(2), 222, 230
(7), 231(5), 452, 468.
488, 637(7), 638(4);
XIV, 163, 243, 399;
XV, 32
Sarah, V, 86, 89
William, XIII, 70
WORMINGTON, Abraham,
VIII, 570
WORRALL, James, XIII, 293
WORSHAM, John, VII, 224.
227
Thomas, XIV, 267, 321;
XV, 342(3)
WORSHBORNE, James, VII,
224
WORTH, Robert, I, 82

WRAXALL, Peter, I, 513
WRAY, George, VIII, 264;
XIV, 323
George, Junior, XIII,
106
Jacob, VIII, 264
Thomas, XII, 201
WREN, John, VII, 218
James, XIV, 387; XV,
178
WRENN, Thomas, XII, 201
WRIGHT, I, vii
Christopher, VII, 228;
VIII, 570
David, X, 448
Edward, V,200(2);VII,
228
Eve (——) (Reid), XVI,
240(4)
George, VII, 217
James, XI, 172; XVI,
240(3)
John, I, 84; VII, 207;
XIV,279(4); XV,223
Martram,* III, 220(2),
472
Matthew, XVI, 179
Richard, II, 15
Thomas, VII, 202

Tommy, XVI, 179
William, IV, 527; V, 72,
184. 200(2); VIII,
130(2)
William, Junior, XIII,
585
WROE, Original, XII, 672,673

WYAT, Francis, I, 235
Thomas, I, 82
WYATT, Anthony, I, 379, 422,
426
Dudley, IV, 515(2), 516
Francis, I, 3(2), 4(3),
111, 113(3), 114(3),
128, 224, 235, 294
George. I, 3
John, VII, 218; XII,
229; XIV, 389
Joseph, XIII, 315; XVI,
268, 403
Nicholas, II, 330
Peter, XIV, 399
Thomas, VII, 21
WYCH, James, VI, 239
WYCHE, James, VII, 230
Nathaniel, XV, 343(2)
WYLIE, Hugh, XVI, 403
WYNCOOP, XV, 271
WYNNE, Edward, I, 84
Peter, I, 83
Robert,† I, 429, 527; II,
147, 148, 149, 161,
163, 179, 195, 196(2),
213, 223, 225, 226,
228, 248, 249, 263,
276, 285, 292, 302,
310, 325, 519
Thomas, I, 83
WYTHE, George, I, vii(3),
viii, 36; VI, 437, 524;
VII, 13, 76, 276, 289,
353, 466, 468, 568,
647; VIII, 146, 213,
365, 378, 578; IX, 70,
175(2), 176; XI, 548;
XIII, 147, 542; XIV,
360; XVI, 34

X

XAVENAUGH, Charles, VIL
326

Y

YACOME, Filey, VII, 196
YADLEY, Richard, VII, 180
YAGER, John, Junior, XIII,
558
Nicholas, VII, 22
William, VII, 23
YANCEY,* Charles, VII, 22,
214; XI, 508; XV, 99,
120, 182, 340(2);
XVI, 149, 155, 179
Jechonias, XVI, 179
Joel, XVI, 100, 149
John, VII, 213
Layton, XV, 128(3)
Lewis Davis, XIV, 336
Robert, XIV, 336; XV,
121
Stephen, XI, 508(2),
509(2)
William, XVI, 338
YARBOROUGH, Jeremiah, VII,
207, 211
Joel, VII, 23
YARDLEY, Benjamin, IX, 420
YARDLY,† Argoll, I, 288, 372,
384, 408
YARLY, Francis, I, 379
YATE, Francis, XVI, 233
YATES, Charles, XV, 43, 58
Elias, V, 195, 196
George, VIII, 130
John, VII, 207
Thomas,† II, 85(3)
William, VII, 205
YEAXER, Adam, VII, 407
YEARDLEY, I, 122
George, I, 3(5), 4, 85,
111, 114(2), 115, 119,
121, 122, 128, 142,
145(3)
Temperance, I, 145(2)

YEATES, XV, 443
Francis, IV, 28
Thomas, Junior, VII,
214
YEDLEY, Richard, VII, 179
YEO, I, 289
Hugh, II, 198
Leonard, II, 197
YEOMANS, Simon, I, 87
YERBURY, II, 328

YOAKUM, George, VIII, 275
Margaret, VIII, 275
YORK, II, 426
YOUNG, Daniel, VIII, 129;
XIV, 322
Edmund, VIII, 129
George, VII, 220; VIII,
130(2)
Harmer, VII, 23
Israel, VII, 209
James, VII, 179, 180,
187(2), 188, 195;
XIII, 169. 175, 599;
XVI, 130
John, VII, 180, 184, 185,
187, 191, 216; VIII,
126; XIV, 322
Nicholas, XVI, 36(4)
Peter, VII, 224
Robert, VII, 189, 190,
191, 192, 193; XIV,
387
Thomas,§ II, 370, 375
(2), 377, 546(2)
William, I, 84
YOUNGER, John, VII, 23
YOUNGHUSBAND, VIII, 423
John, XI, 154(3)
YOWELL, James, XIV, 277
Thomas,|| II, 379

Z

ZANE, Ebenezer, XII, 297,
514, 639; XIII, 282;
XIV,158,424(2); XV,
166, XVI, 242, 316
Isaac, XII,625,661; XV,
274
Jonathan, XIII, 565;

XVI, 54, 242
ZIGLAR, Christopher, VII,214
ZIMMERMAN, Reuben, XV,
176
Stophel, XIII, 583
ZOUCHE, Edward, I, 81, 90

www.ingramcontent.com/pod-product-compliance
Lightning Source LLC
Chambersburg PA
CBHW021443090426
42739CB00009B/1618